MEMORIAL FICTIONS

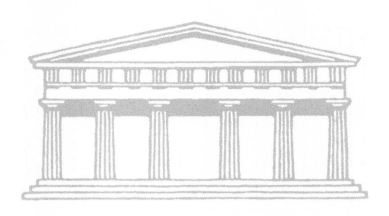

MEMORIAL FICTIONS
Willa Cather and the First World War

STEVEN TROUT

UNIVERSITY OF NEBRASKA PRESS
LINCOLN AND LONDON

Portions of the introduction and chapter 1 first appeared as "Willa Cather's
One of Ours and the Iconography of Remembrance," in
*Cather Studies 4: Willa Cather's Canadian and Old
World Connections,* ed. Robert Thacker and Michael A.
Peterman (Lincoln: U of Nebraska P, 1999), 187–204.

LC Control Number: 2002018114
ISBN 0-8032-4442-8 (cl.: alkaline paper)
ISBN 978-0-8032-1837-6 (pa.: alkaline paper)

CONTENTS

ILLUSTRATIONS

ACKNOWLEDGMENTS

Like almost anyone involved in Cather studies today, I owe an immense debt to Susan J. Rosowski, whose enthusiasm and encouragement gave me the confidence to complete this project. Kind words from other members of the Cather community, especially Joseph Urgo and Richard Harris (the most gentlemanly scholar I have ever met), also convinced me, for better or worse, that a specialist in war literature turned novice Catherite might bring a helpful perspective to *One of Ours*, one of the most controversial novels of the 1920s, and *The Professor's House*, one of the most intensely analyzed.

At Fort Hays State University I am blessed with talented colleagues who are also fine editors—namely, Kristin Maple-Bloomberg, Robert Rook, and Bradley Will. All three took precious time out of their busy semesters (and even busier vacations) to critique this manuscript at various stages. To Bradley Will, proofreader par excellence, who scoured the entire text for stylistic infelicities and grammatical gaffes, I am indebted beyond words. From off campus, my friend Jim Barloon provided comments and corrections that strengthened the final text considerably.

Thanks go as well to the various faculty members and administrators at Fort Hays State University who approved my recent sabbatical leave. Without this block of uninterrupted time, which enabled me to make extensive use of materials housed in the Willa Cather Pioneer Memorial and in the Archives and Special Collections Department of the University of Nebraska–Lincoln Libraries, this book would never have been written. To the chair of my department, Albert Geritz, who cheerfully endorsed my sabbatical application despite the nightmarish staffing and budgetary problems that release time often creates, I am especially grateful.

Other individuals aided me directly in my research. Carolyn Herrman, head of the Interlibrary Loan Department at the FHSU Forsyth Library, processed my almost daily requests for obscure World War I volumes and tactfully ignored my habit of keeping materials long past their due date. In addition, Christie Green of the Liberty Memorial Fund in Kansas City, Missouri, shared her considerable expertise on the Liberty Memorial and kindly sent me copies of several rare pamphlets devoted to the monument's design.

My fondest memories related to this book all have their origin in Red Cloud and Lincoln. At the Webster County Historical Museum in Red Cloud, curator Helen Mathew gave me a personalized tour of artifacts related to the First World War and supplied invaluable information on war memorials and veterans' posts in the region. Equally helpful and friendly, Dorothy Mattison tirelessly searched the archives of the Willa Cather Pioneer Memorial for items of interest and patiently waited (for several hours at a time) while I studied Dr. Frederick Sweeney's diary, as well as several files related to *One of Ours*. In the Archives and Special Collections Department of the University of Nebraska–Lincoln Libraries, I enjoyed working with an extraordinarily attentive and knowledgeable staff—the finest, in fact, that I have ever encountered in a research library. Carmella Garman and Tom Mooney guided me through the immense Bernice Slote and Philip L. and Helen Cather Southwick Collections, made countless photocopies, and, best of all, offered many wise suggestions regarding the direction of my research. Katherine Walter kindly answered my queries regarding permissions and proper citations. At the Nebraska State Historical Society, Chad Wall showed great consideration as he assisted me with the society's extensive collection of Willa Cather–related photographs, several of which appear in this volume.

Finally, I must thank my wife and two daughters (our resemblance to the St. Peter household is uncomfortably noted) for bearing with me on days when Willa Cather's fiction entertained my thoughts to the exclusion of everything else, including several home-repair projects that I can postpone no longer. This book is dedicated to Maniphone, Madeline, and Natalie, who have made my professor's house such a happy one.

MEMORIAL FICTIONS

INTRODUCTION

Military conflict frames and in many respects defines Willa Cather's life and career. Born in 1873 into a family that included numerous Confederate veterans, Cather spent her childhood in Frederick's County, Virginia, a region of divided loyalty (in some cases brother had literally fought against brother), and her adolescence in Webster County, Nebraska, where the rites of the local GAR Post ensured that the War between the States remained a source of legend and high ideals. By the time of her death in 1947, one year after the demise of her futurist contemporary H. G. Wells (1866–1946), Cather had witnessed two world wars and seen a host of technological horrors unleashed against modern armies and civilian populations. The novelist's seventy-four years extend from the final volleys of the age of black powder to the detonation of the atomic bomb—from the last of the Indian wars to the beginning of the Cold War.

Transformed during Cather's lifetime by applied science and the emergence of "total warfare" (the practice of mobilizing an entire population to defeat the enemy by any means necessary), military violence held a lasting appeal to her artistic imagination. For example, long before Cather examined the "War to End All Wars" in *One of Ours* and *The Professor's House*, she produced two works inspired by her maternal uncle William Seibert Boak, who at age nineteen was mortally wounded at the battle of Manassas. In "The Namesake," a poem Cather composed in 1902 that was subsequently included in her first book, *April Twilights* (1903), the male speaker offers a Housemanesque meditation on his dead uncle, a "lad" who "flung his splendid life away / Long before I saw the day," and in lines that anticipate Claude Wheeler's libidinous zest for battle, gushingly declares his desire to join the fallen:

> I'd be quick to quit the sun
> Just to help you hold your gun,
> And I'd leave my girl to share
> Your still bed of glory there. (26)

Cather's short story, also titled "The Namesake" (1907), focuses on an expatriate sculptor who becomes cathartically reconnected to his homeland while studying an ancestor's heroism in the American Civil War. Captivated by the memory of his boy uncle, who died while leading a charge on an enemy fort, the story's Jamesean protagonist, Lyon Hartwell, shakes off his earlier indifference to "race and blood and kindred" (146) and dedicates his artistic career to the production of patriotic war memorials. Reminders of the Civil War, whose commemorative culture Cather experienced in both its pro-Southern and pro-Northern manifestations, also appear throughout her mature fiction. There is the coroner in *My Ántonia*, "a mild, flurried old man, a Civil War veteran, with one sleeve hanging empty" (73), and of course Captain Forrester in *A Lost Lady*, who presumably earns his memorable title while "serving in the Civil War" (42). Even in *The Song of the Lark*, a text that seems far removed from the world of Grant or Lee, the conflict makes its inevitable appearance as the Moonstone Drama Club stages *The Drummer Boy of Shiloh*, part of which "took place in Andersonville prison" (86).

But it was the First World War, a now mostly forgotten conflict (at least in the United States), that had the greatest impact on Cather, both artistically and emotionally. Already colored by her intense affection for France and her conviction (shared by millions of Americans at the time) that Imperial Germany threatened to destroy "Civilization," the war became even more personal for Cather when her first cousin Grosvenor P. Cather was killed at the battle of Cantigny on 28 May 1918. Feelings between the two cousins had never been particularly warm. Cather found G.P. inarticulate, unsophisticated, and openly jealous of her success. However, as an escapee from Red Cloud, now settled (more or less happily) amid the whirl of New York City, Cather could identify with the desire for wider experience that G.P., once a sailor in the U.S. Navy, expressed during their last meeting in 1914. Seemingly condemned to an obscure destiny in the Webster County hamlet of Bladen (population: 498 [Faber 81]), the thirty-one-year-old Nebraskan represented the kind of failed adventurer Cather herself might have become had her flight from Nebraska depended less on formidable talent and unyielding willpower. Despite the dislike Cather apparently felt for her cousin, she nevertheless felt a connection to him, a sensation that intensified tenfold following his death as a volunteer officer in the American Expeditionary Forces (AEF). In the summer of 1918, she stayed with G.P.'s mother, Franc Cather, and read the wartime letters that Lieutenant Cather had regularly sent home, first from stateside training camps, then from the dugouts and trenches of the Western Front.[1] Fascinated and moved by the sense of exuberant self-fulfillment that her cousin described, Cather decided to write a novel about a young man, a similarly dissatisfied Nebraskan, who finds release and then death amid the Great Adventure. Nearly four years of agonizing writing and rewriting followed as Cather struggled to complete the bulkiest of her major works and fact-check each and every detail in her rendering of the AEF at war, a subject Cather knew she would have to capture with absolute plausibility or risk offending Army veterans and offering an easy target to book reviewers.

The work of fiction that finally emerged from this long and difficult creative process stands among the most controversial American novels of the 1920s. Thus, before outlining my own interpretation of Cather's contribution to the literature of the Great War, a brief history of the critical debate over *One of Ours*—one of *two* novels Cather wrote in response to the conflict—is in order. From the beginning, *One of Ours* touched a nerve. H. L. Mencken blasted the book's allegedly fanciful depiction of military heroics. Sinclair Lewis bemoaned its descent into sentimentality. And Ernest Hemingway even coined an especially cruel term to capture the novel's supposed failings as a portrayal of war. In *One of Ours*, he wrote to Edmund Wilson (who also delivered a negative notice of the novel), the

Great War had been "Catherized" (105)—in other words, distorted and romanticized by a woman writer hopelessly out of her depth. Until fairly recently academic evaluations have not been particularly kind either.[2] In his 1960 study of Cather's fiction, *The Landscape and the Looking Glass*, John H. Randall III asserted that the novel had dated quickly, like a Jazz Age Victrola, and appeared embarrassingly "overblown to a reader who has lived into the nineteen-fifties" (171). Four years later Dorothy Van Ghent confessed in an essay on Cather that she wished *One of Ours* could be "quietly buried without remark" (99). And finally, in perhaps the most damning evaluation of all, Stanley Cooperman's 1967 study of American World War I literature cast *One of Ours* as the literary equivalent of a Liberty Loan poster from 1917. Unable to confront the antiheroic realities of the Western Front, the novel falls back on "the stereotypes of war rhetoric, the picture of clean-cut American boys marching to save the world" (30). Nor was it possible, Cooperman claimed, to read this distasteful element of the novel ironically: "[W]here the naïveté of [John Dos Passos's] *Three Soldiers* represents dramatic irony, the naïveté in *One of Ours* represents Miss Cather herself" (188). According to Cooperman, only the link between Claude Wheeler's sexual frustration and his appetite for battle, a presumably unconscious connection on Cather's part, made the novel worthy of study.

Cooperman's influential appraisal of *One of Ours*, with its patronizing references to "Miss Cather" and echoes of the scathing contemporary assessments offered by Mencken, Lewis, and Hemingway, faced little opposition until the publication in 1975 of David Stouck's *Willa Cather's Imagination*. At this point, one might say, the world of criticism on *One of Ours* broke in two. For Stouck, the novel denounced by so many as a work of naive patriotism represented a sophisticated, even cunning piece of "satire" aimed at both the shallow values of contemporary Middle America *and* the militaristic delusions of its protagonist. As for the novel's allegedly preposterous treatment of the First World War, "The author's stylistic intention," Stouck contended, "was not to describe the war in a realistic manner, but to reflect the romantic aura that for so many men gathered around the experience" (92). As Cather studies exploded in the 1980s, ignited by feminism and the proliferation of new theoretical approaches, other critics reached similar conclusions. For example, two major articles in 1984 — Frederick T. Griffith's "Woman Warrior" and Jean Schwind's "'Beautiful' War in *One of Ours*" — helped bolster Stouck's argument that Claude Wheeler's vision of the "War to End All Wars" was most certainly *not* Willa Cather's.[3] Griffith placed the second half of the novel "within the realm of Claude's illusions" (265) and explained that Cather could not have provided the unbroken string of naturalistic horrors that critics such as Mencken and Lewis expected of war fiction without being unfaithful to her chosen point of view. Similarly, Schwind argued that "[f]ar from extolling Claude's 'fulfillment' on the battlefield, [*One of Ours*] insists that Claude dies doubly duped . . . the boy who has been 'terribly afraid of being fooled' all his life is as fatally 'fooled' by his romantic ideals as he is lovingly 'fooled' by Sergeant Hicks" (56).

Still more support for the ironic reading of *One of Ours* came in 1987 from James Woodress, Cather's foremost biographer. In *Willa Cather: A Literary Life*, Woodress claimed that the harsh response by many reviewers (and subsequent critics) stemmed from inattentive reading: such reviewers "did not read carefully to see that Cather had no illusions about the war" and "simply ignored the fact that the novel is told mostly from Claude's point of view" (326). In her influential study of Cather's romanticism published one year before Woodress's widely read biography, Susan J. Rosowski likewise added to the growing body of criticism bent on resuscitating *One of Ours*. Her discussion of the novel stressed Claude's "willed blindness" and noted constant ironic discrepancies between the protagonist's enthusiasm and the often horrific scenes that confront him on the battlefield. For Woodress and Rosowski, *One of Ours* focuses not on the Great War but on Claude's limited perceptions of his quixotic experiences, which reach their climax in his mock-heroic journey over there.

Typical of what Joan Acocella has described as "the unreliable-narrator school of Cather criticism" (41), the readings put forward by defenders of *One of Ours* hinge on the assumption that throughout the text Claude serves as an ironic center of consciousness, one whose misjudgments and romantic excesses are simply passed along to the reader, without explicit judgment or commentary, by the limited third-person narrator. Not everyone shares the view, however, that Cather's sentiments toward the First World War bear little or no resemblance to Claude Wheeler's. Not everyone perceives the ironic subtext that David Stouck first unveiled. Indeed, in criticism published since the mid-1980s, opinion on the novel remains as starkly divided as the opposing trenches on the Western Front. Among the naysayers, for example, we find Hermione Lee, who considers *One of Ours* a "painful and unsatisfying book" (179), due largely to its unsuccessful mythologizing of the Great War, and Guy Reynolds, who contends that after loading the novel with a number of shockingly gory scenes, Cather then seemingly felt entitled to "present the idealistic glory of war without apology" (121). In contrast, Merrill Maguire Skaggs emphatically asserts that "the central fact about *One of Ours* that one must see in order to read it intelligently at all is that the book is bathed and saturated in irony" (40). Clearly, as students of Cather's fiction, we have not yet agreed whether this troublesome novel is one of ours or not. Despite Skaggs's enviable confidence, there are still plenty of readers (including, I suspect, some who have read the text "intelligently") who would eject it from the Cather canon as a hopelessly dated period piece, one whose portrayal of personal liberation through war, if read without the expectation of irony, is entirely offensive.

Given Cather's current stature as a major American writer, one might assume that the eighty-year-old debate over *One of Ours* matters little to our general understanding of her achievement. Yet Cather's creative encounter with the First World War differed sharply from those of other famous literary noncombatants, the vast majority of whom—including Edith Wharton, Upton Sinclair, Thomas Hardy, John Galsworthy, George Bernard Shaw, and H. G. Wells—wrote of the conflict long after producing the works upon which their reputations rest. In 1918, when the American military presence on the Western Front reached its peak, Cather was already an established, critically acclaimed author generally recognized as one of the premier literary talents in America. Behind her stood *O Pioneers!*, *The Song of the Lark*, and *My Ántonia*. But her greatest works—*A Lost Lady*, *The Professor's House*, and *Death Comes for the Archbishop*—were still to come. And all would appear less than ten years after the armistice. Thus, the First World War intersected with Cather's career at a critical moment. *One of Ours* was not in any way peripheral to her artistic and professional development: the novel took her nearly four years to write; demanded more painstaking research than any of her earlier works; won her a wider audience than she had previously enjoyed (as well as the Pulitzer Prize); earned her a considerable amount of money; and placed her, a woman writer trespassing on the supposedly masculine territory of war fiction, at the center of a longstanding debate over what constitutes, to quote Tim O'Brien, a "true war story" (76). In short, Cather's most problematic and perhaps least popular novel stands at the very center of her oeuvre; it cannot be "quietly buried without remark."

Nor, as I will argue in the following chapters, should we wish to do so. This study offers an extended reexamination of *One of Ours* and *The Professor's House* and, in regard to the former, attempts to explain why such a serious and sophisticated work falls so far afield of what readers have come to expect of modern war fiction. By placing *One of Ours* within a number of hitherto unfamiliar contexts, I have tried to occupy a critical no-man's-land between Cooperman's interpretation and that of Stouck. The divergent, even diametrically opposed readings that *One of Ours* has accommodated during its critical history suggest that the novel is far more modernist than most critics have assumed and therefore largely indifferent to the rhetorical strategies whereby more traditional novels communicate their themes. Indeed, with its plethora of internal contradictions, unstable point of view, and overall thematic nebulousness, the text has much in common with a Conrad novel. Ultimately, the novel neither glorifies American participation in the Great War nor consistently satirizes martial idealism. Rather, the text engages the reader in a complex and unsettling analysis that simultaneously conveys the attractions of military conflict (especially for a now frontierless America) and its dehumanizing barbarity. Like Conrad, whose modernist fictions generate more questions than answers, Cather demonstrates that the "truth" about war is more elusive than we think, its motivations and satisfactions more deeply rooted in the American psyche than we would care to admit.[4]

The quietly avant-garde nature of *One of Ours* becomes especially clear when we consider the wealth of cultural references in the text and the ambiguity-generating purposes for which Cather uses them. The novel achieves its disturbingly conflicted treatment of the First World War in part by summoning other cultural responses to the conflict that the text seemingly endorses one moment and jarringly subverts the next. Thus, my reading links the novel to an eclectic assortment of cultural artifacts drawn from its milieu including war memorials, unit histories, panoramic photographs, military citations and awards, and World War I–era postcards. By the same token, the analysis of *The Professor's House* that concludes this study argues that Cather's 1925 novel—or, more specifically, its sweeping evaluation of the First World War as "the great catastrophe" (236)—is no less tied to now forgotten contexts, especially the debate among postwar historians over historical relativism (a theoretical orientation produced partly by an unthinkable world war) and the controversy sparked in the early 1920s by so-called living memorials (functional structures such as the Marselluses' "Outland") that supposedly honored the dead by benefiting the living. Like Joseph Urgo and Guy Reynolds, whose studies have so effectively illuminated the presence of distinctly American myths in Cather's introspective art, I prefer to regard Cather as a writer not in retreat from her age but deeply, if ambivalently, connected to its ideological preoccupations and material culture.

Focused on what I have termed the iconography of remembrance—a pattern of imagery embraced by millions of Americans in the 1920s in order to produce an uplifting interpretation of the nation's one hundred thousand war dead—chapter 1 situates *One of Ours* within the culture of American military commemoration and argues that the text represents, at least on one level, a war memorial in prose—a memorial both to its hero and, less directly, to G. P. Cather. In particular, I parallel Cather's cathartic struggle to complete the novel with several equally urgent commemorative efforts from the same period: the construction of the Liberty Memorial in Kansas City, Missouri, one of the most elaborate World War I monuments in the United States; the interment of the original Unknown Soldier in Arlington National Cemetery, a ceremony that subtly revealed a lack of consensus in America over the true meaning of the Great War;

the reburial, amid considerable military ritual and fanfare, of G. P. Cather in Bladen, Nebraska; and finally, the activities of the Society of the First Division, an organization devoted to memorializing, in concrete and in print, the more than four thousand First Division soldiers (including Lieutenant Cather) who died on the Western Front.

In chapter 2 I seek to contextualize a much different dimension of Cather's text—Claude Wheeler's progress from miserable Nebraskan to exuberant *American*, a transformation that reflects Cather's prescient awareness that the Great War signaled, especially for the carefully indoctrinated citizen soldiers of the AEF, the advent of a more homogenized American worldview. The chapter begins with a discussion of Claude's infatuation with France, then considers how his cross-cultural yearning ultimately gives way to an overwhelming sense of solidarity with other Americans. Drawing on the reenvisioning of the AEF recently offered by historian Mark Meigs in *Optimism at Armageddon*, I suggest that *One of Ours*, not unlike Dos Passos's *U.S.A.*, adroitly analyzes the intersection of the Great War, which brought millions of American soldiers into a shared vision of their homeland, and the emergence of a truly national culture, a phenomenon made possible not only by the military melting pot of the AEF but by technological advances in media (such as cinema), ubiquitous consumerism, and the new science of public relations as practiced in both the government and private sector.

For Cather's harshest critics in 1922 (all of them male), whatever insight *One of Ours* offered into the cultural dynamics of America's first world war mattered little given the sheer preposterousness of the novel's scenes at the front lines. But is Cather's portrayal of combat, or of World War I Army life in general, truly as distorted as these early critics claimed? James Woodress has already provided an effective rebuttal to attacks on the novel's verisimilitude by citing numerous similarities between the protagonist's adventures in France and those of Harry S. Truman, another discontented farm boy who found the First World War exhilarating (see "A Note on *One of Ours*" 4). Claude Wheeler's idealism, it would seem, was hardly anomalous. Building on this argument, I contend in chapter 3 that Cather not only captured in Claude a sensibility shared by many enthusiastic doughboys (thousands of whom later became members of the ultra-patriotic and anything but disillusioned American Legion) but also managed to evoke, through the combat situations that Hemingway found so laughable, many of the most famous legends of the war. Indeed, a careful reading of the war chapters in *One of Ours* reveals that Cather calculatingly drew on situations that were part of almost any front-line soldier's experience — entering the trenches for the first time, liberating a French village, tracking down a sniper, joining the Meuse-Argonne Offensive (where more than one million Americans saw action), and so forth — *and* those that became the inspiration for popular folklore, especially the ordeal of the Lost Battalion, which is echoed throughout the final battle in which Claude loses his life. Here again *One of Ours* emerges as an expansive examination of then-recent history and the cultural myths used by Americans to understand it.

In chapter 4 I shift the focus from *One of Ours* to *The Professor's House* and argue that the First World War stands much closer to the thematic center of this cryptic text than most critics have acknowledged. Indeed, the nihilistic "vacuum" into which Outland vanishes constitutes "the thing not named" in *The Professor's House*. In keeping with the artistic practices outlined in Cather's essay "The Novel Démeublé," the war haunts the text as an all-important but nearly invisible phantom whose ghostly significance extends even to scenes that do not contain any references to the conflict itself. Thus, I argue that St. Peter's encounter with Horace Langtry, for example, evokes professional disagreements that indirectly have their origin in the Great War. Likewise, the professor's lecture on the role of science and technology in modern history (in a scene that similarly avoids any explicit mention of modern warfare) reveals a host of sinister implications once placed alongside Tom Outland's disturbing journey from the Blue Mesa to the Western Front. While *One of Ours* explores the complexity of martial idealism, and so vacillates in its depiction of the Great War, *The Professor's House* offers a vision of the conflict uncompromising in its bleakness.

In addition, I contend that if *One of Ours* represents, at least on one level, a war memorial in prose, then *The Professor's House* trenchantly analyzes the activity of memorializing itself. Cather's most intensely studied novel can be seen, in this respect, as a sequel to her most disparaged one. *One of Ours* focuses on a young man moving ever closer to his fatal destiny on the battlefield. *The Professor's House*, on the other hand, probes the aftermath of such a destiny (almost as if Cather had taken the final chapter of *One of Ours* and expanded it into an entire novel) by examining the multiple, often ironically conflicting legacies left by a lost youth for his survivors. How, the novel asks, are the war dead, those permanently in the Outland, to be commemorated by the living? Ultimately, the characters' inability to agree on an answer to this question—or to conceive of a stable myth that explains Tom Outland's extraordinary life and shadowy death—reflects the failure of American culture in the 1920s to assimilate the contradictory realities of the Great War into a coherent pattern of meaning.

For too long both *One of Ours* and *The Professor's House* have received only passing mention in studies of World War I literature. Lingering doubts about the artistic merits of *One of Ours*, traceable to the animosity it provoked in influential male reviewers (most of whom, ironically enough, had never been to war), have largely prevented its serious consideration alongside World War I "classics" such as *All Quiet on the Western Front, Good-bye to All That, Testament of Youth, A Farewell to Arms, Three Soldiers,* and *The Enormous Room*. Indeed, for evidence of the tenacity with which the novel's contemporary reception still clings to its reputation even after two decades of sympathetic revision, one need only consult Patrick J. Quinn's recent article, "The Experience of War in American Patriotic Literature." Here one reads that *One of Ours* represents a belated variation on the "formulaic romanticism" (760) used by wartime writers such as Arthur Guy Empey to stir up hatred for the Hun and to boost enlistment. In the case of *The Professor's House*, generally regarded as one of Cather's finest novels, different obstacles have thwarted a full appreciation of the work's richness as a statement on industrialized warfare. In particular, the way Cather establishes the First World War as a spectral presence in her text—as "the thing not named"—threatens, at times, to obscure its significance altogether. One often wishes, for the sake of Cather's war-related themes, that fewer "furnishings" had been hauled out of view. When examined more closely, however, Cather's analysis of the First World War in these two novels emerges as a major achievement, one worthy to stand beside her groundbreaking treatment of Nebraska settlers in *O Pioneers!* and *My Ántonia* and her haunting evocation of a more remote and less personal past in *Death Comes for the Archbishop* and *Shadows on the Rock*. In a paradox of the kind that abounds in *One of Ours*, the ugly "catastrophe" of war inspired some of Cather's most beautiful, if unsettling, art.

I

AMERICANS LOST

Perhaps nothing better symbolizes the prominence of war in the life and works of Willa Cather than the concrete obelisk that stands in the northwest corner of the Red Cloud city park, across the street from the house where Cather lived from 1884 to 1890, now a national landmark. Constructed in 1949, just two years after Cather's death, and situated presumably to command the attention of local townspeople and literary pilgrims alike, the obelisk is a veterans' memorial upon which appear the names of every Webster County citizen (including the novelist's cousin, G. P. Cather) who died in the First or Second World War, the Korean War, or the Vietnam conflict. "By building and using the Veterans' Memorial," wrote the author of the program distributed at the monument's dedication ceremony in 1951, "we are remembering our heroic dead by helping the living" ("Dedication of the War Memorial" n. pag.). Separated by just a few yards, these two shrines—one a monument to the mythmaking power of literature, the other an effort to impose a lasting, affirmative interpretation on the sacrifice of young men— create a striking juxtaposition that conveys the proximity of Cather's art to the cultural forms through which Americans have paid tribute to our "heroic dead" for over two centuries.

Indeed, to visit the sites associated with Cather's formative years

in Red Cloud is to encounter the indelible imprint of military commemoration on small-town America. The largest monument in the
Red Cloud cemetery, for example, is the statue of a Civil War infantryman (not unlike one of Lyon Hartwell's fictional creations)
erected in 1904 by the local GAR Post and dedicated to "the memory
of the Unknown Dead of the Union Army and Navy." In addition,
the stretch of state highway that approaches Red Cloud from the
south, passing the Willa Cather Prairie and the signpost announcing
one's arrival into "Catherland," is designated a "Memorial Highway"
by the American Legion. And even if Willa Cather had never achieved
fame as a writer, at least one prominent institution in Red Cloud
would still bear the Cather name—the G. P. Cather Post of the
American Legion, which, like all legion posts, honors through its
title an especially distinguished local casualty. Vintage World War I
tributes to military sacrifice also appear in the Willa Cather Pioneer
Memorial, a stone bank building once owned by Silas Garber (the
model for Captain Forrester in Cather's *Lost Lady*) that now contains
Cather exhibits and a research archive, and in the Webster County
Historical Museum, a converted mansion on the western edge of
town. Inside the memorial's walk-in vault hangs the document presented to G. P. Cather's parents in 1922 announcing the inscription of
their son's name "upon the State Roll of Honor." In the museum one
may view the American flag that draped G.P.'s coffin when his body
was returned from France and reburied amid lavish ritual outside his
hometown of nearby Bladen in 1922.

In this chapter I explore the relationship between *One of Ours*
and the culture of martial remembrance and mourning so much in
evidence amid the literary landmarks of the Nebraska Catherland.
In telling the story of a crusading American soldier who finds fulfillment, then death amid the maelstrom of the First World War,
Cather drew from sources of imagery that were ubiquitous in the
1920s but all but forgotten today—namely, the public monuments
and memorial texts that honored the nation's war dead. In other
words, rather than reviving, as Stanley Cooperman suggests, the
"war rhetoric" (30) of propaganda posters from 1917–18, *One of
Ours* both employs and deconstructs patterns of meaning used by
countless Americans in the 1920s to *remember* the war and to make

sense of the more than one hundred thousand Americans who died in it.

The idea of relating Cather's work to such a context may at first seem eccentric. But the period during which Cather wrote *One of Ours* (1919–22) was one of frenetic, sometimes dangerous cultural mythmaking as the United States sought desperately to understand both the war it had supposedly won and the nature of the rapidly changing society that had emerged from it. Everywhere in the culture of the day there was a desperate desire for clear-cut meaning, which sometimes translated into scapegoating and intensified racism. For example, as the nation vacillated between celebrating its part in the Great War and retreating into a new era of isolationism, the excessive belligerence whipped up by almost two years of Hun-hating propaganda found postwar release through the paranoid fictions of the Red Scare and through the activities of the suddenly "respectable" Ku Klux Klan, which broadened its appeal in the 1920s by targeting immigrants as well as African Americans. Revealingly, in 1923, the year Cather won the Pulitzer Prize in the novel category, the Pulitzer for "meritorious public service rendered by a newspaper" went to the *Memphis Commercial Appeal* for its "courageous attitude" toward the Klan, whose membership in the 1920s soared into the millions ("Nebraska Authoress").

The period also saw a wave of military commemoration on an unprecedented scale—even vaster than that which followed the Civil War—as millions of Americans sought (just as Cather did by writing her novel) to interpret what had in fact been a bewildering national experience. While American Legion halls, each a monument in its own right, appeared on virtually every Main Street in the country, concrete doughboys sprang up in front of virtually every county courthouse and city hall. Bridges, parks, and sports arenas (including the Memorial Stadium dedicated in 1923 at Cather's alma mater, the University of Nebraska) paid homage to the war dead. Pershing Street, or Pershing Boulevard, became a ubiquitous feature on American street maps.

At the same time in France, where the vast desolation of the Western Front invited memorializing on an even grander scale, Pershing himself presided over the work of the American Battlefield

Monuments Commission, whose gargantuan, neoclassical shrines overlooking such blood-soaked regions as the Marne and the Argonne might lead one to conclude that the United States single-handedly won the Great War. So too might the boastful pages of the innumerable company, regimental, and divisional histories (texts that might more accurately be called memorial volumes) that poured out during this period, in some cases while their authors were still serving with the Army of Occupation in Germany or awaiting demobilization in France. Written with an audience of soon-to-be-nostalgic comrades in mind, such volumes describe a war that bears little resemblance to the set of tragic horrors Cooperman later saw at the heart of American World War I literature. Here the dead are honored as "our noble fallen," while cartoons, patriotic verse, and uplifting artwork distract the reader's attention from the command blunders and pointless wastage that such volumes often parenthetically describe. And finally, there were even plans in the early 1920s for what would have been the most grandiose gesture of military commemoration in American history—the so-called Victory Highway, the first paved, transcontinental roadway in the United States, complete with war-related statues and plaques at each county line and shade trees representing fallen soldiers (see Richmond).

Such a plethora of tributes to American military sacrifice and achievement would have been far more understandable following the Second World War (a conflict that, paradoxically, attracted far fewer commemorative gestures). After all, in 1945 Americans could claim with good reason to have led the Allied powers to victory—perhaps not in terms of casualties (that terrible distinction fell to the Soviet Union, with more than nineteen million dead) but in terms of military technology, culminating in the atomic bomb, and industrial power. In contrast, no matter how enthusiastically Americans celebrated on 11 November 1918, almost everything about American participation in the First World War soon thwarted a sense of achievement unalloyed by feelings of ambivalence or doubt. For example, while American factories during the Second World War produced enough war material to support more than eleven million servicemen and women, spread out on opposite sides of the globe, the U.S. Army of 1917–18 was forced to borrow much of its equipment from the other Allies. The Army Tank Corps, then in its infancy, relied on French vehicles. American pilots flew French planes. American machine gunners operated French and British weapons. Even the helmets and uniforms worn by the doughboys came, in many cases, from the British. Though quick to move its economy onto a wartime footing, the United States never became in the First World War the industrial powerhouse that it would develop into in the Second World War.

Nor, despite the predictably exaggerated assessments of American military performance later offered by Pershing and other American commanders, was the short-lived American presence on the Western Front necessarily decisive. While one million American soldiers fought in the six-week battle of the Meuse-Argonne and endured a poison gas–filled hell equal in misery to the worst campaigns of the Second World War, their contribution to the Allied victory in November 1918 remained questionable, even dubious. As David Kennedy points out, despite Pershing's faith in the innate superiority of the American rifleman, American troops, undertrained and often incompetently led, aided the Allies only insofar as they added to the total number of bodies brought to bear on Germany's exhausted forces (204). At its heart, the First World War remained for the doughboys what it had been for the British and the French: a war of attrition generally lacking in decisive and dramatic moments. And as if these military vagaries were not enough, the immediate aftermath of the Great War only deepened the sense of ambiguity and contradiction surrounding the conflict. Woodrow Wilson's humiliating concessions at Versailles, where Allied statesmen made the Second World War all but inevitable, followed by the refusal of the U.S. Congress to support the League of Nations, called into question whether the world would ever be made safe for democracy. In addition, while the nation spent millions on war memorials, men disabled during the Great War received little if anything from the newly created Veterans' Bureau, an organization so corrupt that its exposure during Senate hearings in 1923 was second only to the Teapot Dome scandal in outrageous revelations (see Severo and Milford 247–63).

Thus, the United States' frenetic effort to memorialize the Great War perhaps derived less from confidence and conviction than from bewilderment and doubt—a theory that helps explain both the gigantism (ironically, American monuments in France often dwarf British and French ones) and the overly insistent symbolism that pervade the commemorative iconography. Viewing American World War I memorials as expressions of the nation's urgent desire to impose order on a particularly complex and contradictory national experience also opens a new perspective on *One of Ours*, the alleged failures of which have long been approached less as reflections of Cather's culture than as evidence of its author's personal limitations. In the following discussion, then, I maintain that "Cather's difficulties in gauging the true 'national significance' of the war" (123)—which Guy Reynolds astutely places at the heart of the novel—were far from unique, a point that becomes clear when we set Cather's personal need to understand the Great War by writing what amounts to a war memorial in prose alongside commemorative projects that involved thousands, in some cases millions, of Americans. In the first section of this chapter I discuss two such public endeavors, the creation of the Liberty Memorial in Kansas City, Missouri, and the reburial of the Unknown Soldier in Arlington National Cemetery, and then I examine how the tendrils of World War I commemoration found their way into the Cather family—and into the very soil of Webster County, Nebraska. In the second section I argue that Cather's subject in *One of Ours,* a life cut short in battle, invited a then popular discourse of military remembrance and mourning, a discourse that the novel intricately weaves into its modernist and ultimately cryptic rendering of war.

1. Commemoration and the American War Dead

Almost forgotten today—except by the voters of Kansas City, Missouri, who recently approved a sales-tax increase to pay for repairs to its crumbling structure—the Liberty Memorial is perhaps the most imposing World War I monument ever built in the United States. Consisting of a 217-foot tower, twin Memorial Buildings (one a museum, the other a hall designed for patriotic meetings), and thirty acres of grass and gardens, this massive shrine to the four hundred Kansas City residents who lost their lives in the Great

War sits high on a hill just south of Union Station where, until the arrival of the city's first true skyscrapers, it virtually dominated the downtown landscape (see fig. 1). The structure was so ambitious and imposing, in fact, that the dedication of the site in 1921 (just one year before the publication of *One of Ours*) attracted an assembly of world-famous military leaders whose names read like a who's who of the First World War: General Pershing was present, as were Gen. John J. Lejeune, the Marine hero of Belleau Wood, Marshall Ferdinand Foch, supreme commander of the Allied Armies, and Adm. David Beatty, commander of the British fleet at the battle of Jutland. Representatives from Belgium, Italy, and Serbia added to the throng of dignitaries who posed for photographers before the stone slab marking the location of the future tower. Thousands of American World War I veterans, on hand for the national American Legion Convention (also held in Kansas City that year), filled the areas slated to become gardens and lawns. The dedication of the finished structure, which cost nearly two million dollars, took place on Armistice Day 1926 and was rendered especially auspicious by the presence of President Calvin Coolidge, who delivered a speech following the solemn tolling of 11:00 A.M., Armistice Hour.

Located not in New York or even Chicago but in the kind of midsized, Midwestern city Sinclair Lewis captured so unsparingly in *Babbitt*—one of the novels, incidentally, that lost to *One of Ours* in the 1923 Pulitzer competition—the Liberty Memorial seems an unlikely candidate for such national, even international, attention. But the sheer scale of the undertaking combined, perhaps, with its resonant location at the center of the so-called American heartland made the monument something greater than a tribute to lost Kansas City residents: as evidenced by the popularity of the memorial as an image on travel postcards from the 1920s and '30s, the site quickly became one of the city's leading tourist attractions, inspiring visitors to reflect not only on the four hundred individuals honored directly, but on American losses in general.

Like all such monuments, the memorial's message to the grief-stricken is consolatory—but in a way far removed from that of the Vietnam Memorial in Washington DC, where visitors can actually *touch* the names of the dead and see their own faces intimately

Fig. 1. The Liberty Memorial in Kansas City, Missouri.
A postcard from the 1930s.

reflected on the black surface. In contrast, the Liberty Memorial emphasizes not the connection between the living and the dead but the distance between them—between the ordinary human beings who visit the memorial, who cannot help but be awed by it, and the superhuman heroes whom it commemorates. For example, inside the museum building, whose ceiling soars to nearly thirty feet, the names of the dead appear not at eye level or near the ground as they do on the Vietnam Memorial but on bronze tablets mounted far above the viewer's head. Indeed, everything about the Liberty Memorial conveys a sense of distance and immensity, as though its architects sought to squelch the ambiguities of the Great War through the sheer mass of their design. The stone terrace surrounding the tower, for instance, is nearly three hundred feet long, while the sides of the cavernous Memorial Buildings follow the steep incline of the hillside, forming sheer cliffs of concrete. Even the doors on the buildings are scaled to fit the memorial's titanic proportions: more than ten feet high and cast in bronze, they require an appropriately Herculean effort from visitors. And then there is the unseen memorial, equally colossal, hidden underground. Gigantic vaults, almost like bunkers from the Western Front, honeycomb the hillside and contain, in addition to extensive archives, one of the largest collections of World War I artifacts in North America.

Through its larger-than-life dimensions, the memorial lifts the war dead beyond the realm of ordinary experience, its acres of funereal concrete and bronze creating the impression of an enormous sepulcher, a crypt for titans. Set against the ambiguities of America's participation in the First World War, however, the structure's gigantism appears excessive, as though its designers, unable to find a human image that captured the event in its totality (as the statue of the flag raising on Iwo Jima attempts to do for the Second World War), concluded that architectural vastness suggested ad infinitum would in itself convey the essence of the Great War for Civilization. This sense of overcompensation also pervades the artwork that decorates the structure. Indeed, the Liberty Memorial is a monument not only to the First World War but to allegorical excess. Enormous stone sphinxes—one representing the past, the other the future—flank the stairs leading to the monument, while the "Guardian Spirits" of Honor, Courage, Patriotism, and Sacrifice gaze down from the top of the tower, their sword-bearing figures suggestive of Joan of Arc (a figure of considerable importance in *One of Ours*) and the spirit of Columbia. Likewise, the enormous frieze that faces Pershing Boulevard depicts through allegorical figures the progress of humanity from barbarism to civilization and presents the victorious conclusion of the Great War as the dawn of a utopian era—a considerable irony considering that the frieze was added to the monument in the 1930s, a time when many Americans feared that the "War to End All Wars" merely represented the prelude to an even bloodier conflict.

Perhaps the memorial's strangest and most telling feature, however, is the mural, titled *Le Pantheon de la Guerre*, that covers the walls of Memory Hall. This mural has a curious history. Created by two French artists, Pierre Carrier-Belleuse and Auguste-François Gorguet, who worked on it continuously from 1914 to 1919, the painting originally covered more than five thousand feet of canvas and depicted with photographic accuracy almost every imaginable political leader, military commander, and distinguished front-line foot soldier and aviator from the Allied nations in the Great War, all magically set against panoramic vistas of the actual battlefields. Displayed in Paris until 1927, the mural then passed into American hands, turning up, among other places, at the Chicago International Exposition of 1933 and then on the walls of a Baltimore barroom before finally being acquired by the Liberty Memorial Association (Meigs 221–23). In the artists' original conception, the United States was represented as one of several partner nations, its crowd of khaki crusaders and black-coated statesmen occupying a portion of the canvas that was surprisingly generous given the nation's late entry into the conflict and its debatable military contribution. Once transported to a monument at the heart of the American Midwest, however, the *Pantheon* underwent a predictable editing consistent with the memorial's overly emphatic celebration of American triumph: in the painting's final form, as Mark Meigs points out, "the figures representing the United States hold center stage" while the heroes of the other Allied nations are in the periphery (223). Trimmed and rearranged to serve the needs of its American audience, the mural captures perfectly the anxiety-driven willfulness with which the memorial, like all American World War I monuments, imposes its vision of superhuman sacrifice and achievement on a problematic set of realities. And like the memorial's gigantism, which ironically makes the structure seem remote from the mourners it sought to console, and its strained symbolism, which likewise lacks a sense of intimacy, the *Pantheon* fails to convey the clear and confident meaning that its American editors had in mind. Despite the best efforts of the memorial's staff, French soldiers and other exotic Europeans still appear scattered throughout the foreground, often distracting the viewer's attention from the American figures, while the entire canvas seems, thanks to its rearrangement, unbalanced and without a clear focal point.

Originally "shipped to the United States in a crate nine feet square at the ends and fifty-two feet long" (Meigs 223), *Le Pantheon de la Guerre* made its journey to the United States at a time when even more bizarre cargo arrived from France almost daily—namely, the exhumed remains of more than forty-five thousand American soldiers, an oceanic migration of the dead then unprecedented in history. Among others, former president Theodore Roosevelt, whose son

Quentin remained buried where he fell in France, opposed this removal of the dead, arguing that American KIAS (or, just as likely, doughboys who succumbed to influenza while serving overseas) would naturally wish to remain among their comrades in the sacred soil of the nation whose liberty they had vowed to defend. In the early 1920s, however, pressure from organizations such as the Bring Home the Soldier Dead League became too great, and in cities and towns across the United States the reburial of soldiers killed years earlier on the other side of the Atlantic became one of the defining rituals of the era. Indeed, so important was this gesture to the nation's ongoing assimilation of the Great War that in 1921, the same year as the Liberty Memorial's site dedication, the U.S. government created one of the most resonant public monuments of the twentieth century—the Tomb of the Unknown Soldier or, as it is known today, the Tomb of the Unknowns.

From the beginning, the tomb attracted a profusion of archaic ceremonial trappings that, like the gigantism of the Liberty Memorial, suggest an urgent effort to force the Great War into coherence. For example, the anonymous body housed within the monument was selected through a romantic, quasi-spiritualistic ritual held in the heart of the former American sector on the Western Front. The scene might have come straight from Arthur Conan Doyle: in the presence of military delegations from France and the United States, a blindfolded enlisted man, Sgt. Edward Younger, walked three times around the remains of four unidentified Americans and signaled his choice by laying a bouquet of white roses on one of the coffins (Meigs 147). Once transported to Washington DC, the soldier selected by Sergeant Younger became the focus of ceremonies that "rivaled the funeral of a president or general" (Piehler, *Remembering War the American Way* 119). More than ninety thousand citizens filed past the Unknown Soldier's coffin, which was placed in the rotunda of the Capitol on 9 November, while President Harding, the chief justice of the Supreme Court, the secretary of war, and General Pershing all bestowed the Unknown Soldier with ceremonial wreaths honoring his hypothetical courage and loyalty. Even more grandiose rituals followed. On Armistice Day, a procession consisting of the "president, all members of Congress, cabinet members, state governors, and high-ranking foreign representatives" (119), together with Congressional Medal of Honor winners and American Legion officials, accompanied the casket on its journey to the Memorial Amphitheater of Arlington National Cemetery. Crowds numbering in the hundreds of thousands lined the route. At 11:00 A.M., shortly before the Unknown Soldier's reburial, millions of Americans responded to President Harding's request for a nationwide observance of two minutes of silence.

As Mark Meigs notes, the consolatory appeal of the Unknown Soldier stemmed, paradoxically, from his lack of a specific identity: the soldier enshrined at Arlington could be anyone's missing son, husband, or father and, for that matter, could be claimed as the representative of any racial, ethnic, or religious group in the United States (147). Thus, African American veterans, so ill-used during the war, joined the ceremonies on 11 November, as did representatives from such diverse organizations as the Jewish Welfare Board, the Knights of Columbus, and the National Catholic War Council. Perhaps the most dramatic display of inclusiveness came when, at the invitation of the federal government, Crow chief Plenty Coups placed a wreath on the tomb. The chief "also presented a magnificent eagle-feather bonnet and a decorated croup stick to honor those killed in World War I" and in his address (delivered in the Crow language) expressed his hope that "there will be peace to all men hereafter" (Britten 160). Variously identified, depending on the group bestowing the honors, the Unknown Soldier was everyone and no one—both Jew and Gentile, Protestant and Catholic, white and black, European and Native American. Thus, he was "essentially a void" (Meigs 147).[1] Unlike the allegorical artwork of the Liberty Memorial, designed to steer awestruck visitors at every turn, the nameless body housed within the tomb invited mourners to define his significance for themselves. This perhaps explains why the monument (which now contains additional unknowns selected after later wars) continues to resonate with the American public, attracting over four million visitors a year, while the once famous Liberty Memorial has fallen into obscurity and neglect (Meigs 147).

But what of the thousands of *identified* bodies (nearly half the nation's war dead) also returned to the United States for reburial in the 1920s? What did their posthumous homecoming signify to Americans at the time? And what does this macabre phenomenon, which turns out to have a special relevance to the Cather family, tell us about the milieu within which Cather researched and wrote *One of Ours*? The desire on the part of immediate family members to see their dead brought home is understandable enough. However, such a large-scale removal of bodies that had in some cases already been exhumed and reburied several times (and whose mass transportation on French trains and then on merchant vessels posed serious health concerns) also points, once again, to a widespread sense of uncertainty, at least in the 1920s, surrounding the ultimate meaning of American participation in the Great War. Indeed, the return of America's "fallen," to use the popular euphemism of the day, addressed more than anything else the nation's need for an affirmative vision of wartime loss no longer tied to the now suspect ideals for which America had originally fought. In France, American gravesites symbolized, by their very presence, the cost of American intervention in a European conflict, an intervention whose progressive aspirations appeared increasingly dubious in light of the Treaty of Versailles and the ineffectuality of the League of Nations. However, once separated from "over there" and reintegrated into the geographically and culturally familiar, the dead could be redefined, less as martyrs to Wilsonian internationalism (although the image of America as the chivalrous defender of France remained a vital component in stateside commemoration) than as members of an American military tradition that upheld duty and self-sacrifice for their own sake. Buried in family plots alongside Civil War veterans and often beneath stone monoliths that resemble miniature Liberty Memorials, their graves dutifully decorated each Armistice Day with wreaths of poppies and American Legion emblems, the dead could retain an uplifting meaning even without the dawning of the Brave New World that they had gone to France to create.

Among the lost Americans whose remains made their way to the United States in the 1920s was Willa Cather's Nebraska cousin (see fig. 2). Not everyone in the Cather family approved of the return of G. P. Cather's remains. Apparently sharing Theodore Roosevelt's conviction that America's fallen should remain in France,

Franc Cather, for example, revealed in a letter to E. H. Prettyman, G.P.'s former sergeant, that she disagreed with her daughter-in-law's decision to have the body sent home. "I would like," she wrote, "to say just what I think but better not."[2] Despite the reservations of the deceased's mother, on 3 May 1921, more than two thousand people gathered in the tiny town of Bladen, located on the northern edge of Webster County, to witness what the *Bladen Enterprise* proudly called "the final chapter in the heroic career of Lieut. G. P. Cather, first Nebraska officer to pay the supreme sacrifice upon the battlefields of France" ("Impressive Military Funeral"). The ceremony began in the Bladen Opera House, where the hero's flag-draped coffin was displayed alongside his eleven military medals, which included a posthumously awarded Distinguished Service Cross, the nation's second-highest decoration. Photographs of the event show the Opera House stage almost covered in commemorative paraphernalia (see fig. 3). American flags, a souvenir pennant that recognizes G. P. Cather's service in the Mexican Border Expedition of 1916, photographs of the deceased, and an almost suffocating array of floral decorations surround the casket, suggesting, again like the gigantism and excessive allegorizing of the Liberty Memorial, an anxious effort to fill in the interpretive vacuum created by the Great War. Following musical performances by Legionnaires and a sermon by a former army captain, the mourners formed a procession, which included eight flower girls dressed as Red Cross nurses, and slowly walked behind the horse-drawn hearse that carried the coffin to Bladen's East Lawn Cemetery. For the editors of the *Bladen Enterprise*, this solemn march eastward, in the direction that America's soldiers had sailed and then launched their triumphant offensives three years earlier, almost seemed to transport its participants to the Western Front itself. The paper noted that the "sun glinted upon the guns of the firing squad . . . and above all was the tread of marching feet." For a moment, the sounds and sensations of the procession eerily resembled those of an American unit moving up into the line.

But as the *Enterprise* article makes clear, the consolatory significance of the ceremony stemmed precisely from the fact that it was not held in France. Lieutenant Cather had come home, and now his death could be properly situated within American military traditions

Fig. 2. G. P. Cather in uniform.
Courtesy of the Nebraska State Historical Society.

Fig. 3. The G. P. Cather funeral in Bladen, Nebraska.
Courtesy of the Nebraska State Historical Society.

and aligned with the needs of his community. After the deceased's relatives took their places in the Opera House, the *Enterprise* noted, they were followed by "the uniformed soldiers and sailors of the late war, a few old Civil War veterans, and several Spanish American War soldiers." Three generations of citizen soldiers helped to usher a fellow warrior into the pantheon of American military heroes. In a sermon titled "What Is Life" the main speaker, Capt. Fred O. Kelly, spoke less of making the world safe for democracy than of the example set by Cather for his family and neighbors: "To die for others, as did Lieut. Cather, was all that he could possibly do. . . . It is indeed the supreme sacrifice. Although we can in no way measure up to what he did upon the field of battle, we can at least live a clean, upstanding life. . . . [O]ur efforts in this direction should be tireless. It is no more than should be expected of us."

To ensure further, as the *Enterprise* put it, "that the story of [G. P. Cather's] bravery and gallantry will be handed down through history," the American Legion subsequently erected an elaborate headstone in his honor (see fig. 4). The monument remains the chief attraction in Bladen, the one reason why non-natives (Cather enthusiasts mostly) turn off the state highway to visit this dwindling town with its all but abandoned Main Street. The soldier's face, modeled in bronze and copied from the oval portrait that appears beside his coffin in photographs of the Opera House service, looks toward Bladen. The inscription, however, emphasizes the deceased's exotic destiny on the other side of the Atlantic:

> Lieut. G. P. Cather
> August 12, 1883
> Killed in Action
> At the Battle of Cantigny, France
> May 28, 1918
> Co. A 26th Inft. First Div.

The final three lines of this inscription (designating the battle in which he died and the unit with which he served) are customary on military headstones, but they also hold a special significance and help explain why G. P. Cather's fate attracted a variety of commemorative gestures that go far beyond the lonely graveyard in Bladen. Heralded

Fig. 4. The G. P. Cather monument,
East Lawn Cemetery, Bladen, Nebraska. Photograph by author.

by newspapers at the time, which made far more of the incident than its scale or strategic value warranted, the battle of Cantigny was the first American battle of the war. And by the standards of World War I carnage and stalemate, it represented a remarkable, if localized, victory. On 28 May 1918, following a one-hour bombardment by nearly four hundred pieces of artillery, infantrymen from the First Division (the first American unit to arrive in France and by the end of the war one of the most respected and experienced) climbed out of their trenches, advanced across no-man's-land, and successfully occupied the ruined village of Cantigny, part of a swath of French countryside recently captured by the Germans during their massive spring offensive. For the next two days the doughboys managed to beat back a series of German counterattacks and endured an almost constant barrage of high-explosive and poison-gas shells hurled at them from three sides.

Like the Little Round Top–style military action with which Cather concludes *One of Ours*, the battle lacked little in the way of drama. But its successful outcome was never in doubt. Under constant pressure to disband his autonomous American force and to feed his troops into the depleted ranks of the French and British armies, Pershing staged the battle more for the benefit of French observers than anything else, and he made sure that the attack was too well rehearsed and too modest in its objectives to fail. Moreover, as Edward Coffman points out in *The War to End All Wars*, the German division facing the Americans received only a third-class rating in terms of morale and fighting ability from the intelligence section of Pershing's staff (158). With a more committed enemy, the battle of Cantigny might have turned out quite differently. As it was, the attack resulted in approximately 1,000 American casualties (G. P. Cather was one of 45 officers killed), as opposed to 1,400 German losses, a questionable figure that likely reflects the U.S. Army's pressing need to prove its ferocity to France and Great Britain.

Still, for Americans in 1918, the name Cantigny took on a luster that never quite faded even after the AEF, which grew tenfold by the time of the armistice, plunged into much larger and far bloodier battles. A museum devoted to the First Division, located outside of Chicago, is still known today as the Cantigny Memorial, and to the men of the First Division who went on to participate in one harrowing campaign after another (more, in fact, than any of the twenty-eight other American combat divisions that served in the First World War), the battle represented a special distinction: as a period postcard produced for the First Division by the YMCA boasts, the so-called Big Red One earned its title not only by arriving in France ahead of everyone else but by being "first to shoot at Germans, first to attack, and first to suffer casualties." (The postcard also implies, with perverse pride, that the division earned its nickname by suffering more casualties than almost any other organization in the AEF—21,612, to be exact.) Survivors of the battle of Cantigny later wore a special clasp on their Victory Medal designating their service in America's first battle of the Great War and received from the French the *fourrage* (a green and red braid worn over the left shoulder), an honorary piece of regalia bestowed upon few American soldiers.

Because its circumstances guaranteed instant public attention— Willa Cather's cousin was, after all, the first Nebraska officer to die overseas, a casualty in the U.S. Army's premier engagement—G. P. Cather's fate provides a rich case study in what one might call the "sense-making mechanisms" of military discourse and commemorative ritual. Indeed, almost from the moment the lieutenant died, an ever-tightening web of uplifting interpretation seized upon his memory (that is, shaped that memory to suit the ideals of the army and the needs of the bereaved) and, in a manner that culture critic Elaine Scarry has identified as typical of military discourse, sought to conceal the gruesome realities of his death. For example, in accord with the standard practice of the day, men who had served with G. P. Cather—including the commander of his regiment, none other than Theodore Roosevelt, Jr.—quickly wrote to his wife, Myrtle Cather, and offered predictably glowing testimonials of the novice officer's abilities as well as details pertaining to his demise. Subsequently reprinted in the *Bladen Enterprise*, their letters memorialize G.P.'s earnestness, courage, and concern for his men.

By far the most vivid tribute to G. P. Cather came, however, from a Red Cross worker named Anne Taylor, who wrote to Myrtle Cather from Paris on 18 October 1918. In a hospital in France Taylor had encountered a wounded soldier, Sgt. E. H. Prettyman, who served under Cather at Cantigny. Amazingly, when asked if he could relate any information about G.P.'s final moments, Prettyman "reached under his pillow and pulled out some bits of paper. These," Taylor explained to Myrtle Cather, "were the last orders your husband had given him."[3] The sergeant then told Taylor of Cather's death in dramatic detail:

> "It was May 28, the night after we took Cantigny. We were in the trenches in the wood, and the shelling was awful. It was raining shells. We were loosing many men. The Lieutenant

wouldn't keep off the top of the trenches, but kept out there to look after the men. He worried more about them than about himself. I begged him not to go.

He was down at the post—it was in the afternoon, but in the excitement, I couldn't tell just what time—and he was talking to some men there, trying to cheer them up. There were no dugouts and the tranches were 4 feet deep. We lost 19 men out of 42. He turned around to walk away from the trench—going forward—when a shell burst in front of him. He was thrown way back into the trench, on his back. A piece of shell had gone in just above his heart, killing him instantly. . . . That was his only injury. He hadn't suffered an instant, and was not disfigured."

With a literary flair that Cather would have appreciated, Taylor neatly framed the sergeant's words, presumably quoted from memory, with descriptions of the speaker, "a very intelligent sensitive boy." "It is evident," Taylor remarked, "that he loved [Cather] as few men love their officers. He was very much moved when he told me about what had happened—and more than once there were tears in his eyes."

Had Cather included in *One of Ours* the scene of a sergeant producing the final orders of his commanding officer from beneath a hospital pillow, H. L. Mencken or Sinclair Lewis would probably have seized upon the episode as yet another example of the novel's preposterousness. But Taylor's letter is tangibly real: it is stored in the Willa Cather Pioneer Memorial Archive, still in its yellowed envelope, and folded within it are several handwritten orders (dealing mostly with nighttime work details in no-man's-land), each torn from a French pocket diary and addressed to Sergeant Prettyman by none other than G. P. Cather. That Cather studied this document along with the numerous letters that Franc Cather later received from Prettyman himself seems certain given the many parallels between the sergeant's account and Claude Wheeler's fictional demise.[4] Like Lieutenant Cather, Lieutenant Wheeler coolly exposes himself to enemy fire by standing on the parapet of a trench and dies instantaneously from a chest wound. Moreover, Taylor's touching portrait of Prettyman's grief, three months and several battles after losing his first commander, perhaps inspired Cather's portrayal of the affectionate relationship between Claude Wheeler and his own second in command, Sergeant Hicks.

Although she may have mined Taylor's letter for evocative details, Cather likely understood that such testimonials typically derived less from the facts than from the well-meaning agenda of the officials who offered information to the bereaved. By tracing the correspondence between several American families, each seeking information on the fate of a missing loved one, and authorities in the AEF and the Red Cross, Mark Meigs has demonstrated that accounts of an individual's death in battle were frequently contradictory and unreliable (164–65). Burdened with the time-consuming and painful duty of writing to the relatives of dead men and confronted with the impossible challenge of reconstructing an individual's fate at a moment when eyewitnesses were desperately concerned with their own survival, officers in the AEF understandably turned to generic fictions: none of the soldiers whose families they consoled was ever frightened or incompetent; none died from anything more horrific than a small wound to the head or chest. In this way, bereft families received what the army thought they wanted—heroes who "fell" without pain or regret.

As a member of the Home Communication Service of the Red Cross, the title designated at the beginning of her letter, Anne Taylor likely felt a similar pressure to spare the Cather family the full details of G. P. Cather's demise. And although the inclusion of Lieutenant Cather's final orders substantiates what Taylor learned in her encounter with Sergeant Prettyman (as does the close resemblance between her transcription of Prettyman's story and the version he later supplied firsthand to Franc Cather), some of the details in her letter seem dubious.[5] Prettyman's statement, for example, that he "begged" his commander not to expose himself to danger is especially suspect given the high level of formality that World War I officers, even "90-day wonders" like Cather, typically observed when interacting with enlisted men. It is also interesting to note that the sergeant protests too much when emphasizing the mercifully sudden nature of Cather's death. After establishing that G.P. died "instantly" from an implausibly clean wound located "just above the heart,"

Prettyman returns to the topic a few lines later and stresses once again that "he hadn't suffered an instant, and was not disfigured." Taylor then reinforces this most likely sanitized account in the closing section of the letter, which she addresses to Myrtle Cather in her own words: "It must be something to know how wonderful he was at the moment when he died, and that he didn't suffer."

Thus, as remarkably detailed and vivid as Taylor's letter is, its purpose was far from strictly informational. On the contrary, by constructing G. P. Cather's death (an arbitrary, probably gruesome event, witnessed in the obscurity of battle by a handful of terrified men) as a lesson in courage and the selfless bonds between soldiers, the document represents an early contribution to the culture of commemoration that would later produce the Liberty Memorial and the Tomb of the Unknown Soldier. An accomplished writer, doubtless well practiced in the art of providing plausible consolation, Taylor knew how to put an uplifting spin on tragedy: G. P. Cather was gone, but his family could take solace not only in his macho indifference to danger and fatherly concern for his men but also in the sentimental portrait Taylor so skillfully drew of a "sensitive boy," himself terribly wounded, who still clung to the memory of his first commanding officer.

While Taylor's letter offers an intimate variety of commemoration, relying on "human interest" and specifics (whether real or invented) to present wartime loss in a heroic but individualized fashion, the military organization to which Cather belonged memorialized him in a quite different way. In February 1919 while the First Division served as part of the Army of Occupation in Germany, its officers formed a society dedicated to fostering future ties between First Division veterans and to commemorating the unit's contribution to the Allied victory. Job number one, not surprisingly, was the creation of monuments on the battlefields where the division had fought. Through "initiation fees and . . . a contribution of one hundred thousand francs from the Salvation Army" (Society 251), the Society of the First Division was able to afford five such shrines, including the one eventually erected (but apparently no longer standing)[6] at Cantigny, a concrete shaft covered with the names of the men killed in the battle and surmounted by the image of an eagle

Fig. 5. A First Division battlefield memorial in France.
Courtesy of the Society of the First Infantry Division.

perched on an artillery projectile (see fig. 5). In contrast with many of
the First Division's other commemorative projects, the monument
offered little, apart from its symbolic American eagle, in the way of
patriotic or chivalric iconography. Instead the structure relied for
its effect on the dense columns of names (including G. P. Cather's)
that stood out starkly on its face. Noticeably absent was any sort of
rhetorical exhortation or Liberty Memorial–style allegorizing.

In his study of British monuments and cemeteries along the Western Front, historian Thomas W. Laqueur has emphasized their "hy-
pernominalism" (160), the way that row upon row of etched names
or acre upon acre of identical headstones convey the immensity of
British sacrifices without addressing the question of whether such
colossal suffering occurred for a reason.[7] The Cantigny monument
displayed a similarly evasive strategy when it came to the aims and
results of American intervention in the Great War; however, the
memorial's phalanx of names conveyed its own meaning, testifying

to the ferocity of the battle and reflecting the First Division's under-standable, if perverse, pride in its losses. After all, the Big Red One endured more casualties in this one battle, a relatively small-scale affair, than many American divisions suffered during the entire war. Moreover, unlike the personal and specific commemoration pro-vided (at least in theory) by the soldiers and Red Cross officials who wrote to the bereaved, the monument offered a collective vision of death that was not without its own variety of consolation. Grouped by company and thus defined entirely in terms of their organizational placement, the names of the dead formed a monolithic display of unity, encouraging viewers to consider the victims not as individuals forced by circumstances to don their uniforms but exclusively as soldiers—as if military experience and membership in a crack unit like the First Division automatically effaced everything else that defined a man's personality and character. Indeed, in *History of the First Division during the World War, 1917–1919*, an elegantly formatted volume published by the Society of the First Division in 1922, the illustration preceding the division's official list of war dead (more than sixty pages long) carries this notion to a sentimental extreme. Titled *The Chosen Corp*, the illustration depicts an army of phantoms, like the Angels of Mons, marching ever onward in the clouds above a French cemetery. It was as soldiers, and only as soldiers, that the dead would live on.

As the history of G. P. Cather's commemoration makes clear, the death of an American soldier in the Great War triggered an elaborate process of affirmative interpretation carried out in many different forms by a variety of agencies. Despite the best efforts of organizations such as the American Legion, the Red Cross, and the Society of the First Division, however, the physical reality of G. P. Cather's death, together with the charnel-house conditions of the Western Front, sometimes evaded the sense-making apparatuses of commemoration and, like the vengeful specters of Abel Gance's *J'Accuse*, suddenly came home to the living. By far the most credible and painful section of Sergeant Prettyman's testimony, for example, is where he describes with sudden matter-of-factness the hasty burial of his commanding officer: "I sent three men out to dig a grave, in the rear of our trench. There was so much shelling, there was nothing else to do. No way of getting back to any town. I wrapped him in his blanket and buried him there, with two other men of the platoon beside him. I tore up an ammunition box and made a cross and put it at the head of his grave. I put his name on the cross and nailed to it his identity tag. Then we made a map of the place, so that the grave could be found." With disarming directness, the sergeant lays out the horrors that his account otherwise masks: crouching in their trenches under an enemy barrage, G. P. Cather's comrades had little opportunity to form the kind of heroic tableau featured in nineteenth-century genre paintings of expiring officers. Cather's body was trundled into a hole at the back of a trench. There was nothing else the men could do. Prettyman's concern for precisely marking the location of the grave also speaks volumes regarding the grisly realities of the World War I battlefield, a shell-churned moonscape where thousands of bodies simply disappeared. Indeed, as Willa Cather prepared to travel from Paris to Cantigny in 1920, a trip that she undertook partly to photograph G. P. Cather's gravesite for her aunt (and partly to absorb details for her novel), she quickly learned of the way that modern warfare not only pounded landscapes beyond recognition but also obliterated the identities of the bodies buried within them. The expedition required, in fact, some detective work on Cather's part. Perhaps expecting to find G. P. Cather's grave at the former front line, still at the site where Sergeant Prettyman had ordered it dug, Cather learned from a register (prepared by the bizarrely titled Society for the Care of American Dead) that her cousin's remains had been moved from the Cantigny battlefield to the Villiers Tournelle Cemetery, about ten miles away. She also discovered, probably with dismay, that someone had listed G. P. Cather's name as "Cacher" on the headstone marking his new resting place—an error that Cather promised, in a letter to her father, to correct.[8] Whether a graves registration official had misread the dog tag left behind by Sergeant Prettyman or whether artillery fire had damaged the crude wooden cross marking the grave (or perhaps hit the grave itself) remained unclear.

Whatever the case, enough doubt lingered regarding the identity of the remains contained in Lieutenant "Cacher's" plot that when the coffin purportedly carrying G. P. Cather reached Bladen on 29

April 1922, three men—the deceased's father, George Cather, the local undertaker, and a dentist from nearby Blue Hill, Nebraska—visited the train station where the casket was held overnight. As C. D. Samsel, the Burlington agent who admitted the men into the depot, later laconically reported to Mildred Bennett, they "opened the casket for identification, and it proved OK to be Captain GP Cathers body" (qtd. in Faber, "'All the World Seemed Touched with Gold'" 176). A more sensitive observer would have recognized in this scene a mixture of grotesquery and heartbreak of the kind that Cather created in her most memorable fiction—in the account, for example, of the coroner's investigation following Mr. Shimerda's suicide in *My Ántonia*. Ironically, after all the official commemoration lavished on G. P. Cather's demise and despite such colossal expressions of uplift as the Liberty Memorial, the mass graveyard of the Western Front still managed to extend its horror into the heart of the American Midwest. On the eve of G. P. Cather's "Impressive Military Funeral" (as the *Bladen Enterprise* called it), the climax of a memorializing effort that had worked since 1918 to construct an affirmative interpretation of the lieutenant's death, the deceased's father was still left with the terrible task of determining for himself whether G. P. Cather had indeed come home—or whether an unknown soldier had taken his place.

2. One of Ours *and the Iconography of Remembrance*

Had it not been for G. P. Cather's death, Willa Cather probably would never have written a novel dealing so extensively with the First World War. Yet the nature of Cather's fascination with her cousin remains elusive. Critics generally agree that Cather had little affection for G.P., and in her letters to Dorothy Canfield Fisher (with whom she renewed a long-severed friendship while writing *One of Ours*), the novelist validates this view, indicating that the artistic vision inspired by her cousin meant more to her than the man himself. There are marked dissimilarities between Cather's protagonist and his supposed model as well. For example, Lieutenant Cather was thirty-five at the time of his death, a man of relatively broad experience who had already seen much of the world during stints in the U.S. Navy and the National Guard, and who flung himself into military service in 1917 because, according to one Webster County resident, he enjoyed "chasing wars" (Faber, "'All the World Seemed Touched with Gold'" 17). Moreover, G.P.'s fondness for automobiles (an attribute Cather unflatteringly foists upon Enid), his passion for collecting head-mounts of wildlife killed on hunting trips, and his award-winning skills as a competitive marksman are all in complete contrast to Claude's pastoral and even proto-environmentalist sensibilities. Though G.P. expressed a Claude-like dissatisfaction with what appeared, when he talked with Cather in 1914, to be his prosaic destiny as a Nebraska farmer, he bore little resemblance to the dreamy romantic whom Cather would send to France.

However, as Rebecca Faber reveals in "'All the World Seemed Touched with Gold,'" an amazingly exhaustive source study of *One of Ours*, while the character of Claude Wheeler ultimately owes more to Cather's imagination than to G.P.'s apparently robust and conventionally masculine personality, Cather nevertheless drew on her cousin's life (and death) for far more details than one might suspect. In fact, Cather scrutinized every conceivable facet of G.P.'s life, displaying at times a kind of literary voyeurism. Even the most painful and intimate section of *One of Ours*, the account of Claude and Enid's disastrous courtship and marriage, owes many of its features to Cather's real-life relations. The appearance of the house in Bladen constructed by G. P. Cather for his bride, G.P.'s serious injury in a gasoline fire (linked, like Claude's accident, to an automobile) and his subsequent convalescence, Myrtle Cather's teetotaling fundamentalism and Enid-like absences from her spouse, even the rumor (no doubt passed around Bladen with gusto) that Myrtle sometimes locked her husband out of their bedroom—all these details take their place in Cather's devastating portrait of a couple floundering in delusion and incompatibility. Likewise, Cather drew the essential outline of Claude Wheeler's military service from G. P. Cather's letters to his mother, which the novelist examined during her visit to Webster County in the summer of 1918 and lifted several important details from the testimony supplied by Anne Taylor.

Thus, whether she liked G.P. or not, Cather *studied* him with a cathartic intensity reminiscent of the familial monomania that

Lyon Hartwell displays in "The Namesake." Indeed, in her almost obsessive contemplation of a lost relative, Cather seems to have copied her own fiction. In "The Namesake," Hartwell takes a hiatus from his artistic career and spends a year in Pennsylvania brooding over his namesake's heroic legend and periodically ransacking the family home in search of relics that will bring the color sergeant's personality to life. This period of meditation on the subject of military sacrifice ultimately revives the sculptor's long-dormant sense of himself as an American, as one of ours. But nationalism is not the only thing summoned by Hartwell's musings. Following his climactic discovery of the color sergeant's effects, the sculptor feels an almost supernatural sense of connection with his ancestor: "I came to know him as we sometimes do living persons—intimately, in a single moment" (140). In several passages the story teasingly implies that Hartwell has contacted his ancestor's ghost. While pacing in the garden, for example, the sculptor detects an avuncular presence: "Sometimes, in the dim starlight, I have thought that I heard on the grasses beside me the stir of a footfall lighter than my own, and under the black arch of the lilacs I have fancied that he bore me company" (144). Likewise, near the end of the story as the "realization" of his uncle floods Hartwell's consciousness, he describes his moment of epiphany almost as if he has glimpsed a phantom: "Oh, I could *see* him, there in the shine of the morning, his book idly on his knee, his flashing eyes straight before him" (145–46 emphasis mine). In much the same way, Cather became so absorbed by the story of G.P. during her own period of sustained reflection on war that in a letter to Canfield Fisher she presented the experience as a commingling of souls: part of Willa Cather, she wrote, was now buried with G.P., while part of him would accompany the novelist to her own grave.[9] For Cather, composing *One of Ours* was almost a spiritualistic experience, a literary séance. As James Woodress writes of Cather's "blood identity" with her cousin in *Willa Cather: A Literary Life*, "During the first winter working on the book she never knew when he would come to her—at the symphony, at the tea table—and she got so she had to be alone in case he appeared" (304).

Whether Cather realized that she was acting out a scenario described in "The Namesake" is unclear. However, enough parallels exist between Cather's behavior from 1918 to 1922 and Lyon Hartwell's introspective odyssey to warrant reading *One of Ours* as a kind of war memorial in prose—as a literary counterpart, in other words, to the Civil War monuments that Hartwell completes following his own cathartic inquiry into the meaning of a lost family member. This is not to say, however, that *One of Ours* memorializes G. P. Cather exclusively or in a manner likely to elicit only one interpretation. As the contrasts between Claude Wheeler and G.P. indicate, Cather's protagonist evolved (as any successful character must) into a unique personality who allowed the novelist to explore, in an ultimately inconclusive and highly modernist manner, the theme of heroic idealism. For the imagery with which to convey this idealism Cather turned to the commemorative culture of her day—to the public monuments and memorial texts that sought with increasing difficulty to perpetuate an affirmative vision of American intervention. A careful reading of the novel reveals the pervasive presence of what I have termed the iconography of remembrance, a pattern of images that runs throughout the various memorials we have considered.

One motif linking the novel to this iconography is Cather's emphasis on eastward movement—or Manifest Destiny in reverse. *One of Ours* might have been called "The Journey Eastward." Cather opens the novel, suggestively, at sunrise and sends her protagonist (whose bedroom naturally faces the east) first to Lincoln, where he awakens to the artistic richness of Europe, then to France, where he dies defending a sense of culture and sophistication all but forbidden on the practical American plains. Moreover, the titles of the final three books create a triptych that conveys this theme of eastward flight: "Sunrise on the Prairie," "The Voyage of the *Anchises*," and "Bidding the Eagles of the West Fly On."

As these titles suggest, *One of Ours* offers a new myth of American destiny and places it in a new direction—not west on the frontier but east in the Old World. As Joseph Urgo writes, the novel "situates itself on a liminal moment in American history . . . when the nation made its turn away from hemispheric isolation toward involvement in a major European war" (145)—and away from preoccupation with the vanished frontier toward the notion of the New World triumphantly rescuing the Old. Early in the novel, as the sun sets behind Denver, Claude sees "the statue of Kit Carson on horseback pointing westward," but the era of endless possibilities closer to the Pacific has now, literally, entered its twilight: "[T]here was no West, in that sense, anymore" (100). More than any of Cather's novels, *One of Ours* signals the death of the American frontier and all its attendant mythology. Mechanization and intolerant, evangelical Protestantism (the ironically satanic, spark-emitting automobile that Enid drives to and from her temperance meetings unites the two) have taken over the prairie where Claude's father once encountered Indians and buffalo. And in place of the vibrant, ethnically diverse setting presented in *O Pioneers!* or *My Ántonia*, with its rich blend of first-generation immigrants and frontier free spirits, the first half of Cather's war novel confronts us with an increasingly consumer-oriented and homogenized American Midwest, a place of cultural conformity, big business, and the emergence of everything associated with the appropriately constrictive term "Bible belt." Like James Joyce's Stephen Dedalus—or, for that matter, Tom Outland, the similarly thwarted young American in Cather's *Professor's House*—Claude ultimately flies eastward from a suffocating homeland, and again like Dedalus he seeks the destiny promised by his name. In Nebraska, Claude realizes, people pronounce his name as if he were a clod of dirt. Only in France will the Gallic beauty and romantic potential of his title be understood.

Though this notion of war as a means of delivery from an oppressive peacetime America is understandably absent in patriotic memorials, which typically portray the Great Crusade as an extension of domestic virtues abroad, the imagery of triumphant eastward movement is virtually universal—and not only in monuments constructed by Americans. Perhaps its most spectacular and stirring incarnation appears in the French shrine to the Lafayette Escadrille, a squadron of American aviators who served with the Allies prior to the American declaration of war. Located near Paris, the shrine features a series of enormous stained-glass windows that depict an American eagle outlined with biplanes crossing the Atlantic, soaring above Mont-Saint-Michel, and driving eastward toward the enemy in the skies above Château-Thierry and Hartsmannswillerkopf. The monument literally bids "The Eagles of the West Fly On." It is not surprising that the Society of the First Division also adopted the motif in selecting the artwork for its *History of the First Division during the World War*. The volume features sketches of troopships resolutely pitted against the stormy Atlantic, troop columns streaming eastward across no-man's-land, and in one particularly evocative pen-and-ink drawing, a Gallic rooster encircled by the sunrise with an American flag waving in the background. Another World War I unit history, that of the 110th Engineer Regiment (made up primarily of National Guardsmen from Kansas and Missouri), even parallels Cather's conception of the Great Crusade as an antidote for the closing of the frontier. Inspired by the engineers' period of training near Fort Sill, Oklahoma, once a frontier outpost, the regimental historian suggestively titled his work *The Sante Fe Trail Leads to France*. Manifest Destiny had indeed reversed itself. Nor did the planners of the Liberty Memorial fail to utilize directional symbolism, though they did so in a manner perhaps more consistent with prewar conceptions. As the "Description of the Memorial" prepared in 1929 by the monument's chief architect explains, "[T]he entrance to the court from the south is guarded by two colossal sphinx-like figures typifying Memory and the Future, which conceal their faces with their wings; *Memory faces east* toward Flanders Fields and the seat of war, *the Future faces west* where 'the course of Empire takes its way,' and is veiled as the Future is veiled" (Magonigle 28 emphasis mine).

As an inevitable extension of this emphasis on longitudinal movement, sunrises and sunsets abound in American memorials from the 1920s, especially unit histories. And given Cather's fondness for twilight effects, displayed most famously by the image in *My Ántonia* of the plow encircled by the sun, it comes as no surprise that *One of Ours* shares this feature. Paul Fussell has adroitly analyzed the importance of sunsets and sunrises in English World War I literature, linking the often sinister significance of these atmospheric phases to the daily routine of trench warfare. For instance, dawn, the traditional harbinger of renewal and relief, ironically became on the Western Front a time of danger, as troops exposed themselves to enemy fire during their morning stand-to (a period when soldiers peered en masse into no-man's-land). In the work of such war poets as Siegfried

Sassoon, Wilfred Owen, and Isaac Rosenberg, the reddish skyline announcing the arrival of day becomes equated with the blood of soldiers (and especially in Owen's work, with Christ's misery on the cross).

But for Americans who journeyed straight into the morning sun to reach a battlefield half a world away, sunrise and sunset carried different meanings. American troopships bound for France typically departed New York harbor in the early hours of the morning, just in time for their cargoes of soldiers to see "dawn's early light" strike the Statue of Liberty, an image that appears in countless World War I memoirs (and in *One of Ours*) and that thousands of veterans recalled with fondness for the rest of their lives. Moreover, as a Miltonic symbol of victory over the forces of darkness, sunrise became an irresistible component in the iconography of remembrance. For example, a commemorative medal issued in the spring of 1919 to every homeward-bound member of the American Eighty-eighth Division (a unit that, ironically, saw virtually no real fighting) features the figure of a helmeted American infantryman set against a French landscape. Near the soldier's feet rest a German helmet and the smashed barrel of a German field gun, the symbols of Teutonic defeat. To his left, partially veiled by French poplars, a rising sun breaks over the horizon, illuminating the scene of American triumph and metaphorically announcing the onset of a new era (see *The 88th Division in the World War* 97). Sunset, on the other hand, signified the American soldier's distant home and became during the First World War less an image of frontier promise (into which cowboy heroes proverbially ride) than one of lost comfort and domesticity. Countless sketches and cartoons in American unit histories depict the doughboy's homesickness during evening taps, his loneliness and fears as the sun sinks below the horizon. Sunset also meant loss, as a mournful illustration featured in the history of 353rd Infantry (known as the "All Kansas" Regiment) indicates: as a pair of bereaved parents gaze westward from their Kansas farm, they see the wispy figures of three American soldiers silhouetted against the prairie sunset (see fig. 6). One of the phantoms, presumably the couple's son, lifts his hand in farewell. Positioned near the beginning of the roll of honor (like *The Chosen Corps,* the similarly sentimental soldiers-in-clouds

Fig. 6. Untitled illustration from the
History of the 353rd Infantry Regiment.

painting featured in the history of the First Division), the illustration
is accompanied by a verse caption that further emphasizes the appeal
of sunset as a symbol of military sacrifice:

> I have no pity for the dead,
>> They have gone out, gone out with flame and song,
> A sudden shining glory round them spread;
>> Their drooping hands raised up again and strong;
> Only I sorrow that a man must die
> To find the unending beauty of the sky. (Dienst n. pag.)

Throughout *One of Ours*, Cather displays her own sensitivity
to "the unending beauty of the sky" in a manner reminiscent of
D. H. Lawrence, whose novel *Sons and Lovers*, filled with atmospheric
leitmotifs, perhaps influenced Cather's bildungsroman.[10] Ironically
beautiful, sunsets in *One of Ours* usually signal disappointment or
ruin. For example, after Claude fails to convert Ernest Havel, the
rational realist, to his romantic vision of life, the narrator notes
that "the sun had dropped low" (46), an image of negation, of the

darkness that continually closes in on Claude's quest for "something splendid" within his Nebraska existence. Watching the two young men "moving along the crest of the hill against the golden sky," Mrs. Wheeler sees that they "were arguing . . . and probably Claude was on the wrong side" (47). Likewise, when Claude displays his partially constructed house to his fiancée (who is chaperoned, ironically, by Gladys Farmer, the woman Claude should have married), an especially ominous sunset emphasizes the stillborn condition of Claude and Enid's imminent matrimony. As the couple bickers over their future sleeping arrangements, an early warning sign of Enid's frigidity, the narrator literally alerts us to the darkness approaching on the horizon: "The flat fields turned red, the distant windmills flashed white, and little rosy clouds appeared in the sky above them." The mismatched pair watches "the light die out of the sky" (147). Claude's hopes will be dashed once more. Much later in the novel, as Sergeant Hicks stands on the deck of his homeward-bound transport, bitterly contemplating the "way in which glittering honours bump down upon the wrong heads in the army, and palms and crosses blossom on the wrong breasts," he gazes, appropriately enough, into "the twinkle of the red sunset upon the cloudy water." For Hicks and the other veterans who have witnessed firsthand the realities of the Great Crusade, "The sun is sinking low" (367).

In contrast, the many sunrises in *One of Ours* signify Claude's progress toward the "something splendid" he seeks and, at least in his own mind, finally attains. The novel is filled with evocative scenes set in the early morning: Claude's announcement, made before breakfast, that he has decided to enlist; Mrs. Wheeler's final glimpse of her son "vaulting down the hill as fast as he could go" (214) in order to catch his morning train; Claude's first vision of France as "a great grey shoulder of land standing up in the pink light of dawn" (258). Moreover, as John Anders points out, even Claude's death occurs at sunrise, "the time of day when he makes his personal discoveries and when Cather's story of his life begins" (95). Although associated with military sacrifice, evening, with its connotations of grief and loneliness, would have been inappropriate for the protagonist's heroic exit: Claude dies without regret, recklessly perched (like G. P. Cather in Anne Taylor's letter) on the parapet of a trench, and he perceives with joy, not fear, the columns of advancing enemy soldiers revealed by the morning light. The final sunrise of Claude's life illuminates his own "unconquerable" men standing behind him "like a rock" (366). No longer an outsider, Cather's protagonist could ask for nothing more.

Perhaps the single most memorable sunrise in *One of Ours* occurs in the lushly romantic account of Claude's departure at dawn from New York harbor, an episode played out in reverse 146 pages later during Sergeant Hicks's disenchanted reflections, which he makes near the same body of water. Indeed, in her version of a scene that resonates throughout the American experience of the First World War, Cather provides a tour de force of luminous imagery. The account opens with a blurred sunrise straight out of an Impressionist painting. The sun appears as "a red ball, streaked with purple clouds," and to the disappointment of the Midwesterners who crowd the deck of the *Anchises* searching for skyscrapers in the mist, the buildings of Manhattan first take shape as Monet-like "shadows of grey and pink and blue" (220). Then, with a sudden breeze, the air clears: "Blue sky broke overhead, and the pale silhouette of buildings on the long island grew sharp and hard. Windows flashed flame-coloured in their grey sides, the gold and bronze tops of towers began to gleam where the sunlight struggled through" (221). Cather completes this breathtaking panorama with the Statue of Liberty, which looms out of the ocean "so much nearer than [the soldiers] had expected to see her, clad in green folds, with the mist streaming up like smoke behind" (221). Signifying Claude's dawning awareness of his nation's power and majesty, this ecstatic vision of New York (the American city that, above all others, personified modernity in 1918) marks a pivotal moment in the protagonist's metamorphosis into one of ours—in his journey from rural isolation to contentment within an American collective. As the clouds literally part, the Nebraska rube (or "hayseed" as Claude thinks of himself) receives a vision of the promised land, now a world power, that he will represent overseas.

Beyond its recurring emphasis on eastward movement and its symbolic manipulation of sunrise and sunset, *One of Ours* also shares with the commemorative culture of its day a distinct variety of medievalism. Given the belief held by millions of Americans in the

1920s that the United States had come to the rescue of civilized
Europe and defeated a nation of barbarians ("Huns") who disre-
garded the rules of civilized warfare, chivalric motifs pervade the
iconography of remembrance. The United States Victory Medal,
awarded in 1919 to every American participant in the Great War,
displays on its face the image of Civilization, a winged, Valkyrie-like
Amazon armed with a sword. Anticipating the "Guardian Spirits" of
the Liberty Memorial (which were modeled, as the structure's chief
architect explains, from figures at Chartres Cathedral [Magonigle
25]), the medal presents a chivalric figure that is at once militant
and maternal. Likewise, the official certificate given after the war
to veterans wounded overseas depicts the robed figure of Columbia
knighting a kneeling soldier whose steel helmet (adopted, ironically,
to deflect such thoroughly modern projectiles as high-power bullets
and shrapnel) gives him a conveniently medieval appearance. The
rhetoric of the document matches the flamboyance of its visual
image. Its caption reads, "Columbia Gives to Her Son the Accolade
of the New Chivalry of Humanity." In the same vein, an illustration
from a book on the history of the Seventy-seventh Division, the
New York unit that included the famous Lost Battalion, captures
the so-called Spirit of the Argonne in the form of a Yankee colossus
who, outfitted with a sword, helmet, and shield, bears down on
diminutive Huns (see fig. 7).

In *One of Ours* Claude first imbibes the romance of the Middle
Ages and receives his first impressions of the country where he will
lose his life through the legend of Joan of Arc. As a child, Claude
discovers an old picture of the Maid of Orleans dressed in her armor
and learns the "essential facts" of her story from his mother, who subsequently parallels the medieval heroine by combining belligerence
(inspired by the German "rape" of Belgium) with saintly faith. Later,
after momentarily escaping from his oppressive denominational college to study European history at the University of Nebraska, Claude
writes a thesis examining the Maid's testimony during her trial.
Significantly, the project becomes "for a time . . . the most important
thing in his life" (53). Throughout Claude's adolescence and early
adulthood, Joan of Arc stands literally at the center of his conception
of France, a deeply romantic vision that Cather renders through a

Fig. 7. *The Spirit of the Argonne.*
Courtesy of the 77th Infantry Division Association.

string of phrases linked by ellipses: "[A]bout [Joan of Arc's] figure there gathered a luminous cloud, like dust, with soldiers in it . . . the banners with lilies . . . a great church . . . cities with walls" (54). Joan of Arc's story also demonstrates, at least to Cather's protagonist, "that ideals were not archaic things, beautiful and impotent; they were real sources of power among men" (339). As he prepares his thesis, Claude suddenly marvels at the way in which "a character could perpetuate itself . . . by a picture, a word, a phrase" and "be born over and over again in the minds of children" (54).

Characters in Cather's fiction often experience such visionary moments or epiphanies—as Jim Burden does throughout *My Ántonia*—while constructing personal myths that bestow a sense of order and meaning on their lives. But Joan of Arc is an icon whose significance extends far beyond Claude's individual history and the parameters of Cather's text. In fact, the Maid of Orleans played a significant role in the way that grieving Americans looked back on the Great War, embodying both the spirit of France for which the doughboys fought and in many cases sacrificed themselves and the virtues of the chaste Christian soldier, a creature the YMCA (whose somewhat less-than-popular field canteens and wholesome entertainments the American army heartily endorsed) had tried its best to manufacture in France. Once again, if we open the *History of the First Division during the World War*, we see that Cather's text shares an iconography that must have appealed to nostalgic veterans and bereaved family members alike. The frontispiece, for example, portrays an American soldier on horseback flanked by medieval nobility, including Richard Lion-Heart (whose tomb several of Cather's soldiers visit in Rouen). To the soldier's right, hovering near his divisional banner and leading him forward with an inverted sword, is Joan of Arc (see fig. 8). Another painting, titled *The Gold Star* (a reference to the ribbon pin that signified participation in a battle), illustrates this frothy mixture of medievalism, martial regalia, and the militant Christianity associated with the French saint. Here, beside the profile of a helmeted American youth, a crucifix appears, superimposed on a medieval broadsword (see fig. 9).

Like the stained-glass windows of the Lafayette Escadrille shrine, these paintings capture the spirit of Claude's war experience, at least as he perceives it. Through their heraldry and evocations of medieval heroes and heroine, such illustrations place the American soldier triumphantly within the traditions of Europe. In the same way, Claude discovers a sense of belonging—of connection—with the Old World that culminates in his idyllic afternoon with Mme. Olive. The antithesis of Claude's born-again wife, who leaves him to join her missionary sister in China, Mme. Olive is also a modern Joan of Arc, still elegant and cultivated but exhausted by war. Claude's rapport with her is instantaneous. He becomes "almost lost to himself in the feeling of being completely understood, of no longer being a stranger. . . . Two people could hardly give each other more if they were together for years" (316). Appropriately, it is shortly after this profound encounter that Claude contemplates the inscription on the graves of unknown French soldiers ("Soldat Inconnu, Mort Pour La France") and realizes the depth of his own devotion to France: "A very good epitaph, Claude was thinking. Most of the boys who

Fig. 8. The frontispiece from the
History of the First Division during the World War, 1917–1919.
Courtesy of the Society of the First Infantry Division.

Fig. 9. *The Gold Star*. Courtesy of the Society of the First Infantry Division.

fell in this war were unknown, even to themselves. They were too young. They died and took their secret with them—what they were and might have been. The name that stood was *La France*. How much that name had come to mean to him, since he first saw a shoulder of land bulk up in the dawn from the deck of the *Anchises*" (318–19). Claude's reflections in this scene signal the importance of military commemoration both as a shaping influence behind Cather's treatment of the First World War and as a subject in the narrative. Carried to France by a narrative that repeatedly betrays its own indebtedness to American war memorials, Claude achieves his most intense appreciation of military sacrifice by gazing at a forest of monuments to bodies without names, each a miniature Tomb of the Unknown Soldier.

However, while Claude stands transfixed, lost in his enjoyably bittersweet contemplation of the anonymous human beings who have been blown to pieces for *la France*, a curious thing happens. Standing at Lieutenant Wheeler's side and gazing at the same graves, Sergeant Hicks suddenly becomes, much like Ernest Havel, an articulate foil to the romantic protagonist. The sergeant's words stress not the significance but the ultimate meaninglessness of military commemoration: "'Somehow, Lieutenant, 'mort' seems deader than 'dead.' It has a coffinish sound. And over there they're all 'tod,' and it's all the same damn silly thing. Look at them set out here, black and white, like a checkerboard. The next question is, who put 'em here, and what's the use of it?'" (319). "'*Who put 'em here, and what's the use of it?*'"—Sergeant Hicks's question, which seeks to circumvent the game of rhetorical hide-and-seek that Elaine Scarry reveals in the euphemistic, pain-denying usages of military discourse (of which the phrase "unknown soldier" is a classic example), naturally fails to register with his commanding officer: "'Search me,' [Claude] murmured absently" (319). Oblivious to Hicks's insight, Claude proceeds joyfully to his death forty pages later without questioning for a single moment whether the "Huns" that his "unconquerable" soldiers slaughter deserve to die or whether the defense of an inconsequential position on the Western Front, rather unheroically called "The Snout," warrants the virtual annihilation of his company.

Like the intimations of horror that managed to reach all the way from France to G. P. Cather's family in Nebraska, somehow eluding the net of military mythmaking and patriotic uplift, Hicks's unanswered question marks a momentary breakdown in the iconography of remembrance. As it turns out, there are many such breakdowns—counterattacks, if you will—when the nihilism that such iconography sought to dispel creeps back into the novel, complicating its portrayal of war. Thus, before considering the implications of the parallels between *One of Ours* and American war memorials, both architectural and textual, I will turn briefly to several episodes that undermine the affirmative vision of the Great Crusade that Cather's novel seems to endorse in so many respects. Many critics have viewed such episodes as evidence of an ironic subtext undergirding the entire novel. However, I view them as integral features of a text that eludes easy classification. More than anything, the tension created throughout book 5 between Cather's affirmative, even quasi-patriotic iconography and these sudden moments of bleakness suggests that *One of Ours* is neither a celebration of the First World War (as Stanley Cooperman argues), nor an ironic unmasking of military romanticism (Merrill Maguire Skaggs's reading). In a manner that would please neither war propagandists nor pacifists, *One of Ours* examines instead the paradoxical nature of war and the idealism it inspires. Disturbingly, and in a manner far removed from works more securely positioned in the canon of American World War I literature, the book refuses to leave the reader with any easy answers regarding the ultimate meaning of military courage and sacrifice.

Perhaps one of the best examples of an episode that runs at cross-purposes with the iconography of remembrance occurs when Claude and several fellow officers bathe in a shell hole. The scene opens innocently enough as yet another display of the indomitable good humor (and inevitable good looks) that Cooperman finds so offensive in Cather's crusaders. But then Claude retrieves a grisly relic from the bottom of the makeshift swimming hole—a German helmet "coated with rust and full of slime." The men scramble out as "big sleepy bubbles" rise to the surface. Claude has unwittingly "opened a graveyard" (296). Instances of the grotesque or the macabre are not unusual in Cather's fiction; they are the norm. One thinks of Pavel

and Peter in *My Ántonia*, renowned throughout their native Russia
as "the men who had fed the bride to the wolves" (40); Henry
Atkin's horrific rattlesnake bite (straight to the forehead) in *The
Professor's House*; the unfortunate French missionary in *Shadows on
the Rock* who is served a human hand during an Indian feast; or
the "sunken tree" (169) in *Lucy Gayheart* that holds the drowned
heroine in its death grip. However, the bathing scene in *One of Ours* is
more sinister than these seemingly arbitrary moments of horror. As if
lifted from one of Siegfried Sassoon's wartime shock poems or from
the pages of *All Quiet on the Western Front*, the episode ominously
juxtaposes the naked physiques of young soldiers with corpses. War
is a matter of turning healthy young men into bloated cadavers at
the bottom of a muddy hole. And although killed Hollywood style
by a wound to the chest, Claude's body will ultimately undergo the
same corruption.

Similarly, when Claude and Sergeant Hicks encounter a sixteen-
year-old English soldier, already a veteran with more than two years
of experience on the Western Front, they receive a chilling lesson
in the kind of mass slaughter that the United States might well
have experienced had it entered the conflict sooner. The boy calmly
describes how his Pals Battalion (a unit made up entirely of men
from the same business or community) was massacred at the 1916
battle of the Somme: "'We couldn't even get to the wire.... We
went over the top a thousand and we came back seventeen'" (304).
While John Anders may correctly argue that the boy's narrative
describes a modern version of the Sacred Band (a brotherhood of
ancient Greek warriors united by homosexual love who impressed
even their enemies with their courage and loyalty), it is a version
that Cather constructs ironically. The Sacred Band, killed to the
last man at the battle of Chaeronea in 338 B.C., was annihilated
through the kind of close-quarters, man-to-man combat described,
for example, in Homer's *The Iliad*; Cather's Pals are mowed down
before they can even reach the enemy's trenches. As the boy's story
makes disturbingly clear, Claude's opportunity to make his exultant
last stand on the Snout, a demise he regards as glorious and necessary,
is as much a matter of luck as it is a testimony to the protagonist's
courage. As Cather would have understood through her numerous

interviews with wounded veterans, most American soldiers killed in action during the First World War met their end either while hiding in foxholes, praying that the enemy's artillery shells would land elsewhere, or in situations similar, if smaller in scale, to the massacre in no-man's-land experienced by the Pals Battalion on the first day of the Somme. For example, following their triumph at Cantigny, the infantry regiments of the First Division were cut to pieces while suicidally advancing across open wheat fields at the battle of Soissons. Claude—and the reader—would likely feel differently about his fate had he been ordered, like so many victims in the Great War, to advance straight into a machine gun without any hope of affecting the outcome of the battle.

By far the most subversive moment in Cather's text, however, comes during Mrs. Wheeler's reflections in the final chapter, a section that seems to negate the entire mythic structure of Claude's eastward flight and heroic fulfillment. Indeed, Mrs. Wheeler's thoughts strike a sour note not entirely dispelled by the final sentence of *One of Ours*, which describes Mahailey's faith in a God "located not so very far above the kitchen stove" (371). In his mother's eyes, Claude died deluded, "believing his own country better than it was, and France better than any country can ever be" (370), and is lucky to be removed from a world where "desolating disappointment" awaits the noblest of heroes. Better a soldier's death in France, Mrs. Wheeler reflects, than disillusionment and suicide, the bitter fate suffered by those veterans who found "they had hoped and believed too much." Claude is at least "safe" from the realization that his fellow crusaders, unconquerable in battle, ultimately failed to make the world safe for democracy, "that nothing has come of it all but evil" (370).

By closing the novel with Mrs. Wheeler's perverse declaration that for idealists such as her son death represented a kinder fate than life in postwar America, Cather does more than simply undermine her own version of the iconography of remembrance; she also turns a key component of World War I propaganda completely inside out—namely, the cult of patriotic motherhood. In his final letter to Franc Cather, dated (appropriately enough) 12 May 1918, Lt. G. P. Cather included a YMCA pamphlet that vividly conveys the symbolic role assigned to American mothers during the First World

MOTHER'S DAY
1918

Fig. 10. Cover illustration from *Mother's Day 1918*.
Courtesy of the Archives and Special Collections Department,
University of Nebraska–Lincoln Libraries.

War. Titled *Mother's Day, 1918*, the pamphlet consists primarily of hymns to motherhood by Rudyard Kipling and Jessie Pope, as well as other predictably jingoistic poets, and features on its cover a scene curiously anticipatory of the relationship between Mrs. Wheeler and her warrior son: an American officer, helmet in hand, kneels at the feet of a knitting matron, whose stoic expression conveys her realization that the defense of Civilization must take precedence over maternal feelings (see fig. 10). In other words, women of America say, "Go." A letter from a presumably fictional mother to her son included in the pamphlet reinforces this subordination of personal affection to national need: "Betty says to tell you that Jack Ellis sails next week;—I know just how his mother will feel for those ten days while he is crossing. But she wouldn't have had him stay home, any more than I would have had you!"

The utilization of mothers as motivational icons did not stop there. As historian G. Kurt Piehler reveals, for the first time in American military history, the United States government also turned to mothers in its promotion of an affirmative vision of death in battle. "In order to sustain morale on the home front," Piehler writes, "the Women's Section of the Committee of National Defense urged women not to wear black when mourning the loss of a son killed in the nation's service. Instead, the Women's Section convinced many families to display a distinctive Gold Star emblem to express their sacrifice of a son to the nation" ("The War Dead and the Gold Star" 171). Embroidered on small flags and hung in the windows of thousands of American homes in 1918, the Gold Star signified the willingness of American mothers to see their personal tragedy as meaningful civil action; the symbol encouraged the friends and neighbors of the bereaved to view them less as victims than as heroines who had willingly sacrificed their greatest treasure for the good of the nation.

Following the war, two organizations sought to perpetuate this image of the American mother as the ultimate patriot—the American War Mothers and the American Gold Star Mothers Association. Like the American Legion, neither group had any patience with pacifists or with those who would paint the Great War for Civilization in nihilistic hues. Founded during the period when Cather wrote *One of Ours* and "open to all mothers who had a son or daughter who had served in the First World War," the American War Mothers "insisted that America had not been mistaken in entering the conflict and challenged those women who equated motherhood with pacifism, arguing that the great lesson of the First World War remained the ongoing need for military preparedness" (Piehler, "The War Dead and the Gold Star" 175). Likewise the more exclusive American Gold Star Mothers Association, created in 1928 expressly for bereaved mothers such as Mrs. Wheeler, "supported preparedness and wanted the First World War remembered as a noble crusade" (177).

Through their message that military action was a sad but necessary response to national threats, both organizations offered women who had lost their sons a way of making peace with tragedy. But Claude's mother will have none of it. Patriotism offers her no solace. In the months that follow Claude's death, "when human nature looked to her uglier than it had ever done before," Mrs. Wheeler reflects that "it seemed as if the flood of meanness and greed had been held back just long enough for the boys to go over, and then swept down and engulfed everything that was left at home." She is thankful only that Claude died still believing "the cause was glorious" (370). There is no Gold Star at the close of *One of Ours*, literally or figuratively. Instead, Cather shifts the final sentences as far from commemorative iconography as they can go and concludes the novel not with Claude's presence on some official roll of honor or with the kind of posthumous military homecoming created for G. P. Cather but with a heartbreaking scene featuring the two women who loved him most. We watch as "while working at the table or bending over the oven," Mrs. Wheeler and Mahailey suddenly "think of him together, as one person" and as Mahailey offers her conventional but heartfelt assurance that Mrs. Wheeler will see her boy "'up yonder'" (371). Like the final chapter of Virginia Woolf's *Jacob's Room*, which closes with the similarly domestic image of Betty Flanders sorting the contents of her dead son's closet and holding up his empty shoes, Cather's ending eschews the various official interpretations of Claude's demise and instead emphasizes his absence, the reality of his nonexistence.[11] The novel's epic vistas of American crusaders crossing the Atlantic and taking their place on the Western Front collapse into this intimate scene of quiet grief set in a Nebraska farmer's kitchen, far from the nearest war memorial.

· · · · · · · · · ·

What, then, does an understanding of Cather's extensive borrowing from the culture of World War I commemoration add to our understanding of *One of Ours*? What are we to make of the incidents in the text that openly subvert this imagery? The parallels between Cather's imagery and what I have termed the iconography of remembrance suggest that *One of Ours* is much more than the character study of a solitary lost Nebraskan. In the process of telling Claude's story, Cather presents — and simultaneously deconstructs — a version of the Great War that millions of Americans in 1922 still affirmed amid such shrines as the Liberty Memorial and the Tomb of the Unknown Soldier. Through its emphasis on the eastward pursuit of a new frontier, its inspiring sunrises and funereal sunsets, and its preoccupation with the age of chivalry, especially the legend of Joan of Arc, Cather's text indeed constitutes a war memorial in prose, a textual counterpart to the patriotic statues created by Lyon Hartwell for American Civil War battlefields.

However, as we saw in the first section of this chapter, the meaning of American World War I memorials was unstable from the start, always threatened by the incongruities and anticlimaxes that lurked within the actual experience of the conflict. Witnessed directly by only one American soldier in four (half of the American army — more than two million men — never even made it to France) and complicated by such inconvenient realities as the AEF's questionable military performance and the devastation wrought by the 1918 influenza epidemic (which killed more American soldiers than Germans did), the Great War for Civilization proved a slippery subject for the designers of uplifting American monuments. As a result, unintentional expressions of uncertainty appear everywhere in the culture of World War I commemoration: in the anything but consoling gigantism of the Liberty Memorial; in the intentionally vague symbolism of the Tomb of the Unknown Soldier (a subtle concession to the fact that war failed to generate a central affirmative myth); and in the often grotesque disparity between the medieval imagery that decorates unit histories like the *History of the First Division during the World War* and the thoroughly modern mass carnage they describe. In the same way, Cather's version of the iconography of remembrance continually betrays its own limitations and contradictions. The notion of chivalry, for example, hardly fits the grim tale of the annihilated Pals Battalion. Cather's Sacred Band is no match for the modern machine gun. In addition, the instances of Hun depravity Cather presents in book 5, including a Prussian sniper's presumably intentional murder of a French child, seem inexplicable in light of the gentleness and decency that Claude associates with his German American neighbors back in Nebraska. In depicting the paranoid hostility directed against immigrants like Gus Yoeder or Mrs. Voigt, Cather exposes the dark side of the crusader mentality that her imagery so often celebrates. Written during the Red Scare, *One of Ours* unsparingly reveals a potential at home for the brutality and atavism that Claude perceives within his demonized enemy.

Such contradictions ultimately do more, however, than simply mirror the perplexities of America's first world war or expose Cather's personal ambivalence toward martial lore (as already evidenced by "The Namesake"). They call for a rethinking of Cather's most controversial novel, especially its relation to literary modernism. Indeed, if we suspend the reigning critical view that *One of Ours* belongs in a separate category from such openly experimental texts as *The Professor's House* or *Death Comes for the Archbishop*, we can see that Cather's highly ambiguous treatment of the relationship between idealism and action, especially as it relates to war, shares many of the features of Joseph Conrad's *Lord Jim* (1900), a protomodernist narrative devoted to the same subject and likewise famous for eliciting conflicting interpretations. Like *One of Ours*, *Lord Jim* tells the story of a frustrated idealist who finally achieves his romantic fulfillment— though at the cost of his own life and at the end of a personal quest shrouded with contradiction. Again like *One of Ours*, Conrad's novel breaks into two halves, each of which seems to come from a completely different writer. The first emphasizes, in a manner similar to Cather's rendering of Claude's misery on the plains, Jim's painful sense of the incongruity between his actions, or lack thereof, and his conception of himself as a would-be hero, as someone destined, in Claude's words, to achieve "something splendid in life." For much of this section, Conrad paints a largely negative portrait of Jim's romantic nature, especially his inability to unite idealism with action. Paralyzed at a crucial moment by his self-absorption and excessive imagination, Jim does not just miss his chance to be a hero, he leaves five hundred people to die, and during his subsequent wandering from one colonial outpost to another he broods with infinite self-pity over the way that circumstances have conspired to thwart his self-actualization.

In much the same way, Claude lives in a state of psychic impotence throughout the Nebraska chapters of *One of Ours*, continually failing to assert himself. Mirroring Claude's consciousness, the imagery in this section is often cruelly deterministic. In a scene worthy of Thomas Hardy, for example, Cather uses a shed full of smothered pigs, ironically left under the protagonist's care during a Nebraska blizzard, to suggest Claude's similarly suffocated condition. And when Claude learns that he must give up his studies in Lincoln, the only place on the utilitarian plains where he is allowed access to high culture, he feels "as if a trap had been sprung on him" (57). But Claude mostly creates traps for himself, blundering into his disastrous marriage, for instance, after the girl's father all but warns him away and after witnessing ample evidence of Enid's sexual frigidity and limited interests. Nor does Claude ever stand up to his insensitive father or break from the rigid conventions of his community.[12] He is too timid to drink beer with Ernest Havel, and when Gladys Farmer displays her unspoken affection for him, he backs away: "[A] boy whose wife was in China could hardly go see Gladys without causing gossip" (190). All in all, Jim and Claude make a rather pathetic duo.

Ironically, however, both of these seemingly impotent dreamers go on to become remarkable men—Jim, in the remote Indonesian settlement of Patusan, where he puts an end to ethnic violence and becomes a celebrated White Lord; Claude, on the front lines of the Western Front, where he becomes an effective military leader. Indeed, while the first half of each novel seems to attack its protagonist's quest for "something splendid," demonstrating that his unwillingness to settle for a common existence is self-destructive (and in Jim's case potentially destructive to others), the second suggests that life sometimes accommodates romantic aspiration. In Patusan, Jim's imaginative capacity, the very feature of his personality that crippled him during the *Patna* episode, enables him to conceive of a swift end to anarchy. Moreover, Jim's drive to achieve his idealized self, egocentric though it is, paradoxically makes him a relatively just and benevolent leader. The character's conception of himself as a storybook hero prevents him from ever becoming a sadistic despot like Kurtz in Conrad's *Heart of Darkness*.

By the same token, when the United States enters the Great War midway through *One of Ours*, Claude suddenly discovers that his idealistic yearning *fits* the national mood, a point Cather reinforces by presenting the protagonist's individual experience of the conflict through patriotic iconography shared by millions of Americans. Claude's longing for something noble, which brought him only alienation in peacetime, now animates an entire army, drawing in even pragmatists like Leonard Dawson and sophisticated intellectuals such as David Gerhardt. Like Jim, Claude is now at the right place at the right time, and as Gladys Farmer gazes at him during their final conversation, he almost seems to have become a war memorial already, the ultimate doughboy cast in a heroic stance. After their meeting she reflects on "how often she would see him standing here by the window, or moving about the dusky room, looking at last as he ought to look,—like his convictions and the choice he had made. She would never let this house be sold for taxes now. She would save her salary and pay them off. She could never like any room so well as this. It had always been her refuge from Frankfort; and now there would be this vivid, confident figure, an image as distinct to her as the portrait of her grandfather upon the wall" (211–12). Claude's "vivid, confident figure" becomes, at least in Gladys's mind, an icon akin to the portrait of the color sergeant that haunts the Hartwells' parlor in Pennsylvania. The "chump" or "hayseed" has been magically transformed into a timeless symbol of the exuberant American warrior—a change no less amazing than Jim's progress from humiliated outcast to all-powerful White Lord.

Nor does the protagonist's death in either novel mark the collapse of his idealism. On the contrary, both characters view their demise as the climax of their self-realization. By willingly handing himself over to Doramin, Jim dies content, believing "with his exalted egotism" that his self-sacrifice will validate once and for all his heroic self-image, and he gives little thought to the people, such as Jewel and Tamb'Itam, who will be left shattered by his departure. In the same way, Claude mounts the parapet of his trench with suicidal eagerness, as if realizing unconsciously that the halo of enchantment surrounding his military experience will not last indefinitely. By offering himself to the enemy's machine guns amid the kind of Alamo-like last stand celebrated throughout American military history (and especially during the First World War with the legend of the Lost Battalion), Claude ensures that his death is consistent with his personal quest for transcendence *and* with the cultural myths that define his romantic perceptions of the Great War for Civilization. Both idealists die, if anything, joyfully—at sunrise of course—but whether their self-sacrifice represents a victory over life or a pathetic retreat from it remains a mystery thanks to the multiplicity of subjective perspectives that both novelists employ.

In *Lord Jim*, Conrad complicates any judgment of the protagonist through his avant-garde narrative technique. Inaugurating the arrival of literary modernism, the text literally enacts the death of the omniscient narrator. One hundred pages into the novel, the third-person point of view suddenly vanishes, giving way to a string of conflicting subjective testimonies—surrounded by two and sometimes three sets of quotation marks—that Conrad forces the reader to subject to almost legalistic scrutiny. As a reading experience, *Lord Jim* is simultaneously fascinating and maddening. Just as one set of witnesses seems to establish a stable assessment of the protagonist, a new set, possessing additional information and informed by a different set of values, enters the text, complicating what has come before it. Thus in the final analysis, neither the sympathetic view of Jim offered by Marlow and Stein nor the harsher verdict articulated by characters such as the French Lieutenant or Gentleman Brown achieves authority—which is precisely the point. Focused on the paradoxical benefits and dangers of heroic idealism, *Lord Jim* also deals finally with the complexity of moral judgment and the inscrutable nature of truth, themes that the novel makes its reader experience directly—and uncomfortably.

Though more conventional on the surface, *One of Ours* is also a novel of conflicting voices, a text that continually offers disparate assessments of idealism and warfare, no one of which is necessarily more reliable than the others. Against Claude's search for the splendid, Cather sets Ernest Havel's satisfaction with the ordinary; against Mrs. Wheeler's view of the Great War as a Christian crusade against Evil (sustained until the death of her son), Sergeant Hicks's disturbing conclusion that "mort" and "tod" mean the same thing.

Indeed, the only truth teller in *One of Ours* is the spring at the head of Lovely Creek, whose "soft, amiable bubbling" Cather likens to a "wise, unobtrusive voice, murmuring night and day, continually telling the truth to people who could not understand it" (127). Even Mrs. Wheeler's sour reflections in the last chapter, which many critics perceive as Cather's final word on the Great War, betray their subjectivity. One notes the qualified language with which the narrator records them: "Human nature *looked to her* uglier than it ever had before . . . it *seemed as if* the flood of meanness and greed had been held back just long enough for the boys to go over" (369–70 emphasis mine). In addition, the catalog of postwar suicides that Mrs. Wheeler contemplates tells only part of the story. True, Lost Battalion commander Maj. Charles W. Whittlesey drowned himself in the Caribbean soon after the war and probably inspired Cather's reference to former heroes who "slip over a vessel's side, and disappear into the sea" (370). As readers in 1922 would have been well aware, however, the two most celebrated American heroes of the Great War—Alvin York and Eddie Rickenbacker—thrived in the postwar years and remained exuberantly patriotic, so much so in the case of York that he later assisted with the World War II propaganda film (starring Gary Cooper) based on his adventures.[13] Though seemingly privileged above other assessments of the Great War because of its placement in the final chapter, Mrs. Wheeler's verdict nevertheless reflects and is limited by her need to believe that Claude is better off dead. Had Cather chosen to reserve the last word for, say, Mme. Olive, a different conception of Claude's fate and of the Great Crusade would appear to dominate. War, Cather suggests through her multiplicity of perspectives, is ultimately paradoxical, simultaneously glorious and banal, liberating and destructive. Were war anything else, she implies, human beings would have abandoned it long ago.

Moreover, the often jarring inconsistencies within Cather's narrative point of view create a modernist turbulence similar to Conrad's subjective free-for-all. Neither consistently limited nor omniscient, Cather's third-person perspective wavers throughout between fidelity to Claude's romantic vision and the accommodation of additional perspectives. For paragraphs and sometimes even entire chapters, the novel adheres to Claude's consciousness with almost Jame-sean discipline. Then, without warning, other perspectives suddenly drop into the narrative, sometimes confirming Claude's idealistic conclusions, sometimes raising doubts about them. The French characters whose thoughts Cather momentarily records provide some of the most interesting examples of this inconsistency and the way in which it creates a distinctly modernist effect. For example, when Claude encounters a family of refugees, the narrator suddenly enters the mind of 'Toinette, an eleven-year-old girl, and we receive a vivid impression of the American crusaders as they appear to an outside observer. After Claude addresses the girl in characteristically rudimentary French, the narrator remarks: "She understood him. No distortion of her native tongue surprised or perplexed her. She was accustomed to being addressed in all persons, numbers, genders, tenses; by Germans, English, Americans. She only listened to hear whether the voice was kind, and with men of this uniform it usually was kind" (292). 'Toinette's perception that the voices of American soldiers are usually kind confirms Claude's own idealized vision of the men with whom he serves. But the scene does not end there. As 'Toinette introduces the members of her family, she points to a "white and sickly" baby nursing at her mother's breast and matter-of-factly declares that the infant is a "Boche" (292). Conditioned by atrocity stories, Claude and his companions immediately conclude that the child's mother has been raped; indeed, the platoon's resident sentimentalist, Bert Fuller, nearly breaks into tears, and he controls himself only by muttering repeatedly, "'By God, if we'd a-got here sooner, by God if we had!'" (292). But the reality of the situation is by no means clear, and significantly, the narrator never clears up the mystery by returning to the girl's consciousness. Cather cunningly utilizes 'Toinette's perspective just long enough to add credibility to one of Claude's beliefs but then shuts down this additional point of view at precisely the moment when the reader needs it most. The doughboys' indignation may, of course, be justified. However, as we learn several chapters later when Claude uncovers the details of a tragic love affair between a French curé's niece and a Bavarian officer, consensual relations with the Hun are not unprecedented. Does the scene involving 'Toinette and her family demonstrate, as Stanley

Cooperman would probably allege, Cather's use of propaganda-inspired atrocity lore? Or does the scene reveal, as advocates of the ironic reading of *One of Ours* would likely maintain, that Claude is easily misled?

The important thing to note is that this scene opens itself to both of these possibilities, thus displaying, like so much of *One of Ours*, a Conradian unwillingness to dispel ambiguity. So I return to the image suggested throughout this discussion of *One of Ours* and the culture of American military commemoration—that of Cather's novel as a war memorial. In telling Claude Wheeler's story, Cather relied in part on the kind of imagery used by organizations such as the American Legion, the Red Cross, and the Society of the First Division to commemorate her real-life cousin. Thus, the tensions and contradictions discernable today in structures such as the Liberty Memorial found their way into Cather's text. But the ambiguous nature of America's first world war and the commemorative culture it spawned only partially explain the diametrically opposed readings that Cather's most controversial and slighted novel accommodates. If indeed *One of Ours* is a monument to its hero and less directly to G. P. Cather it is, finally, a *modernist* monument, one that, like the Vietnam War Memorial, remembers the dead but leaves their meaning a mystery that we must solve for ourselves.

2

AMERICANS FOUND

In 1922, the same year that *One of Ours* was published, Frank Holden, a former second lieutenant in the AEF, described his experiences in the Great War in a small volume simply titled *War Memories*. Like many veterans, Holden regretted that wartime necessity had prevented him from truly experiencing and appreciating the land where he had fought. More than anything, he announced in the opening chapter, he wanted someday to return to France—to Paris, that "great paradise of pleasure seekers," to the "little villages where our battalion was billeted," and to sites of Gallic greatness, such as Verdun, "where the French fought as no people ever fought before" (17). Moreover, such an intense longing was, Holden believed, nearly universal among the two million American veterans who seen France in wartime. "Life," he wrote, "sometimes seems strange and queer. . . . How we disliked to be in France during those weary months after the Armistice (except when on leave). That was when we were waiting so long to start back home, when the hours that dragged by seemed like days. But now ask the ex-service man how he feels about going back. More than likely he would say that he would like to go back in civilian clothes and see France in peace time" (15). Such comments, typical of what one encounters in American war memoirs from the 1920s (especially those written by former officers), point on one level to the profoundly cross-cultural nature of the U.S. involvement in the Great War. As Holden demonstrates by expressing his yearning for a new journey through France, American war memories were inevitably linked to thoughts of the alien environment within which members of the AEF spent on average a year of their lives. But at the same time Holden imagines his return visit not as a genuine reencounter with cultural difference, with all its attendant frustrations and vagaries, but as a return to the familiar—to places that have already been assimilated into an American narrative and that symbolize the military greatness of which he has been a part. Though he looks forward to once again "*see*[*ing*] the wonderful French people" (16 emphasis mine)—note the detached perspective of the tourist here—he has little interest in learning more about French culture through direct involvement with others or in wandering beyond the battlefields and billets he visited in wartime. Instead, his itinerary reaches its climax with an excursion into "No Man's Land in broad daylight," followed by the climbing of Montsec (a fortified mountain seized during the battle of St. Mihiel) and a pilgrimage to the graves of American "boys who did not come back" (17–18).

The tension in Holden's remarks—between the desire to discover France anew and the impulse to visit only places inscribed with American meaning—has an intriguing relevance to *One of Ours*, a novel whose presentation of France is nothing if not conflicted. Throughout much of book 5, titled "Bidding the Eagles of the West Fly On," Cather's text celebrates France as an alternative to the oppressive cultural norms that have defined Claude's purgatorial existence on the plains. In France, for example, Cather's protagonist discovers (or at least *believes* he discovers) all that is missing in Nebraska: agriculture practiced in harmony with aesthetics; a reverence for tradition (as opposed to utility and profit); and people who live simply but with a keen appreciation of life's pleasures. In France there are no dyspeptic Baylisses to spoil a good meal or Enids to preach against drink, and no worthless machines, apparently, to clutter one's cellar. Though qualified by Claude's ignorance—Cather's hero never achieves fluency in the French language, let alone more than a superficial knowledge of the French people with whom he briefly interacts—this utopian vision of France nevertheless reinforces the criticisms of Frankfort-style culture established in the first half of the novel. A French paradise, uncorrupted by such ugly Americans as Bayliss Wheeler or Brother Weldon, allows Cather to drive home, by way of contrast, her assault on the mechanization, oppressive religiosity, and anti-intellectualism that she felt were destroying the Nebraska prairie.[1] This emphasis on France as the repository of everything lacking in the American Midwest does not, however, dominate the text indefinitely. As Claude grows ever more content with his life as a member of the AEF, as one of ours, the novel correspondingly shifts its focus from the allure of France to the benefits (at least in Claude's eyes) of a new, more broadly defined America. Indeed, despite the considerable extent to which Cather's own affection for France colors the narrative, *One of Ours* is, in the end, a study not of Claude's escape from American culture and embrace of French models but of his solidarity with the "wonderful men" (366) of the American army. In this sense, Cather's novel is less about a lost American than a found one.

In this chapter, then, I focus on what I have termed the cross-cultural impulse in Cather's novel (the desire, that is, to embrace an alternative, non-American worldview), especially as manifested in such characters as the amnesiac "lost American" and Victor Morse, and the way in which this impulse ultimately yields to other thematic urgencies. Throughout, I have sought to understand Claude's enthusiasm as a Francophile *and* as an increasingly patriotic American soldier, a contradictory mix, by drawing on recent historical writing on the First World War, especially the work of Mark Meigs, whose study of the culture of the AEF first prompted my interest in reexamining the origins of Claude's values and perceptions in book 5. Arguing that the American army of the First World War sought above all else to inculcate its members with a unified, progressive vision of their homeland and of their own attributes as citizen soldiers, Meigs offers a model of the male American war experience that goes a long way toward explaining Claude's transformation from brooding Nebraskan to exuberant American warrior. Moreover, Meigs's examination of the way in which American soldiers became *tourists* during their overseas service illuminates Cather's conflicted presentation of

France, a setting whose meaning for Claude subtly changes during book 5. Once placed beside current research on the AEF, book 5 of *One of Ours*, long regarded as the weakest section of the novel (if not the weakest piece of writing in *any* of Cather's novels), takes on a new and surprising level of profundity, revealing not only Cather's formidable research on the day-to-day activities of overseas soldiers and sustained reflections on the issue of cultural difference, but her prescient insight into the new model of America and Americans that emerged from the Great War.

The kind of complexity I have just outlined may, however, fail to emerge upon a first reading, so intense is the personal affection for France that Cather allows to color her narrative. Indeed, on one level, *One of Ours* stresses the attractiveness of French culture in comparison with the debased American version in precisely the manner that one would expect of a novel written by a devout Francophile and, by the early 1920s, exasperated critic of mainstream American values. For Claude, France is a place of "hazy enchantment" and "purple evenings" where "the smell of wood smoke from the chimneys [goes] to his head like a narcotic" and "everything [has] a noble significance" (332). Even the agricultural details add to his joy. In France, he notes, farmers actually cherish indigenous trees, such as cottonwoods, rather than replace them with something more fashionable and allow ancient groves to exist side by side with cultivated fields. In this anti-Nebraska, beauty means more than maximized yield. So too does tradition—despite Claude's jarring discovery that "American binders, of well known makes" (274) now outnumber thatched roofs. Claude's infatuation with France in general stems largely from his callow estimation of the nation's premodernity, its lingering ties to something older and more noble than the cult of utility and profit that has wrecked the American plains. Not for Claude are the grim realities of French industry, as depicted more than three decades before the AEF's arrival by Emile Zola in *Germinal*, or the sophistication and internationalism of Paris, which by 1914 was the hub of a French empire with vast territories in North Africa and Indochina. Rather, Claude's France is a quaint amalgam of cathedrals, medieval streets, forests, and fairy-tale villages "buried in autumn color" with "wells of cool water that tastes of moss and tree roots" (350). Moreover, Claude unconsciously transforms this already romanticized physical setting into a refuge—like the shelter for game birds that he preserves on Lovely Creek—for everything that his odious brother Bayliss would seek to deny or kill. Here, as in the Erlichs' ironically Germanic parlor back in Lincoln, people know "how to live" (38), and in the gracious dignity of the Jouberts and Mme. Olive Claude reencounters the simplicity and goodness of his own mother and Mahailey. Not unlike Niel Herbert, whose gaze constructs of Marian Forrester what it wants, Claude assembles an image of *la France*, his lost lady, that serves his personal mythology.

Despite the many moments when Cather stresses the ignorance that often underlies Claude's cross-cultural enthusiasm—Mrs. Wheeler, in the closing pages, concludes that her son believed France "better than any country can ever be" (370)—his vision is in some respects as irresistible as it is selective and unreliable. Like Oz, France enters the text as a burst of color after chapters of sepia-toned misery, its poppies and red tiles standing in stark contrast to the gray water of the Atlantic or with Enid's black automobile. In her evocation of France, Cather masterfully plays upon *all* the senses. Along with Claude we experience the smell of wood smoke, the sounds of spoken French (a language that "had to be spoken with energy and fire, or not spoken at all" [287]), the feel of a "wide feather bed" (350) after days of marching, the poignant sight of Mme. Olive's half-ruinous garden "lying flattened in the sun" with its "dahlias and marigolds" and "glistening boxwood wall" (317). Nor in the midst of this tour de force of sensual appeals does Cather neglect the flavors of France. In contrast to the leaden meals joylessly consumed in the Wheeler household or Mrs. Royce's flavorless vegetarian concoctions, the reader now encounters such delicacies as "rabbit stew made with red wine and chestnuts" (350). "Oh, the days that are no more!" exclaims the narrator, lamenting the lost entrées of yesteryear (350). The many epicurean passages in book 5 remind one of Cather's chief and perhaps most revealing extravagance as a wealthy author—her hiring of a personal French cook.

Thus, whatever our suspicions regarding an ironic subtext running throughout the final book of *One of Ours*, it is difficult to avoid being captivated, if only on a sensual level, by Claude's vision. Nor does Cather miss an opportunity to strengthen her often withering critique of Frankfort-style values by juxtaposing them with French models. France is what Nebraska might have been had the Old World sensibility of its earliest European immigrants been left unmolested, had the puritanical Protestantism represented by the temperance movement not taken hold, and had the American passion for the machine not transformed agriculture into mere mass production. France, in other words, stands for genuine civilization, while the culture of Bayliss and Mr. Wheeler represents a "cheap substitut[e]" (30). In France, even a cooked meal is a profoundly meaningful work of art. In Nebraska, on the other hand, the word "literature" signifies pamphlets on hoof-and-mouth disease or propaganda disseminated by the Anti-Saloon League.

Cather's sympathies as a Francophile and correspondingly dour view of twentieth-century Nebraska complement one other most vividly, however, in one of the most subversive characters in *One of Ours*—namely, the lost American, a wounded soldier who achieves an idyllic existence in France after a German bullet conveniently erases his memories of the United States. Thanks to the ferocity of Cather's attack on the American Midwest, this brain-damaged "psychopathic case"—like his probable model, Chris Baldry in Rebecca West's *Return of the Soldier*—actually seems fortunate in his affliction.[2] Freed from the presumably Enid-like "nice girl" who awaits his return and mercifully severed from the "small town" (another Frankfort, one assumes) where he grew up, the lost American, in effect, acts out Claude's fantasies of expatriation by running off to work on a French farm and by entering into a passionate relationship with a young French woman, most likely a member of the country family that "sort of adopted him" (273). "'I've got used to things over here,'" the wounded soldier tells Claude and thus demonstrates that he is not lost at all, except in the sense that he has *been lost* by his own undeserving nation. Even more than Victor Morse, whom Claude admires but cannot "altogether believe in" (267), the lost American symbolizes the rich potentialities offered by the only true frontier left in the novel—the uncharted territory of an alternative culture.

For Claude, emulating the lost American is ultimately out the question. Despite his soul-killing existence in Nebraska, Cather's protagonist is too content with army comradery ever to follow his double across the no-man's-land that separates American and French identity. It is hard to imagine Claude going AWOL and seeking refuge with a French family, as John Andrews (a David Gerhardt turned deserter) does in John Dos Passos's *Three Soldiers*, or imitating the joyfully iconoclastic protagonist of e. e. cummings's *Enormous Room*, who embraces life in a French jail, surrounded by Gallic eccentrics. Unlike these cross-cultural rebels whose rejection of conformity becomes equated with criminality, Claude remains to the end a team player, one of ours. Sensing the lost American's seductive significance, however, Claude still regards this character and the impulse toward cultural redefinition that he represents with a wistful envy, especially in the strange scene in which the lonely Nebraskan first picks the lost American and his French lover out of a crowd, follows them (the word "stalks" also presents itself), voyeuristically spies on their embrace, and then keeps watch over the pair "like a sentinel" (270).

Amid scholarship devoted to Claude's alleged homosexuality (an increasingly popular notion not without support in the text), this episode has received little attention—perhaps because the protagonist's behavior, at least in this instance, simply does not support a queer interpretation.[3] As a close reading reveals, Claude's encounter with the couple is, from the start, defined by heterosexual desire, his envy of the lost American's cultural redefinition accompanied by a vicarious and, given Claude's matrimonial vicissitudes, fully understandable satisfaction in the wounded soldier's enjoyment of a willing female partner. The scene occurs, suggestively, immediately following Claude's dinner with Victor Morse, an alcoholic affair erotically charged in its own way by Victor's offer to introduce Claude to some French prostitutes and by the orgasmic opening of bottles of champagne, a forbidden fruit that Claude, now an ocean away from the Anti-Saloon League, tastes for the first time. Still under the puritanical influence, as Victor puts it, of "'Church and State,'" Claude, the chaste YMCA doughboy, forgoes the opportunity to go "'play with some girls'" and spends his evening in characteristic fashion wandering the streets of St. Nazaire alone, dreamily contemplating the crowds (367). But Claude's long-thwarted sexual desire still finds an outlet amid his new surroundings, albeit in a fashion consistent with the preference for contemplation over action that he consistently displayed in Nebraska. Standing opposite a red theater sign that reads, appropriately enough, "Amour, quand tu nous tiens!" Claude suddenly catches sight of the lost American and his lover, somehow sensing, although he has not yet learned the details of the wounded soldier's mental condition, that the couple is "different." His gaze settles lovingly on the French girl's "young and soft" face, her "wide, blue eyes," and, in a disconcertingly eroticized detail, the "space between her two front teeth, as with children whose second teeth have just come" (269). As Claude shadows the couple ("without realizing what he did") and stands guard over their physical intimacy, the narrator's language continues to suggest arousal: "The girl bent over her soldier, stroking his head so softly that she might have been putting him to sleep; took his one hand and held it against her bosom as if to stop the pain there" (270).

If read as a reflection of Claude's reawakened heterosexual desire, suppressed and denied during his empty marriage to Enid, this scene takes on an interesting significance. One notes, for example, the disturbing coupling of sex and death: "[T]hey clung together in an embrace that was so long and still that *it was like death*"; the girl "might have been *putting him to sleep*" (271 emphasis mine). Such details give credence (though others in the novel do not) to Stanley Cooperman's influential assertion that Claude seeks out combat and ultimately self-destruction as a sublimated form of sexual gratification. More relevant to our present discussion, however, is the way Claude creates an eroticized image of the Other, transposing onto a French stranger all the qualities that he believes American women lack, especially those like Enid. Simultaneously childlike (note again those prepubescent teeth) and maternal (lying across her lap, the lost American resembles the wounded soldier cradled by the Greatest Mother in the World in the famous World War I poster), the lost American's lover is less a woman than a fantasy figure, one shaped through Claude's erotic gaze and made to conform to his often erroneous assumption, formed within twenty-four hours of his arrival in Europe, that France represents the perfect antithesis to Frankfort.

Indeed, the atmosphere of tension that surrounds the couple only intensifies Claude's identification with them. Claude notes "the expression of intense anxiety" on the wounded soldier's face and the "bewildered look" of his lover, and he is so moved by their ambiguous plight that he chivalrously vows to "take their part if any alarm should startle them" (270). While another observer might interpret such signs of stress as weaknesses in the couple's relationship, Claude prefers to interpret their unhappiness as the product of some vague menace lurking nearby. The next day, after he talks with the lost American directly and learns the details of his story from Dr. Trueman, Claude conceives of the wounded soldier and his lover as fugitives from the tyrannical Frankfort values that seek, via the medical authorities of the AEF, to reclaim one of theirs. Believing that he has found the explanation for the couple's anguish, Claude again expresses a chivalrous desire to intervene on their behalf: "He wished that he could do something to help that boy; help him get away from the doctor who was writing a book about him, and the [American] girl who wanted him to make the most of himself, get away and be lost altogether in what he had been lucky enough to find" (273). Although Cather's third-person narrator never directly questions Claude's romantic conclusions in this scene, Dr. Trueman perhaps steps in on the narrator's behalf. When Claude bitterly comments that the lost American is "fortunate" in his inability to remember his American fiancée, Dr. Trueman replies, "'Now Claude, don't begin to talk like that the minute you land in this country'" (273). But Claude ignores the wise advice offered by this true-man—just as he will later ignore Sergeant Hicks's incisive question at the French cemetery. Although content by the end of the novel to pursue his personal fulfillment through military action rather than a romantic relationship, Claude never renounces his erotically charged fascination with this character who has lit out for the new territory (albeit through the uninvited agency of a head wound) by merging with America's Other, by truly going "over there."

Though present for only a few pages, the lost American haunts the final quarter of *One of Ours* as a memorable projection of Claude's deepest longings, both cultural and sexual. But he is hardly the only character in book 5 who dangles before Claude the tantalizing possibilities offered by an alternative cultural orientation. Cather also presents the cross-cultural impulse, albeit in a more comic fashion, in Victor Morse, the preposterous Iowa-Englishman, and in Barclay Owens, whose archaeological discoveries (like Tom Outland's) become a monomania. Simultaneously ridiculous and compelling, Victor is one of Cather's greatest achievements, the one memorably comic figure in a novel otherwise lacking in humor. With his "pale forehead and brilliant eyes and saucy little moustaches" (267), Victor bears a striking resemblance to Charlie Chaplin, and his behavior matches Chaplin's comic exterior, especially his affectation of European savoir faire and patently phony English accent, which fail to fool even as gullible an audience as Claude Wheeler. Cather has considerable fun with Victor's absurdities. For example, although only two years have passed since Victor joined the Royal Flying Corps (RFC), he now uses the pompous phrase "you Americans" when referring to his fellow countrymen. Equally hilarious is Victor's affectedly blasé response when Claude asks for the name of his hometown: "'Crystal Lake, Iowa. I think that was the place'" (227). And then there are the stereotypical English colloquialisms that flow so incongruously from the Iowan's lips—phrases like "I say," "Rather!" "nasty business," and "quite knocked out" (233–34). As much an American "hick" or "yokel" as Claude, Victor talks, ironically enough, like one of the public-school boys turned officers in R. C. Sherriff's English war play *Journey's End*. Moreover, a hint of comic decadence flavors Victor's self-conscious artifice and the Wildian wit that peppers his speech—for example, when he comments on his escape from Crystal Lake: "'I've had a narrow escape, Wheeler; *as a brand from the burning*. That's all the scripture I can remember'" (267). Like the protagonist of "Paul's Case," Victor is both an aesthete (his cultivated persona is his art) and an escapee from the dreary world of Main Street, USA.

As Rebecca Faber points out in "'All the World Seemed Touched with Gold,'" Cather probably drew part of her inspiration for Victor Morse from the published letters of Victor Chapman, an American aviator who flew for the Allies before the American declaration of war and met his death on the Western Front. Cather's copy of Chapman's book, preserved in the Willa Cather Pioneer Memorial Archive at Red Cloud, bears witness to her fascination with the aviator's story: inside the front cover, the novelist pasted several news clippings concerning famous World War I pilots. The differences between Chapman and Morse, however, reveal far more than their similarities. Chapman came from a privileged, New England background; Cather's fighter pilot has literally risen, Dedalus-like, from the same middle-class, small-town milieu in which Claude was raised. Thus, Cather retained some of the attributes of the volunteer flyer she encountered in Chapman's letters while discarding others to create a character who would serve more effectively as Claude's double. Indeed, Cather's pilot is much more than a clown. For all its absurdity, Victor's playacting represents a variation, not entirely comic, on the kind of self-redefinition that Claude finds so attractive in the lost American and that the lonely Nebraskan seeks for himself. Although Victor may be a fraud, the simplistic dichotomy that he draws between Europe and Crystal Lake feeds Claude's own belief that in France he has finally found "something splendid." Victor's rhetoric on the subject is fraught with amusing hyperbole: "'In that part of France that's all shot to pieces, you'll find more life going on in the cellars than in your hometown . . . I'd rather be a stevedore in the London docks than a banker-king in one of your Prairie states'" (250). As for the small-town environment that both men have escaped, the aviator can barely contain himself: "'Where you come from it's nothing—a sleeping sickness. . . . My God, it's death in life!'" (249–50).

Victor's success in rejecting the kind of YMCA–sponsored Protestant morality to which Claude dutifully clings, even at the moments when he most intensely yearns for an alternative to American norms, also makes him a unique figure in *One of Ours*. In Crystal Lake, Victor works as a bookkeeper in his father's bank, and in a brilliant stroke, Cather makes us imagine him literally trapped behind bars— an image that readers who have visited the Willa Cather Pioneer Memorial Museum, housed within an especially forbidding and jail-like bank building, will especially appreciate. Ironically, Victor's most vivid nightmares once he joins the RFC are not of a fiery death (the fate, within two weeks, of most fighter pilots on the Western Front) but of suddenly finding himself back in the bank-teller's cage. As Victor confides to Claude, "'I have bad dreams, and find myself sitting on that damned stool in the glass *cage* and can't make my books balance; I hear the old man coughing in his private room, the way he coughs when he's going to refuse a loan to some poor devil who needs it'" (267 emphasis mine). Victor's hellish cubicle is reminiscent of the cages in the Spanish dungeons at Vera Cruz, which Usher describes to his companions aboard the *Anchises*—"'rusty iron cages where a man couldn't lie down or stand up, but had to sit bent over until he grew crooked'" (236). The bars that surround Victor at work symbolize the suffocating moral conventions that imprison his entire existence, stifling his natural desires and making him grow "crooked." Up to the moment when he suddenly defies his family by crossing the Canadian border and joining the Allied war effort, Victor, like Claude, is the good son who slavishly sacrifices himself to his parents' wishes. He goes into the bank business not because he has any interest in banking but because it is expected of him. Nor does he have any real affection for the "preacher's daughter" to whom he "got himself engaged" (248). Here again parental wishes prevail. Until his twentieth year, Victor remains all that his family and community can hope for—mindful of his obligations to the family bank business, chaste, teetotaling, and superficially content with the small pleasures (such as skating, tennis, and working in "the strawberry-bed") offered by life in a cultural backwater. But then comes the war—Victor's "avenue of escape" (248).

With a wonderful knack for comic insinuation, Cather reveals that the new Victor Morse we encounter aboard the *Anchises* has broken free of his cultural cage in ways that Claude Wheeler cannot begin to imagine. Now beyond the reach of the preacher's daughter, Victor has fallen into the willing arms of Maisie, a middle-aged camp follower, and taken to enjoying frequent "diversions" in French brothels—so much so in fact that he has contracted venereal disease, a secret he reveals (more to the reader than to Claude) when he sends the wide-eyed Nebraskan to procure "palliatives" from Dr. Trueman (250). Confronted with the innocent "Leftenant," Victor becomes an inexhaustible font of salacious advice, recommending that Claude "brush up" on his French: "'I hear your M. P.'s are very strict. You must be able to toss the word the minute you see a skirt, and make your date before the guard gets onto you'" (235).

When Claude wonders aloud whether "'French girls haven't any scruples,'" Victor humorously replies, "'I haven't found that girls have many, anywhere'" (235). All this from a young man who was warned by his father just two years before to avoid women "who ask the time without an introduction" (248). Victor's teetotaling days have ended as well. The model son who had never been inside a saloon before his enlistment now boozes past dawn, filling his shipboard compartment with the "heavy smell of rum" (224). The bookkeeper who agonized over his ledgers now drunkenly misplaces an entire trunk—and then, in a marvelous parody of an English snob, berates his bath steward for failing to locate his belongings.

Like the fugitive protagonist of "Paul's Case," who knows that his brief taste of the lush life must end in discovery and death, Victor justifies his childish hedonism with reminders of his own imminent demise. "'Women,'" he explains to Claude, "'don't require . . . fidelity of the air service. Our engagements are too short'" (268). "'In the air service, we don't concern ourselves with the future. It's not worthwhile'" (248). But Victor's reckless behavior also derives from the role that he has carefully studied and at times overplays: that of the swaggering English airman, whose devil-may-care attitude, unacceptable in any other soldier, reflects his membership in an elite (and for most of its initiates, quickly lethal) branch of the service. Pilots of all nationalities, especially aces (the media darlings of the Great War), carefully cultivated this image, which helps explain why no one aboard the *Anchises*, apart from Claude and his irritated bunk mates, finds Victor's antics especially surprising. For example, the American volunteers of the Lafayette Escadrille, whom Cather encountered in Victor Chapman's letters, caroused between missions accompanied by their own unique and sometimes dangerously frisky mascot, an African lion named "Whiskey." Alcohol flows through the aeronautical history of the Great War, regardless of nationality. What is most striking about Victor's transformation then is the extent to which he masters the peculiarly English nuances of his chosen persona. For example, although his accent still needs work, he has made considerable progress in the art of English understatement, an ironic form of self-expression that also reflects a distinctly non-American way of looking at the world. Asked if "'it makes a fellow feel pretty fine to bring down one of those German planes,'" Victor replies, again in language worthy of R. C. Sherriff's subalterns, "'Sometimes. I brought down one too many, though. It was very unpleasant'" (234). And on the subject of leaves: "'They work us pretty hard. . . . The only Cook's Tour we had was Gallipoli'" (233). Thus, Victor's entry into the ranks of the Royal Flying Corps represents both a hedonistic pursuit of the physical pleasures banned in Crystal Falls and the achievement, at least on some levels, of a different cultural orientation. Victor's makeover, in other words, is more than skin deep—more, ultimately, than just an act. Through boldness and his own variety of fabulous artifice, this Iowa Dedalus achieves what the lost American could presumably accomplish only through the aid of a bullet to the brain—flight from his Midwestern American values and the embrace of an alternative worldview.

The engineer, Barclay Owens, a minor but memorable character, offers still another variation on Cather's cross-cultural theme. Like the lost American's amnesia and Victor Morse's playacting (carried to the point such that the actor has started to become his part), Owens's transformation from xenophobic American technician into loquacious Europhile and would-be expert in classical history suggests an emptiness at the heart of modern American life, one that only an encounter with European cultural riches can fill. In this case, however, the character who is reborn in Europe remains unaware of the barrenness of American culture and of his desire for an alternative until he accidentally stumbles on his own unique "something splendid." Indeed, the Barclay Owens who goes to Spain during the prewar years to work on "the largest dam in the world" is, one suspects, a man who prides himself on his technical expertise as applied in the here and now—a man, in other words, who would feel at home in the practical, nuts-and-bolts environment of Frankfort, Nebraska. In college, the narrator remarks, Owens never showed "the least interest in classical studies," and as his later need for a translator reveals, he never bothered to learn a European language. His are "exclusively engineering brains" (299). Everything changes, however, when Owens suddenly receives a cathartic glimpse of antiquity that prefigures Tom Outland's life-altering encounter with ancient America in *The Professor's House*. While building his dam, the engineer uncovers an ancient Roman camp, and instantly he is hooked. The Roman Empire, from this point on, becomes his idée fixe. Now "an engineer by day and an archeologist by night," Owens orders "crates of books" from Paris—"everything that had been written on Caesar"—and employs "a young priest to translate them aloud" (298). History, or at least the portion of it that Owens adopts as his personal hobby horse, overwhelms the engineer's "easily inflamed imagination" (298). Owens becomes so obsessed with another time and place that he earns the half-affectionate, half-contemptuous nickname of "Julius Caesar."

The engineer's awakening to the fascinations of ancient Rome and his subsequent archaeological monomania might seem little more than a comic digression were it not for Cather's pointed attacks earlier in the novel on the anti-intellectual, humanities-hating tendencies of Main Street. In the utilitarian Middle America of the first half of *One of Ours*, the study of history or art signifies either godlessness or the greatest of all possible sins—impracticality. The denominational college that Claude attends, for example, ignores European history entirely, an omission based on the same neofundamentalist assumptions that Claude attributes to his mother: "The history of the human race, as it lay behind one, was already explained; and so was its destiny, which lay before. The mind should remain obediently within the theological concept of history" (23). Claude manages to study the Middle Ages from a secular perspective only by moonlighting at the state university. Bayliss's sour comments likewise reveal a completely dismissive attitude toward European culture and history. When Claude tells his brother that Julius Erlich is going to study abroad to become a professor (presumably in the humanities), Bayliss replies, " 'What's the matter with him? Does he have poor health?' " Europe, in Bayliss's eyes, is nothing more than a destination for consumptives, academia a vocation for invalids. Such, then, is the anti-intellectual background against which Cather sets Barclay Owens's passion for history. Thus, although comic, his eccentricity emerges as a subtle form of rebellion against American cultural norms. Just as Victor Morse passes into Canada and then on to the Royal Flying Corps, leaving the values of small-town America behind, Owens crosses the border between professional disciplines, between the practical and socially acceptable business of dam-building and the more suspect vocation of historian and archaeologist. Cather also makes Owens something more than just a Tristram-Shandyesque monomaniac (there are echoes of Sterne's Uncle Toby in the engineer's fixation on fortifications) by emphasizing the capacity for action that Owens displays following his immersion in the past. Once the Great War breaks out and work on the Spanish dam abruptly halts, Owens's newfound affection for European history carries over into his committed response to the Allied cause at a time when the vast majority of Americans favored neutrality. In one of the novel's more bizarre and amusing juxtapositions of the Old World and the New, "Julius Caesar" returns home to Kansas, of all places, "to explain the war to his countrymen." The Roman general then tours the American West "demonstrating exactly what had happened at the first battle of the Marne" (299).

Given the romantic lushness of Cather's portrayal of France, the poignance of the lost American as an extension of Claude's deepest yearnings, and the potential for cultural transcendence dramatized even in such comic characters as Victor Morse and Barclay Owens, one would expect Cather's novel to sustain its satire of American mores and to develop in a fashion that could never be mistaken for—to quote the language of the Pulitzer Prize that *One of Ours* received—a celebration of "American manners and manhood." As I have suggested above, *One of Ours* contains the seeds of an all-out attack on American values via the celebration of contrasting French virtues and the emphasis on cross-cultural journeying that if sustained would have placed *One of Ours* much closer to the war fiction of John Dos Passos and Ernest Hemingway. Imagine Claude carrying his fixation on the lost American to the point of desertion, for example, and you have the final quarter of Dos Passos's *Three Soldiers*, with its portrait of cross-cultural rebellion. Likewise, imagine Victor Morse surviving the Great War and returning to his cage in Crystal Lake, and you have Harold Krebs, the tortured protagonist of Hemingway's short story "Soldier's Home."[4] When considered in this way, *One of Ours* suddenly looks as though it belongs much closer to works more securely established in the canon of American World War I literature.

Why, then, does the novel not culminate in an explicit endorsement of one cultural orientation over the other? How is it that numerous readers have interpreted this text, with its withering assault on American values (at least in the first half), idealization of all things French, and celebration of the cross-cultural impulse as a work of naive patriotism? In the previous chapter I suggested that the modernist texture of *One of Ours*—its inconsistent point of view and multiplicity of conflicting perspectives—helps explain the polarized readings that the novel has attracted. An additional answer, however, lies in the simple fact that Claude, whose consciousness dominates the narrative in books 4 and 5, does not experience France as an autonomous, solitary traveler but as a contented member of a mass American army whose vision of itself and of its homeland finally exerts a stronger pull on the protagonist than even that of his beloved France. As the following overview of the culture systematically created within the AEF suggests, the features of Cather's text that prevent an outright endorsement of France over America from materializing are faithful both to Claude's complex personality and to the historical moment that Cather depicts.

What Claude's metamorphosis from potential lost American into exuberant junior officer acknowledges, albeit obliquely, is that for the first time in American military history, the U.S. Army of 1917 and 1918 sought not only to train its soldiers in the military arts but to indoctrinate them in a more expansive vision of their own nation. Indeed, according to historian Dennis Showalter, the importance of the First World War in American history lies not in the actual fighting or even in the American encounter with France but in the discovery made by millions of servicemen that "home" now signified something greater than one's community, county, or state (36). Home now meant America, and for thousands of soldiers from places like Frankfort, Nebraska, the experience of going "over there" ultimately became an education in the awesome power of the United States as a collective force on the world stage and in the advantages of the American way of life above all others.

Consider in this regard the sentiments displayed in the concluding chapter of Carl E. Haterius's *Reminiscences of the 137th Infantry*, a fairly typical World War I eyewitness account, part unit history and part personal memoir. After paying tribute to the "strong hearts, strong minds, and strong wills" of the French people, Haterius shifts in his final paragraph to what he regards as the greatest lesson of his overseas service:

> We have returned home, let us hope at least, bigger, better, stronger men and citizens, and do now realize our forthcoming responsibilities. We now realize that we, you and I, are stockholders in the greatest institution founded upon the sands of the earth. Today, we stand firmer for Democracy, Freedom, Equality, than ever before. . . . Yesterday, we went away, "State citizens" if you please; today we have returned *world citizens*. We see the brotherhood of man not merely in a local way, but in a worldly manner, for we realize that if the world is really to be made safe for democracy, it means that all, each of us, must needs realize our responsibility to our fellowmen. (224)

Among other things, Haterius's verbose mode of expression, abounding in capitalized abstractions and rhetorical redundancies, suggests the extent to which American soldiers internalized the language of Wilsonian Progressivism. Even more revealing, however, is the way this graduate of Bethany College in Lindsborg, Kansas, describes his expanded vision of the world. While internationalism or the "brotherhood of man" ostensibly emerges as his theme, the author assumes that this universal utopia will, of course, derive from the global proliferation of quintessential *American* values and beliefs. What Haterius actually describes here—in the nineteenth year of what we now call the "American Century"—is his wartime awakening to the potentialities of the United States as a world leader, as a model for the rest of the planet. For Haterius, as for thousands of doughboys, the First World War finally represented a lesson more in America culture, as posited by the military and political Progressives who taught this Kansan to write like Woodrow Wilson, than in the French variety.

In fact, the cross-cultural impulse that Cather examines was weak—if present at all—in the vast majority of Americans who joined the Great Crusade. For example, despite the popularity of bicultural romances in silent war films, relatively few American soldiers actually married French women (see Meigs 107–42). Fewer still settled in France or expressed, in later years, a preference for Gallic culture. And for American veterans who later revisited France, perhaps to commemorate the tenth anniversary of the armistice or some similar occasion, the allure of former battlefields and wartime haunts—sites indelibly linked to *American* experience—usually proved irresistible. Most of these veterans followed an itinerary essentially the same as the one Frank Holden imagined for himself in *War Memories*. One searches in vain amid the written artifacts of the AEF and postwar veterans' societies for anything even remotely resembling Victor Morse's declaration that he would rather work as a laborer on the London docks than become a "banker-king" on the American prairie. While vaudeville queried, "How ya gonna keep 'em down on the farm after they've seen Paree?" the voluminous writings left behind by Americans who actually served overseas (including letters, diaries, unit histories, memoirs, regimental newspapers, and the *Stars and Stripes*) almost universally express the conviction that Europe, even "Paree," has nothing on America.

As Mark Meigs demonstrates, two factors explain this ubiquitous sense of national pride and the resistance to outside influences that emerged as the defining cultural features of the AEF: first, the War Department's unprecedented attempt to exercise benevolent control over every conceivable facet of its soldiers' lives, and second, the unconscious tendency of Americans who served abroad to pass through foreign cultures not as travelers, attuned to the possibilities for self-enrichment represented by cultural difference, but as tourists and consumers. In a remarkable example of the former, a soldier's private life while off duty, once left to the discretion of the individual, became during the First World War the subject of an intense motivational agenda. Endorsed by the army and beloved by political Progressives such as President Woodrow Wilson and Secretary of War Newton D. Baker, civilian organizations like the YMCA and the Knights of Columbus worked tirelessly to ensure that the doughboy's character remained as spotless as his rifle. Such organizations distributed pamphlets warning of the dangers of venereal disease, constructed reading rooms and other wholesome diversions (designed to counter the not-so-wholesome Victor Morse variety), and in general incessantly reminded the American soldier of his obligations as a full-time ambassador of the greatest nation on earth.

Even the areas to which a soldier could travel on leave became a matter of progressive planning. As if sensing the very subversive quality that Cather assigns to France, the U.S. Army avoided simply turning Americans loose in an unfamiliar culture by establishing specific leave areas where members of the AEF could be provided with American-style amenities, trained to "appreciate" famous examples of European art, and perhaps most important, be spared the inconvenience of dealing with non-English-speaking natives. Victor Morse, in fact, actually refers to this xenophobic practice when he scornfully remarks to Claude, "'I understand the Americans have leased the Riviera,—recuperate at Nice and Monte Carlo'" (233). Genuine cross-cultural interaction, which might have led to a questioning of American values, did not fit the agenda of the AEF. Thus, the resemblance between the American military leave of 1918 and the European bus tour of today is hardly coincidental. With its assumption of passivity, detachment, and recreation-oriented activity, tourism provided the perfect model for an army less interested in exposing its soldiers to a foreign culture than in vigorously promoting its own.

Judging from the behavior of most American soldiers, the notion of the Great Crusade as an elaborate, expense-paid tour of Europe became an especially appealing one. Though homesick and often frustrated by the "Frogs," doughboys dutifully mailed home postcards of famous French cathedrals, castles, and battlefields (along with countless silk articles embroidered with the words "Souvenir de France"), made sure that they were photographed in front of famous European landmarks (such as the Eiffel Tower and Notre Dame), and whenever possible seized the opportunity to learn the sorts of touristy facts and figures covered in Baedeker travel guides. The general staff of the Eighty-ninth Division, one of the units assigned to occupation duty following the armistice, even created a special booklet designed to assist members of the division as they took in the sights along the Rhine. Titled *Historical Sketch of German Area Occupied by the 89th Division,* the booklet described for its readers (mostly draftees from Kansas, Missouri, and Nebraska) the architectural and scenic wonders of an area previously accessible to only the wealthiest of American travelers. However, fraternization with the modern-day denizens of this region "rich in legend, lore, and fables" (3) was, of course, forbidden. Nor, predictably, does the booklet ever suggest that American visitors have anything to learn from German culture.

In their diaries and personal memoirs, World War I soldiers often slip into language that comes straight out of guidebooks, thus demonstrating once again the extent to which members of the AEF internalized the kinds of discourse and concomitant worldview with which the U.S. Army and its civilian allies bombarded them. For instance, in the diary of a Nebraska machine gunner who served with the Eighty-ninth Division, a Baedeker-like voice suddenly takes over when the author describes his seven-day leave near the French Alps: "March the 9th [1919] John and I took the lake trip offered by the YMCA. They had chartered the largest boat on the lake, carrying about 250 passengers. Lake Bourget, one of the main charms, is less than two miles from Aix. This beautiful sheet of water is 11 miles wide and 13 miles long, while 500 feet is its greatest depth. The outlet was formerly in the south, but in the year 1248 a landslide occurred from Mt. Granier" (Stricklett 174). Then a few paragraphs later he writes: "Hannibal's Pass on the Chambery-Lyon road, built by the ancient Romans, was pointed out by the guide. Hannibal came over it on his way to Italy in 218 B.C. To the right of this pass rises Mt. Charoz, on which one sees two little hamlets almost hidden from sight up among the cliffs" (175). And so forth. In a presumably unconscious regurgitation of guidebook prose, the author illustrates a way of responding to foreign lands that bears little resemblance to the intense cultural *engagement* seen in the lost American (and even in Victor Morse) or the sincere historical enthusiasm displayed by Barclay Owens. For this Nebraskan, Europe represented little more than a cavalcade of curious facts, quaint customs, and scenic wonders, none of which ever prompted him to think critically about his own background. The important thing was recording the details—the depth of the lake, the date of the landslide, the location of Hannibal's Pass—for the future edification of the folks at home. Such is the mind-set Cather captures when she depicts a group of soldiers, led by Sergeant Hicks, touring the churches of St. Nazaire. Utterly monolingual, oblivious to non-American cultural practices, and unable even to use French currency, Hicks and his comrades make an especially amusing band of ugly Americans. But they have learned the ethos of tourism well, as Cather perceptively indicates: "It was in their minds that they must not let a church escape, any more than they would let a Boche escape" (264). Like the present-day American tourist who slogs from one predictable postcard destination to another, dutifully videotaping everything, Cather's soldiers understand that there are sights they *must* not miss.

In their personal writings, the accidental tourists of the AEF also demonstrate that modern sightseeing—a feature of twentieth-century American life that one can actually see taking shape during the First World War—carries with it an obligation to *buy things*. Tourists, by definition, are also consumers. Indeed, in the diary of Dr. Frederick Sweeney, the New Hampshire physician whose experiences formed the principal basis for the *Anchises* episode of *One of Ours*, Cather encountered many illustrations of this truism. Following his perilous Atlantic crossing, Dr. Sweeney was assigned to Base Hospital #65 near Brest where he endured a tour of duty that was equal parts boredom and horror. While the subjects of mud, loneliness, and the lingering effects of his own bout with the Spanish flu dominate many of his wartime entries, the human wreckage he saw produced by American battles in the fall of 1918 appears as well. For example, in a passage that leaves little doubt as to whether Cather encountered the full hideousness of war while researching her novel, Sweeney describes the wave of American casualties that swamped his hospital at the height of the Meuse-Argonne campaign. On 9 November 1918, he writes: "They put 80 [wounded men] in my two wards, over 800 coming to Base Hospital #65. Most of them are Western boys and their wounds are very bad. Two of them had their eyes shot out, or one eye each, arms and legs off, and about every conceivable injury or wound."[5]

However, such sobering realities never squelched Dr. Sweeney's desire to acquire mementos of his service in the Great War. For example, on the very day that the doctor records his sobering visit to a nearby AEF cemetery—"1,650 graves since Oct. 1st [1918]"—he writes, "Got an officer's helmet German [*sic*] as souvenir today to take home. Also a smoker's set made from 105 in. shell." Several days later Sweeney mentions that he "[b]ought 5 napkin rings [made] from French shells." The acquisitiveness of American soldiers in the First World War, enhanced by their high rate of pay (in comparison with other Allied troops) was legendary; hence the amusing scene in *One of Ours* in which Hicks and company, again exemplifying the crass insularity of the typical American tourist, descend on a French cheese shop, ignore the regulations in effect to prevent wartime shortages, and swiftly devour everything in sight. In another overt departure from Claude's point of view, the narrator momentarily enters the mind of the shop proprietress, whose perception of the voracious Americans as cultural and economic marauders tempers her delight in overcharging them. In her eyes, the freewheeling Americans are part of an "invasion" that because of its emphasis on consumerism has "threatened everybody's integrity" (264).

Inevitably, along with the U.S. Army's largely successful mission to educate its men on American superiority, the pleasures of tourism, and the American way of consumer consumption came an emphasis on conformity, on molding the individual to fit the mass culture that the military now helped to define. The themes of cooperation and the subordination of the individual to the group appear everywhere in the cultural artifacts of the AEF, nowhere more strikingly than in World War I–vintage panoramic photographs. Among the most popular souvenirs of the era, these yard-long images typically depict an entire company, approximately two hundred identically Stet-soned young men, lined up on bleachers or arranged in an oblong formation outside their barracks. As intended, the individuals are almost indistinguishable. What such photographs convey as their "subject" is the collective power of the group, the sense of strength and solidarity created by bringing so many interchangeable figures together within the same frame. In a variation on this approach, some World War I photographs taken from towers or balloons depict divisional insignia constructed out of the living bodies of thousands of soldiers. The photographic record left behind by the AEF illustrates how far the U.S. Army had come by 1918 in its pursuit of military homogenization (and the symbols thereof) since the days of the Civil

War daguerreotype, with its emphasis on individual flair and exotic, nonregulation props.

The footlockers or suitcases full of wartime keepsakes that many World War I veterans cherished for the rest of their lives also speak eloquently of a standardized experience. Regardless of their prewar background, soldiers collected the same kinds of booty from dead or captured Germans; wore the same aluminum dog tags (each stamped with the soldier's serial number, another World War I–era innovation that bespeaks the impersonality required by modern war); purchased the same commercial postcards; wrote on the same YMCA stationery; recorded their monthly earnings (minus war-risk insurance premiums and Liberty Loan contributions) in the same regulation pay book; carried the same collection of official U.S. Army song lyrics (as well as the standard-issue New Testament with khaki cover); and shaved with the same recently introduced Gillette safety razor. In a truly surreal expression of World War I–style impersonality, the U.S. Army and its civilian partners even standardized the personal correspondence that flowed homeward from the AEF. After all, the army was confident in this new age of mass culture that it already knew what the boys wanted to say. When American soldiers first arrived in France, for example, they dutifully signed and addressed a small card, subsequently mailed to their families, that read simply, "The Ship on Which I Sailed Has Arrived Safely Overseas." Even more bizarre was the postcard designed by the YMCA for soldiers to fill out as soon as they landed on the east coast. Faked to look like a personal note, complete with appropriately generic greetings and written in bogus cursive, the card must have been an invaluable aid to the soldier suffering from writer's block: "Arrived today in the good old U.S.A. It certainly looks good to me. Feeling fine and dandy. Sure anxious to see you" (see fig. 11). If the Great Crusade was ultimately about the making of Americans, then very few patterns—linguistic or otherwise—were used as molds.

For the vast majority of American soldiers in the First World War, this incessant emphasis on collectivity and conformity simply did not lead to the kind of disillusionment that Dos Passos presents in *Three Soldiers*, as his characters realize their servitude to "the vast

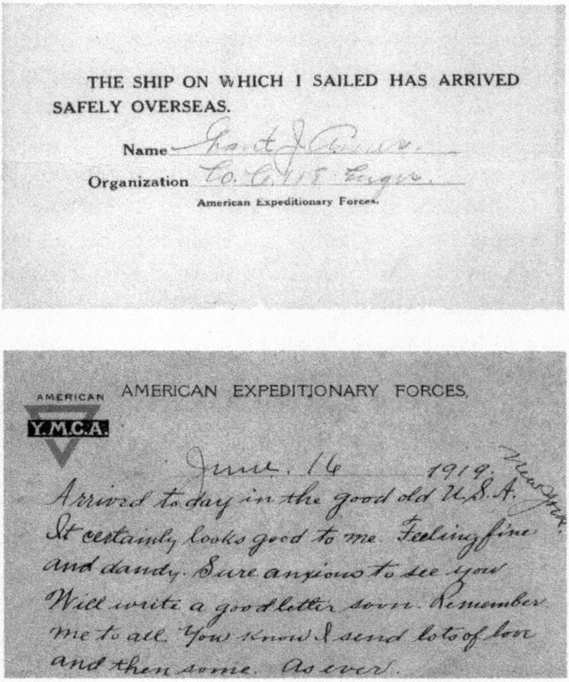

THE SHIP ON WHICH I SAILED HAS ARRIVED
SAFELY OVERSEAS.

Name *Grant J. Co....v.*

Organization *Co. C. 118 Engrs.*

American Expeditionary Forces.

AMERICAN AMERICAN EXPEDITIONARY FORCES.

Y.M.C.A.

June 16   1919.
Arrived to day in the good old U.S.A.
It certainly looks good to me. Feeling fine
and dandy. Sure anxious to see you.
Will write a good letter soon. Remember
me to all. You know I send lots of love
and then some. As ever.

Fig. 11. Standardized correspondence
created by the Red Cross and the YMCA (author's collection).

machine" and are ground "under the wheels." On the contrary, as
their personal writings indicate, most members of the AEF felt a
general sense of purpose and belonging—even when the conduct
of American military operations seemed dubious—that Mark Meigs
aptly characterizes in the title of his study of AEF culture: *Optimism
at Armageddon*. American attitudes toward the Great War for Civilization may have soured to some extent following the Versailles
conference, and the contradictory realities of the Great Crusade may
have prevented the formulation of enduring myths within the postwar culture of military commemoration. However, for soldiers *at the
time*, the worldview continually reinforced by the U.S. Army with
its emphasis on American solidarity and global leadership, together

with the emerging values of mass American culture as exemplified by tourism and consumer consumption, offered a welcome conceptual framework for the otherwise bewildering experience of world war.

Indeed, the lessons taught by the AEF often penetrated the inner lives of its members to an extent that they themselves probably did not realize. Dr. Sweeney's diary again provides an especially compelling example of how soldiers turned to the models with which the army provided them in times of stress. While marooned at Base Hospital #65 for months following the armistice, Dr. Sweeney fell into a state of profound depression and made several attempts to wrangle an immediate discharge, behavior that perhaps explains his initial hesitancy to share his diary with Cather. Filled with home-sickness and gloom, his entries for this period are, if anything, even darker than those describing the maimed bodies produced by the Meuse-Argonne campaign. But in his entry for 8 March 1919, the darkest day of all, the physician heals himself through a revealing rhetorical formula: "This has been an awful lonesome day for me, one of the worst I ever put in in my life. Sometimes I am afraid I am going to lose my nerve but I never did yet nor shall I now, even if I stay here until I die. *I am a soldier*!" Middle-aged, the head of a family, and a well-paid professional, Dr. Sweeney was hardly a typical American warrior. And yet the doctor's emphatic declaration—"*I am a soldier*!"—betrays a surprising investment in the one-size-fits-all identity that the U.S. Army had handed him and four million other men. While Dos Passos's burnt-out doughboys turn, in their moments of loneliness and misery, to the forbidden fruits of French culture dangled just outside the military machine, Sweeney adopted a more common form of coping with personal unhappiness—by willfully recommitting himself to the ethical and cultural standards of his own group. Despite the pronounced differences in age, family status, and professional training that separated Sweeney from the men who flowed through his ward, he still saw himself as an American soldier, and he remained pledged, even when his personal experience of the Great Crusade became especially bitter, to the ethos of teamwork and self-sacrifice in which he had been acculturated. He, too, was one of ours.

Thus, although Cather never refers specifically to any of the innumerable propaganda posters, training pep talks, silent war films, YMCA pamphlets, martial sermons, regimental newspapers, military stage shows, and patriotic sing-alongs through which a citizen soldier such as Lt. Claude Wheeler would have absorbed the cultural values of the AEF, her novel nevertheless traces the essential trajectory of the male American war experience, presenting a progression from a locally defined identity to membership in a brave new American collective. Or, to put it another way, as a Nebraskan stuck on a farm near Frankfort Claude is miserable, but as an *American* he is filled with a sense of purpose and fulfillment. Even the title of Cather's novel reflects this theme. *Claude*, the title that Cather preferred, would have stressed the hero's moments of cross-cultural yearning by highlighting his Gallic name. But the title *One of Ours*, as it turns out, is truer to Claude's destiny. By the end of the novel Claude's story is no longer that of a French soul trapped in a clumsy American body but of the fusion of individual need and collective action, the perfect meeting of the "one" and the "ours."

The failure, then, of *One of Ours* to sustain its satirical uses of France and its celebration of the cross-cultural impulse has as much to do with the identity-altering environment created within the AEF, which Cather astutely acknowledges through her protagonist's transformation, as it does with the text's (frequently interrupted) fidelity to Claude's point of view. While France beckons to Claude, tempting him to emulate the lost American, a more powerful force ultimately claims his allegiance—the agenda of the army that he so contentedly inhabits. This radical but plausible shift in Claude's perceptions helps explain features of *One of Ours* that might otherwise seem bewildering, especially the way that certain scenes in book 5 appear to retract the attacks on American cultural sterility so effectively delivered in the first half. Examples of this contradiction abound. For instance, while the Nebraska chapters underscore the evils of modern machinery (note that a "gasoline motor-truck" [115] causes the protagonist's plow team to drag him into a barbed-wire fence), Claude achieves fulfillment, ironically enough, in the midst of the most industrialized war imaginable. At one point even the moonscape produced by modern field artillery offers him "reassuring signs"

(289). Likewise, the novel's treatment of mass production does an about-face in book 5. In Nebraska, Claude resists the products offered by his throwaway society and patiently repairs Mahailey's antiquated kitchen knife when the other Wheelers threaten to buy her something more modern. In France, however, Claude's encounters with mass-produced American goods stimulate not irritation but pride. When he sees pieces of American crates used in the shantytowns of French refugees, he feels "cheered" by the familiar company names painted on the boards. The rows of canned goods that Claude glimpses in Mme. Olive's storeroom—"all with American names"—produce a similar response, prompting Claude to reflect patriotically on his nation's "long arm" (311–12).

To some critics, this kind of thematic backpedaling suggests that Cather lost control of her novel—that she allowed her naive enthusiasm for the Great Crusade to weaken the indictment of American vulgarity and anti-intellectualism that *One of Ours* promises in its first half to deliver with knockout force. Critics who posit the existence of a consistent ironic subtext, on the other hand, have interpreted such contradictions as evidence that Claude remains utterly blind from start to finish—first to his own failings then to the extent of his wartime indoctrination. Blind Claude may be, but readings of *One of Ours* that adhere too rigidly to either of these positions ignore the perceptiveness with which Cather attributes her hero's rebirth, however ironic, to the specific cultural agenda of the AEF, especially to the more expansive conception of America that soldiers like Carl E. Haterius later remembered as the most important lesson of their service in the First World War. Thus, the remainder of this chapter considers Claude's growing identification with his fellow Americans, an attitude almost impossible to imagine in books 1 and 2.

More typically examined in terms of its homoerotic overtones, Claude's friendship with David Gerhardt emerges as a crucial catalyst in his awakening to the collective power and potentiality of America. At first sight, the artistic Gerhardt would seem to belong in the category of misfits who turn to Europe for various forms of fulfillment denied in the United States. The product of an Ivy League—and thus Eurocentric—education, Gerhardt speaks fluent French, understands the nuances of Gallic culture (he relates, with equal ease, to both the humble Jouberts and the aristocratic Fleurys), and until the war enjoys a successful career as a classical soloist, performing the works of European masters on his seventeenth-century Italian violin. He is far removed from the typical doughboy tourist. However, like Dr. Sweeney, a man similarly out of step with the rank and file of the AEF, Gerhardt is subtly won over by the value system of his new military environment. In the Fleurys' chateau, where Gerhardt displays a genuine savoir faire that would put Victor Morse to shame, the violinist even offers a variation on Dr. Sweeney's therapeutic assertion of his military identity. When asked by the brother of his dead friend to play the violin, Gerhardt opens his initial refusal with the words, "'But, Lucien, *I am a soldier now*'" (337 emphasis mine). As Gerhardt's behavior throughout book 5 demonstrates, his characterization of himself as a "soldier" in this revealing scene is neither a straightforward statement of fact nor a calculated excuse designed to spare Madame Fleury the painful experience of hearing music performed on her dead son's instrument. What Gerhardt means is that he has renounced his former identity as an artist—a renunciation symbolized by the violent demise of his Stradivarius, "smashed into a thousand pieces" (330) in a car accident—in favor of the military mold. Gerhardt explains his personal journey from artist to infantry officer, a transformation no less remarkable than Claude's, through his own vague, fatalistic philosophy. "'The war,'" he tells Claude, "'was put up to our generation. I don't know what for; the sins of our fathers, probably'" (330). His only hope resides in a vague intuition that all the suffering produced by the Great War will finally "'bring a new idea into the world . . . something Olympian'" (331).

At the same time, however, this Europeanized sophisticate, who seems to have leaped into the trenches straight from the fiction of Henry James, remains bound to American concepts of military duty and honor that he never acknowledges openly—or perhaps even realizes that he has absorbed. When faced with the possibility of evading the draft, for example, Gerhardt conforms to his culture's conception of military service as a masculine obligation. As he explains to Claude, "'I couldn't stand for it. I didn't feel I was a good enough violinist to admit that I wasn't a man'" (329). Ironically, this devotee of high culture implies that fidelity to art, rather than war, would have been the act of a coward—and a sissy.[6] Once in France, Gerhardt further falls into line with the manly ethos of war. We learn, for example, that rather than remain in the U.S. Army Band where he was first posted, Gerhardt requests assignment to a combat unit and receives his promotion to lieutenant only after serving on the front line. This unwillingness to settle for an emasculating "soft job" unites him with his men, mostly Midwesterners, who might otherwise resent having a cultured New Yorker as their superior: "They respected a man who could have wiggled out and didn't" (288). Moreover, when Colonel Scott introduces the officers of Claude's company to their new replacement, he mentions that Gerhardt was given "'his commission for good service'" and that the musician is "'a capable fellow'" (279)—high praise from this former member of the Pershing Rifles. Far from exemplifying the cross-cultural impulse, Gerhardt is in the end an American follower like Claude; were he anything else, the bond between the two men would hardly be so strong.

Through their friendship, Claude and David create a model in microcosm of American power and unity, joining the American West, the former frontier, with New York City, the seat of modernity and the arts. Each offers complementary strengths. Though physically frail, unaccustomed to outdoor work, and flawed by "occasional superciliousness" (288), Gerhardt proves the perfect ambassador, if you will, of Manifest Destiny abroad, and he inspires Claude's envy through his effortless ability to move in and out of other languages and cultural settings, all the while performing his duties as an American officer. More inured to physical labor and possessed, albeit grudgingly, of practical know-how, Claude, on the other hand, brings pioneering energy and enthusiasm to the Great Crusade, as well as humility, openness, and naïveté that complement Gerhardt's confidence and worldly knowledge. While Gerhardt effortlessly masters the diplomatic tasks necessitated by waging war in France, such as negotiating with non-English-speaking farmers for shelter or provisions, Claude proves most adept when it comes to interacting with the men under his command, even handling a "baby" (239) like Bert Fuller with the right mixture of firmness and maternal gentleness. In this pair of American officers, urbanism reconciles with agriculture, east coast sophistication merges with Midwestern earnestness, and art strikes a balance with utility. Ultimately Claude and David, both of whom *could* have followed the example of Victor Morse or the lost American but do not, symbolize a united America ready to take its place as a world power.

Such friendships were not unusual, especially during a conflict that radically modified the traditional American practice (vividly displayed during the Civil War) of tying military organizations to particular regions or states. Indeed, in the rapport between these two dissimilar but complementary men, Cather captures yet another important feature of American participation in the First World War—the way that members of the AEF broadened their knowledge of America through their day-to-day interaction with fellow soldiers of varying ethnicity whose homes were spread out across the nation. The idea of an American military unit as a cross section of the United States is, of course, a standard feature of World War II combat narratives, ranging from Norman Mailer's *Naked and the Dead* to Steven Spielberg's *Saving Private Ryan*. But in Claude Wheeler's war, the kind of education in American regional and ethnic diversity that we now associate with military service was a new development, one not fully anticipated by the War Department. As reflected by Cather's references throughout book 5 to regiments of "Missourians" and "Kansans," state affiliations remained in place for some units for at least part of the First World War. In accordance with the organizational scheme hastily worked out by the U.S. Army in 1917, National Guardsmen who hailed from the same state, for example, typically served together, while so-called National Army Divisions (a euphemism for organizations consisting of draftees) usually drew their initial membership from two or more neighboring states. Thus, to take the approximately 48,000 soldiers (Ayres 23) provided by Nebraska as an example, most of those who belonged to the Nebraska National Guard found themselves assigned to the Thirty-fourth Division, which made it to France but never saw action, while perhaps a quarter or so of those drafted went into the Eighty-ninth "Middle-West" Division where they served in combat, then in the Army of Occupation, with men from Kansas, Missouri, and the Dakotas.

However, the speed with which the United States had to assemble its massive army, which grew from fewer than 200,000 troops to four million in about twenty months, and the devastating casualty rates experienced by American units once they entered the front line soon led to a breakdown in this system. In the interest of reaching France as quickly as possible, the famous Forty-second "Rainbow" Division, for instance, contained National Guard units thrown together from numerous states. Even more dramatic, the suggestively nicknamed "All-American" Division, the Eighty-second, claimed to hold members from every state in the Union. Moreover, units that *did* have distinct regional identities when they set sail for France — note Cather's references in the *Anchises* section to the closely knit "Kansas Band," a veritable Pals Battalion whose fourteen members all enlisted from the same prairie town — quickly lost them once they entered battle and experienced what military experts euphemistically refer to as "wastage" or "attrition." Men from numerous western and Midwestern states, for example, flooded New York's own Seventy-seventh Division when it suffered heavy losses in the Meuse-Argonne Offensive. During the same campaign, Minnesotans poured into the depleted ranks of the "All Kansas" 353rd Infantry, rendering its name a misnomer. As historian Dennis Showalter points out, even the numbering system for World War I regiments (most of them brand-new entities) reflects this new conception of men as material, ready to be shifted as needed within a national military framework. For the first time in American history, regiments bore triple-digit designations, thereby suggesting the dizzying number of individuals involved and the unavoidable impersonality of the system created to accommodate them (32–33).

Arbitrarily mixing together soldiers from different regions and ethnic backgrounds was not without its dangers, as military planners learned when they naively required a regiment of mostly Irish New Yorkers (the "Fighting 69th" of later Hollywood fame) to serve alongside a regiment of Alabamians in the Forty-second Division. In the brawls that ensued, one soldier from Alabama was killed (Cooke, *The Rainbow Division* 15). And there was one sizable contingent of men (numbering more than 200,000) that the U.S. Army never regarded as interchangeable with other soldiers — African Americans.

Though Native, Hispanic, and Asian Americans served alongside whites in the First World War, African Americans found themselves in segregated regiments (assigned mostly to tasks considered too unpleasant for other soldiers, such as the retrieval of bodies) and in some cases were disowned to the point of being officially attached to the French Army. The military's Jim Crow policies, which basically rendered blacks invisible to their white counterparts, explain why African American soldiers never appear in *One of Ours*. Realistically, in the rigidly segregated environment of the AEF, a white junior officer such as Lt. Claude Wheeler would have had little or no interaction with the one group of servicemen deliberately excluded from the Progressive vision of American solidarity. Though probably apocryphal, an anecdote in Dr. Sweeney's diary recorded secondhand on 19 February 1918 may have provided Cather with a vivid measure of race relations at the time, at least as constructed by the myth-generating discourse of military scuttlebutt: "A Negro Officer who had been drinking wine, ordered a white Sgt. to salute him so a French girl would know he was an officer. The Sgt. ignored him and the officer drew a knife and the Sgt. killed him."

Despite the occasional eruptions of violence between soldiers bent on reenacting the Civil War and the systematic marginalizing of blacks, most members of the AEF viewed their overseas experience as an enlightening introduction to American diversity and, more important, commonality. The kind of cultural unity Claude comes to share with his fellow soldiers also draws comment in historical documents from the period. For example, in one of G. P. Cather's letters from France, he writes of the simultaneous ethnic variety and cultural homogeneity that he perceives in the men under his command: "My boys are all good boys. I think they will go through anything with me, and I know my sergeant will take the platoon right on through by himself if necessary. I get to know my boys pretty well. I censor all their mail, and in that way I come to know them. I have Americans, English, Germans, French, Swedes, Italians, Austrians, Poles and Greeks represented in my platoon. However, the majority are Americans" (qtd. in Faber, "'All the World Seemed Touched with Gold'" 141–42). What Lieutenant Cather meant in this context by "Americans" is unclear. However, he likely used this label for second- or third-generation citizens, whose specific European ancestry no longer showed on the surface, or for soldiers whose ethnicity was simply indeterminate. Whatever the case, while emphasizing the diversity represented in his platoon, Cather's cousin managed at the same time to stress the power of assimilation—*most* of his men were "Americans," and *all* of them were "good boys," able warriors, in other words, shaped uniformly by the teachings of their military masters. Moreover, it is telling that even the soldiers whom Lieutenant Cather considered overtly ethnic Americans presumably wrote in English. Otherwise he could not have "censor[ed] all their mail" and "come to know them."

Amid this military melting pot, friendships such as the one Cather depicts between a Nebraska farmer and a New York violinist opened unforeseen vistas on a nation that most Americans at the time perceived primarily in terms of their own immediate neighborhood, community, or county. Indeed, with one-third its present population and a sizable percentage of its citizens still living in small towns, the United States in 1917 was a nation of Frankforts, a demographic reality that made the experience of serving in a truly national army alongside citizen soldiers of varying ethnicity and regional ties all the more memorable. Thus, when viewed in this context, Claude's interaction with an ever-widening variety of American characters in books 4 and 5 of *One of Ours*, culminating in his all-important friendship with David Gerhardt, takes on a new significance and helps, once again, to explain the waning of the cross-cultural impulse in the closing pages of the novel.

In addition to serving as a vital structural link between the Nebraska chapters and those set in France, book 4 in particular charts an important expansion in the range and number of Claude's American acquaintances. Ironically, while at home in the so-called American heartland, Claude spends most of his time by himself. For example, book 3, titled "Sunrise on the Prairie," has an especially lonely atmosphere, as when the protagonist soaks in his outdoor bath tub, dreamily composing his theory of the "children of the moon" (171) until Enid's automobile appears and shatters his solitary reverie. Claude's new role aboard the *Anchises* at the beginning of chapter 4, on the other hand, keeps him in constant contact with an eclectic

but united assortment of fellow countrymen. And in contrast to the
silent stretches of book 3—at one point Claude even feigns sleep
to avoid speaking with his wife—dialogue fills the narrative of his
eastward voyage. The diverse interlocutors include Lieutenant Bird,
a drawling Virginian whose speech (marked by the use of "ain't" and
"I reckon" [226]) vividly evidences his regional roots; Corp. Fritz
Tannhauser, the German American giant who contracts influenza
and deliriously rants "in the language of his early childhood" (241);
the "four Swedish boys from the Scandinavian settlement at Lindsborg" (230); the Marine, Albert Usher, who was left an orphan on
a "lonesome ranch" (228) in Wyoming; the bandmaster from "Hill-
port, Kansas" (224); Claude's bunkmate, Lt. Tod Fanning, formerly
of the Westinghouse Works in Chicago; Captain Maxey, a Nebraskan
whose family originally came from Mississippi; Dr. Trueman, who
presumably hails (like his model) from New Hampshire; and, of
course, Victor Morse, the Iowan turned English flyer. While these
soldiers talk to Claude about their individual pasts, amid various
locales, the narrator stresses their wartime homogeneity. Boarding
the ship, the men form "brown lines" that flow "continuously up
the gangways, like belting running over machinery" (220). Gazing
at the Statue of Liberty, they coat the superstructure of the *Anchises*
with "brown uniforms," clinging to "the boat davits, the winches,
the railings and ventilators, like bees in a swarm." "Two thousand
voices" boom out the words to "Over There" (221). And later, as
Claude gazes at the assorted visages of his shipmates, the narrator
remarks, "Their youth seemed to flow together, like their brown
uniforms" (228). Like G. P. Cather's description of the soldiers under his command, "The Voyage of the *Anchises*" presents Claude's
education in American diversity (at least among whites) and the
promise of a greater America with a truly national culture, ready to
extend its benefits abroad. "In this massing and movement of men,"
he concludes, "there was nothing mean or common" (231).

One measure of just how quickly and intensely Claude comes
to share the sense of national identity that unites this grab bag of
American characters appears when he discovers Corp. Bert Fuller,
the same soldier who later responds so emotionally to the "Boche"
infant, "misconducting himself." At sick call Claude notices the cor-

poral "snivelling and crying like a baby" (239), and in a display of assertive leadership that strikingly contrasts with his impotent behavior earlier in the novel, Cather's hero takes the anguished soldier in hand through a revealing appeal to military esprit de corps: "'If you can't stop that, Bert Fuller, get where you won't be seen. *I don't want all these English stewards standing around to watch an American soldier cry*. I never heard of such a thing'" (239 emphasis mine). At end of their conversation, by which point the lieutenant's mixture of firmness and empathy has produced the desired boost in Corporal Fuller's morale, Claude cunningly modifies his initial concern with face-saving: "'I know it's a little gloomy. *But don't you shame me before these English stewards*'" (240 emphasis mine). Skillfully manipulated, Fuller now understands that "misconducting himself" will reflect poorly on the AEF and, even more important, on Lieutenant Wheeler. While critics have stressed the paradoxically maternal, nurturing quality of the all-male community created aboard the *Anchises*, within which Claude happily functions as a nurse and cheerleader, the masculine, nationalistic ethos that undergirds Claude's conception of soldierly behavior also deserves mention. Just as David Gerhardt eschews his "soft job" in favor of a combat assignment, in order to retain his self-image as an American male, Claude automatically suppresses the supposedly un-manning hysterics displayed by one of his subordinates. Thus, even as Victor Morse outlines for the inexperienced Nebraskan the pleasures, licentious and otherwise, that await him in Europe, Claude has already committed himself to his own culture, especially to its standards of masculine behavior and military esprit de corps. Such are the psychological barriers, ultimately insurmountable, that bar his pursuit of a non-American worldview. In one of his more insightful moments, Claude realizes that entering the war in Europe by volunteering to serve in a foreign army as Victor does (and as Tom Outland, a different kind of fabulous artificer, does in *The Professor's House*) would not have been "the Wheelers' way" (252). To join the conflict, Claude concludes, he needed to be part of an American mass. For all his rebelliousness—mostly manifested in brooding rather than action—he could never have done anything "conspicuous" or "picturesque" (252).

As the action shifts to France in book 5, still more Americans enter Claude's previously constricted social orbit, and his investment in his military identity, already apparent in the scene discussed above, becomes even greater. Offsetting the lost American in terms of their influence on the hero's emerging sense of his identity are Sergeant Hicks, precisely the sort of bluff realist whom Claude would have avoided in Frankfort, and of course David Gerhardt, whose every move convinces Claude that refinement and high culture are less alien to the United States than he had feared back in Nebraska. Cather further establishes Claude's patriot's progress from outsider to joyful team player in book 5 through what we might call the language of American commonality, a set of words and phrases that cue us to Claude's identification with the Americans who surround him. Chief among these is Cather's colloquial use of the term "boys" to signify the men in Claude's unit. "Boys" appears everywhere in book 5: "But they were wise *boys* and knew where dead Prussians most loved to hide" (290 emphasis mine); "The *boys* had lost all their bashfulness about trying to speak French" (252 emphasis mine); "Nobody had fallen out yet, but some of the *boys* looked pretty wilted" (356 emphasis mine). In each of these examples, "boys" conveys not only the pleasing homogeneity of the soldiers under Claude's command, their attractive immaturity and good humor, but also their ties to Lieutenant Wheeler himself, whom the narrator describes as "having his youth in France" (331).

As one of the "boys," Cather's once-alienated protagonist has less and less need for an alternative culture. Thus, despite his ruminations in the middle of book 5 on "how much [*la France*] had come to mean to him" (318), Claude allows his Gallic sympathies to affect his actions only once in the final fifty pages of the novel when he chooses to ignore the overnight love affairs that have sprung up between his soldiers and the women of Beaufort, a village in the Argonne Forest. Apart from this episode, in which Claude unconsciously encourages the creation of more lost Americans, the concluding chapters emphasize the hero's rebirth within the progressive environment of the AEF, while presenting France, once an alluring beacon of cultural difference, as a new frontier slated to be "improved" by the very forces Claude condemned in Nebraska but of which he now enthusiastically approves. Note, for example, that the soldiers who enjoy romances at Beaufort "promise to come back after the war, . . . marry the girls, and *put in water works*" (352 emphasis mine).[7] Like the rest of the world during the "American Century," France will inevitably yield to the "men of destiny" (315) with their modern plumbing. Moreover, by the time Claude embraces his heroic demise, he no longer thinks of *la France* but *exclusively* of his now cemented bond with other Americans. Indeed, although Claude never quite learns how to perceive his environment as a tourist would, France serves in his death scene as little more than a backdrop for American military greatness (or Claude's perception thereof). Revealingly, as Lieutenant Wheeler lays dying, cradled by his fellow Americans, he feels "*just one thing*: that he commanded wonderful men" (366 emphasis mine). And had Cather chosen to continue Claude's story past death, using G. P. Cather as her model, we would see the hero recommitted once more, this time literally, to the land whose greatness he came to perceive only in the midst of a European war.

Ultimately, then, it is perhaps fitting to think of Claude as one of those American soldiers standing shoulder to shoulder, four ranks deep, in a World War I panoramic photograph. And in the distance, barely visible behind the uniform phalanx of men, is a solitary French farmhouse (perhaps the very site where the lost American discovered the compensations of his memory loss), a symbol of the cross-cultural impulse that Claude finally renounces in favor of becoming one of ours.

3

CATHER AND COMBAT

Of the major prose works of World War I literature by English and American women writers, Willa Cather's *One of Ours* alone depicts combat directly and at length.[1] The novel follows its male protagonist all the way from Nebraska to the Western Front where mines, corpses, snipers, and attacks across no-man's-land receive graphic treatment. Unlike Virginia Woolf's *To the Lighthouse*, which places front-line carnage in parentheses (much as Cather's *Professor's House* does), *One of Ours* unflinchingly depicts the dark heart of war—the point of contact between armies on the battlefield. For a woman novelist in 1922, such a candid and sustained portrayal of military violence, a subject then perceived as the exclusive domain of male *eyewitnesses*, was nothing short of audacious, and as it turned out Cather paid dearly for her venture into what Maureen Ryan aptly calls "no-woman's-land." Although positive reviews of *One of Ours* outnumbered negative notices by two to one, the ferocity with which several especially influential male critics blasted Cather's rendering of front-line action established an aura of slipshod artistry and general dubiousness around the novel that, to a large extent, remains in place today. Thus, before reexamining Cather's rendering of combat, the focus of this chapter, a brief overview of this masculine censure is in order, along with some consideration of the contrastingly positive responses Cather received directly from male and female readers alike.

Never one to restrain his notoriously vituperative pen, especially when confronted with what he regarded as patriotic propaganda, H. L. Mencken provided perhaps the most influential negative review, proclaiming in *Smart Set* that the war section of *One of Ours* "drops precipitately to the level of a serial in *The Lady's Home Journal*" (140). Mencken had adored *O Pioneers!* and *My Ántonia*, praising them lavishly in reviews that helped launch Cather's career, but with *One of Ours*, he concluded, something had gone terribly wrong. Cather's war, he wrote with obvious relish, "is fought out, not in France, but on a Hollywood movie-lot. Its American soldiers are idealists engaged upon a crusade to put down sin; its Germans are imbeciles who charge machine-guns six deep, in the manner of the war dispatches of the New York *Tribune*. There is a lyrical nonsensicality in it that often grows half pathetic; it is precious near the war of the standard model of the lady novelist" (141). Sinclair Lewis, another admirer of Cather's earlier fiction, also found the war chapters inauthentic, even embarrassingly preposterous. According to Lewis's notice in the *Literary Review* of the New York *Evening Post*, while "truth does guide the first part of the book," Cather turned to fantasies in the second, creating a "romance of violinists gallantly turned soldiers, of self-sacrificing sergeants, sallies at midnight, and all the commonplaces of ordinary war novels" ("Hamlet of the Plains" 24). And in a letter to Edmund Wilson, which the author of *One of Ours* mercifully never saw, Ernest Hemingway ridiculed Cather's rendering of combat in a remark that has since become one of his most famous critical witticisms: "Wasn't that last scene in the lines wonderful? Do you know where it came from? The battle scene in *Birth of a Nation*. I identified episode after episode, Catherized. Poor woman, she had to get her war experience somewhere" (*Selected Letters* 105).[2]

Perhaps the most revealing example of critical condemnation, however, came from Sidney Howard, whose review in the *Bookman* appeared under the belittling title "Miss Cather Goes to War." Like Mencken and Lewis, Howard regarded books 4 and 5 of *One of Ours* as completely hopeless, little more than "a potpourri of soldier yarns and impressions of Rheims two years after, amalgamated into a 'Saturday Evening Post' version of 'Three Soldiers'" (218). Yet for Howard, the collapse of the novel in its second half conveyed a larger message, one with which Mencken and Lewis implicitly agreed—that women novelists should stay where they belong. "To treat the small facts and the microscopic phenomena of everyday as significant of the dominant energies and emotions of living, this," wrote Howard, "is pretty generally the woman's method of novel writing. . . . And when women disregard it . . . they seem to withhold the best that they can give and offer shoddy merchandise as substitute" (217). Howard regarded books 1 through 3, set in the by then familiar landscape of Cather's south-central Nebraska, as the best that this primarily regional woman novelist could offer: "While Claude sticks to his western lands, the thing is above reproach" (217). The "shoddy merchandise" appeared in the second half of the novel, where Cather wandered too far from her established geographical domain and from her own feminine experience. It was as if Jane Austen had tried to write *War and Peace*. *One of Ours*, Howard concluded, "seems to me a book to show what a woman can write supremely and what she cannot write at all. . . . The pity is that Miss Cather did not know the war for the big bowwow stuff that it is and stick to her own farms and farmer folk" (218).

The absurdity of a woman novelist venturing into the all-male terrain of the trenches also formed the basis for a clever parody of Cather's novel by Christopher Ward that appeared in the *Literary Review* several months after Sinclair Lewis's notice and shortly before *One of Ours* won the Pulitzer Prize (a middlebrow honor that only confirmed the book's shallowness in the eyes of its critics).[3] In Ward's version of the story, Lieutenant Wheeler receives a phone call from Cather minutes before his scheduled death atop the parapet, instructing him on his final actions. The character argues with his creator, whose comments Ward withholds from the reader, over the necessity of his demise. "You want me to do *what*?" cries Cather's incredulous hero. "On the *parapet* when the *attack* comes?" Through Claude's reactions, which grow increasingly desperate as he realizes that Cather is determined to kill him off in an especially ludicrous manner, Ward lampoons what he—along with other male readers—

regarded as the purely fanciful results of Cather's doomed attempt to render military action. For example, Claude points out to Cather the statistical improbability of his fate: "There ain't about six killed in action out of a thousand Americans in this war and I don't see why you pick on me. How'd I get elected?" The protagonist also questions whether his suicidal self-exposure is militarily justifiable. The parapet, he explains, is "no place for an officer to command. Officers are supposed to take care of their selves an' not expose their selves unnecessarily. They got to look out for their men, not try to be heroes or anything." In the end, Claude escapes his creator's plans through a comic ruse, placing a mannequin on the edge of the trench and allowing it to be riddled with the bullets that were intended for him. "What's this for?" asks Sergeant Hicks, as Lieutenant Wheeler quickly conceals his replica. "To fool the Heinies?" "No," replies Claude, "that was for the home folks who read serious novels" (435).

Cather's reckless entry into the masculine arena of front-line action was, however, only one of her transgressions. As Mencken makes clear in his review through repeated references to John Dos Passos's *Three Soldiers* as a veritable touchstone against which all American war narratives must be measured, Cather also committed heresy by appearing to argue that the First World War had actually been an inspiring, even liberating experience for *some* of its combatants. In contrast with the absolute realism achieved in *Three Soldiers*, Cather's sentimental depiction of Claude Wheeler's military adventures, Lewis quipped, might have come from "that sweet singer of lice and mud, Mr. Conningsby Dawson" ("Hamlet of the Plains" 24). And then there was the issue of experience: how could anyone, male or female, purport to describe modern warfare without ever hearing a hostile shot? In Europe, critics with extensive front-line experience rooted out such literary pretenders with inquisitorial zeal. In France, for example, combat veteran Jean Norton Cru compiled a bibliography of French war writing, subsequently translated into English and reprinted under the title *War Books*, that actually measured the veracity of battle scenes in novels and memoirs by setting them against the service records of their authors. Material that proved the product of imagination, rather than firsthand observation, came under Norton Cru's scornful attack.

Likewise in England, military historian turned literary critic Cyril Falls produced his own bibliography of World War I sources, also titled *War Books*, and evaluated the personal writing on the conflict almost exclusively as historical "testimony" or "evidence." *One of Ours*, oddly enough, met with Falls's approval (perhaps because it did not fall squarely into the category of antiwar literature),[4] while *All Quiet on the Western Front*, supposedly filled with inaccuracies, represented "frank propaganda" (294).[5] Such are the standards that Hemingway (many of whose own claims regarding his war experience do not hold up to close scrutiny) affirms when he remarks that Cather, "poor woman," had "to get her war experience somewhere." Literary treatments of war, he implies, properly belong to front-line eyewitnesses—hence the title and focus of the somewhat less than inclusive war-literature anthology Hemingway later compiled, *Men at War*.

With its bold foray into subject material long regarded as a masculine enclave, its refusal to fall into line with the supposedly authoritative version of the Great Crusade provided by Dos Passos, and its substitution of research and imagination for the direct observation of combat, *One of Ours* was almost guaranteed to meet with a hostile reception—and Cather knew it. Indeed, her prepublication campaign to secure positive notices for the book, which included an obviously less than successful attempt to secure Mencken's favor, demonstrates that she understood all too well the literary taboos she had broken. However, as male critics rushed to dismiss the novel and as Cather's friends, such as Dorothy Canfield Fisher, dutifully defended it in praise-laden reviews, perhaps the most revealing contemporary assessments came from a far less predictable quarter— from ordinary members of the so-called reading public who purchased the book and then wrote directly to Cather. The samples of this fan mail that survive, housed in the Willa Cather Pioneer Memorial and in the Archives and Special Collections Department of the University of Nebraska–Lincoln Libraries, describe a broader range of responses than one would expect. One correspondent, in fact, anticipated by more than fifty years the ironic reading of the war chapters now in vogue. For this reader, *One of Ours* constituted above all else an attack on "a mechanized Western Civilization, whose crown of achievement, so far, is a *scientific* world war that killed 40 millions of human beings."[6] Sharing Cather's scorn for "standardization and machinery," the writer noted the terrible irony underlying the protagonist's fate: modern America offered "Claude Wheeler and his kind" just one avenue of escape from its mechanized dreariness—"a moving and terrible death by fire and shell."

Other correspondents, men and women alike, seemed oblivious to any irony and instead stressed Cather's historical accuracy in book 5, the very thing that Mencken and Lewis deemed lacking, or her insight into the generous idealism that had motivated American soldiers. Ironically enough, this group of readers included army veterans who apparently possessed more firsthand knowledge of modern warfare than any of Cather's critics, including Hemingway. A book dealer in Minneapolis who served "in France for over three years, first with the French Foreign Legion, then with the Americans," declared that "the last part of 'One of Ours' is the most perfect picture of the war that I have read."[7] Another AEF veteran emotionally described the novel as an authentic portrait of the U.S. Army and a fitting tribute to the war dead: "As one of Claudes [*sic*] generation— let me say that I have been the comrade of just such spirits as his— who never returned from France. Memory of them stirs the best in one to carry on. 'One of Ours' seems a noble gesture pointing to that memory."[8] Still another former soldier, writing from Washington DC, gratefully described the novel as a Proustian evocation of things past: "I cannot express the emotions you have you have aroused—I have not felt them since I went through Hoboken, Newark & Elizabeth on a troop train & heard the people cheer; not since I talked with men in camp, on the transport, in the billets."[9] Such letters, Edith Lewis later remarked, "might have been written by *Claude Wheeler* himself" (123). Others might have come from Mrs. Wheeler or Gladys Farmer. A Gold Star Mother in Denver, for example, delivered perhaps the highest praise that Cather's verisimilitude ever received: "The last ten pages of your book were written especially for the mothers, and as one of them I thank you. We know:—but I cannot understand how you do."[10] A woman librarian, writing from a military hospital in Virginia, applauded Cather's fidelity to the doughboy's noble nature: "I was with 'Ours' in France, and have been with them in Army,

Navy, and Veterans' Hospitals ever since, so I feel I know them, and I can say that you have drawn a wonderful picture of their spirit and ideals."[11] For readers like these, there was nothing at all inauthentic about the wartime section of Claude's story.

What, then, do we make of a narrative so roundly condemned by some readers on the basis of its alleged naïveté and fancifulness and at the same time embraced by so many others (by enough, indeed, to send the sales of *One of Ours* soaring) as a truthful picture of war? This divided response may, of course, tell us more about Cather's audience in 1922 and the contradictory models of the Great War then competing for dominance within the national consciousness than about the actual text. As David Kennedy suggests, the controversy over *One of Ours* revealed a rift in post–World War I literary culture between the intellectual elite, which viewed the Great Crusade as the Great Sham, and the vast mass of so-called middlebrow readers who, contrary to the mythos of the Lost Generation, retained a largely positive impression of their wartime experience (218–30). But this interpretive chasm also raises a number of intriguing questions about the text itself. Is Cather's rendering of military action really as ridiculous as its most famous male critics allege? Was Elizabeth Shepley Sergeant (one of the few women writers with qualms about the novel) correct in attributing the success of *One of Ours* not to its mimetic value but to the sentimental consolation it supposedly offered to Gold Star Mothers and former soldiers (181)? Or does the book achieve a greater realism than its detractors in 1922 were willing to perceive? And if the novel abandons its realistic trappings at its climax (which I believe it does), why? What themes and preoccupations necessitated the text's departure from the realm of ordinary military experience and its suspension of the clinical language and graphic grotesquery of "authentic" military reportage?

The beginning of the twenty-first century is an especially appropriate moment to consider such questions. At this writing only a handful of the millions of men and women who witnessed the Great War are still alive (by last count, fewer than twenty-five hundred AEF veterans still linger, all centenarians), and in the very near future, perhaps a matter of months rather than years, there will be none left at all. The experiential contours of the Great War as they exist in popular culture and public memory have, therefore, long ceased to derive from the direct testimony of eyewitnesses. Instead, images of "what World War I was like" now come chiefly from narratives that, like Cather's, combine research with overtly imaginative speculation. Pat Barker's Booker Prize–winning World War I trilogy, Timothy Findley's *The Wars*, Sebastian Faulks's *Birdsong*, and Mark Helprin's *Soldier of the Great War* (to cite just a few of the dozens of World War I novels published over the last twenty-five years, all written by people born long after 1918) exercise a creative license in assembling myth out of historical events that would have been unforgivable in 1922. These works, not *Three Soldiers*, are the true contemporaries of *One of Ours*. War literature from the past two decades, much of it informed by Tim O'Brien's postmodern musings on the impossibility of telling a "true" war story, provides us with a different set of standards and assumptions by which to judge Cather's novel.

Moreover, decades of theoretical inquiry into the relationship between literature and historical writing — between fictional and supposedly nonfictional forms of discourse — have now largely dismantled the intellectual framework within which war-literature critics operated in the 1920s. Theorists such as Hayden White have argued that myth manifests itself not only in the work of literary artists but also in the so-called documentary materials from which historians *create* their narratives.[12] Likewise, readerly faith in the attainment of absolute mimesis via the doctrines of literary realism is no longer what it once was. As Peter Widdowson observes in an essay on Thomas Hardy, when regarded from a poststructuralist vantage, the "truths" offered by realism emerge as subjective constructs: "[R]ealism," he argues, "is not just a matter of literary form; it is the common-sense expression of an ideology," one that "presupposes a universe that *can* be made sense of and an always potentially self-determining human subject" (42). In other words, Dos Passos's application of realism in *Three Soldiers* (a mode he radically modified in the *U.S.A.* trilogy) does not necessarily produce a truer picture of the Great Crusade than Cather's more ambivalent and inconclusive approach.

The subsidence of the First World War into the now distant past, the recent proliferation of war novels (by men *and* women) that ignore the experiential "qualifications" once expected of all such texts, and major changes in critical theory allow for a rethinking of Cather's most precarious literary gamble—her depiction of military action. Thus, the following discussion revisits the issue of verisimilitude or authenticity in *One of Ours* and, while acknowledging the various factual errors and artistic weaknesses that surface in book 5, contends that Cather's depiction of battle is more complex than generally recognized. In the first section of my analysis I will argue that Cather's scenes of combat borrow from two antithetical discourses— the shockingly candid and clinical language of naturalistic war fiction *and* the euphemistic parlance of military commendations and awards, a type of expression that quickly encrusted the legend of G. P. Cather. The text's refusal to commit itself fully to either of these discourses ultimately reinforces the ambiguity already created by its inconsistent point of view and contradictory assortment of subjective voices. Moreover, the dual nature of Cather's language in book 5 is complemented by radical shifts in point of view, as the narrative vacillates between *mirroring* the confusion of battle and omnisciently *explaining* front-line action. In the second section I assert that Cather went to great lengths to achieve an impression of universality (at least as far as American World War I combatants were concerned) in her depiction of Claude's front-line experiences. A close reading of book 5 reveals that in more places than not, Cather strayed from the record of G. P. Cather's overseas experiences (even as she mined her cousin's letters for important details) in the interest of creating a more representative version of the American soldier at war. At the same time, however, Cather's concern with surface realism— with creating a recognizable portrait of *typical* military experiences— ultimately gives way to her fascination with military mythos. In particular, the circumstances of Claude's ultimately atypical demise evoke the celebrated story of the Lost Battalion, the single most resonant legend of America's first world war.

1. Cather's Competing Visions of Battle

Fearing exactly the sort of criticism that she eventually received, Cather ironically spent more time and energy researching the First

World War, still underway when she conceived of Claude's story in the summer of 1918, than she would later devote to either nineteenth-century New Mexico or seventeenth-century Quebec, the settings for *Death Comes for the Archbishop* and *Shadows on the Rock,* respectively. As we have already seen, Cather scoured her cousin's wartime letters (as well as those written by David Hochstein, the New York violinist who inspired David Gerhardt), commandeered Dr. Sweeney's wartime diary (despite his understandable reluctance to share such a personal document), studied personal narratives such as *Victor Chapman's Letters from France*,[13] and as Janis P. Stout convincingly argues, gleaned much of her knowledge of wartime France from Dorothy Canfield Fisher's writings.[14] However, Cather did not conduct her research entirely, or even mostly, through texts. She also interviewed veterans at her New York apartment, met with wounded soldiers in stateside hospitals, observed firsthand the wartime behavior of rural Nebraskans (described in her 1919 article, "Roll Call on the Prairies"), and in 1921 actually visited the battlefields of France.

Despite such rigorous preparation, however, factual errors and distracting implausibilities inevitably found their way into the military section of Claude's story. As James Woodress points out, Cather's mistaken notion that American battleships served as convoy escorts was caught, thanks to a tip from Cather's former editor Ferris Greenslet, and corrected in the third printing (*Willa Cather: A Literary Life* 332). But other gaffes permanently eluded not only Cather's editorial scrutiny but that of her new publisher, Alfred A. Knopf, and his staff. Among them are the following: the incorrect dating of the battle of Passchendaele or Third Ypres (which occurred in the summer and fall of 1917, not, as *One of Ours* implies, in 1916); the dispatching of British artillerymen and flyers to Verdun (located well outside the British sector of the Western Front); the placement of a lieutenant colonel at the head of an American battalion (majors commanded AEF battalions); the references to American infantryman still wearing their campaign hats ("Stetsons") months after arriving overseas; the erroneous description of plugs, rather than pins, used as primers on American hand grenades; the strange absence of artillery support as Claude's company advances in phase one of the Meuse-Argonne Offensive (which in fact opened with a barrage that consumed more projectiles than the entire American Civil War); the equally inexplicable description of Claude and his men pursuing rapidly "retiring" (343) German forces in the last week of September 1918 (which does not match the experience of any American unit during this period); the overabundance of free time enjoyed by Claude Wheeler and David Gerhardt (made possible by a less than credible absence of military paperwork and bureaucracy); and the bewildering tactics used by Cather's doughboys when they rush a German sniper with their rifles and bayonets (a method of attack that results in the pointless wounding of Dell Able) instead of using their grenades.

The artificial language that Cather's soldiers speak also undermines the credibility of the war chapters. Purged of both profanity and convincing soldier's slang, their speech, as James Woodress remarks, is hardly that of "men living in an all-male society" (*Willa Cather: A Literary Life* 331). Consider, for example, Claude's quarterback-style instructions, supposedly delivered in the heat of battle, to the private who joins him in the attack on the sniper: "'Now, Willy, we'll both go in at once; you jump to the right, and I to the left,—and one of us will jab him. He can't shoot both ways at once. Are you ready? All right—now!'" (348). Or Sergeant Hicks's stilted outcry at the end of the same scene: offered a souvenir taken from the dead Prussian, Hicks breaks into tears and replies, "'Think I'd touch anything of his? That beautiful little girl, and my buddy—He's worse than dead, Dell is, worse!'" (348). At other moments sentimentality implausibly enters the dialogue. When Gerhardt orders some stretcher bearers "'to make the best time you can'" because the man they are carrying has just died, "Oscar, the pious Swede," replies, "'Them that are carrying him now won't jolt him'" (324).

Far more distracting and disturbing than the false notes struck in the dialogue, however, are passages in which the *narrator's* voice lapses into martial clichés and euphemisms, thus adding to the sense of contrivance that provoked so much hostility in Cather's male reviewers. Several sentences in book 5, all attempting to describe combat, seem purely derivative. When Claude and a small detachment of men stage a nighttime attack on a German machine-gun nest, for example, the narrator suddenly resorts to stock phrases to describe the action: pinned down by enemy gunners who "knew the hill like a book," the Americans "could not retaliate with effect"; the enemy's bullets "bounded on the rocks about them like hail" (321). Likewise, the climactic account of Claude's final battle comes uncomfortably close to the euphemistic world of adolescent adventure fiction. In some respects, the battle for the Snout owes more to G. A. Henty than to D. W. Griffith, as martial clichés infiltrate Cather's ordinarily anything but derivative prose: "suddenly the advance was checked"; "the rifles recovered themselves"; "[Claude] could see the fire take effect"; "the men behind him had become like rock" (366). Typical of the desensitizing military language that Elaine Scarry has analyzed in her argument that military discourse inevitably denies the true product of war (harm to the human body), such statements obscure what they ostensibly describe. For example, a less elegant way of saying that fire "takes effect" is to say that pieces of lead perforate human bodies. Perversely appropriate on one level, Cather's language in this section stresses the egocentric nature of Claude's last stand. Just as the men behind Lieutenant Wheeler are tellingly compared with inanimate matter, with "rock," we see the advancing Germans ("Huns" by this point in the novel) only at a distance, "stumbling and falling" as the Americans fire at them. The only soldier viewed intimately as a person rather than an object in this scene is Claude, whose exultation remains disturbingly and perhaps necessarily divorced from the violence that surrounds him.

However, the notion that Claude's consciousness dictates the narrator's language of combat does not entirely explain the clichéd quality of Cather's depiction of his final moments, especially when one considers that by this point in the novel Claude has already received a thorough education in the horrors of war. Book 5 is filled with imagery that stresses the protagonist's exposure to the physical consequences of military violence—the very thing missing in the euphemistic account of his death. Several chapters earlier, for example, just after the unconvincing description of the doughboys' nighttime attack, Claude tends to a wounded soldier—"a young doctor" from Pennsylvania who volunteered to join the raiding party. At first, while shrouded in darkness, the doctor's condition appears to be stable. The doctor calmly apologizes for using his flashlight, an error that attracted German artillery fire, and displays a strictly professional interest in his own wound. Once Claude strikes a match, however, and illuminates the doctor's body, the scene takes a gruesome turn: "The wounded man had already loosened his trousers, and now he pulled up his bloody shirt. His groin and abdomen were torn on the left side. The wound, and the stretcher on which he lay, supported a mass of dark coagulated blood that looked like a great cow's liver" (323). With keen psychological insight, Cather conveys Claude's unspoken shock as he views this horrific wound through the simile "like a great cow's liver." Confronted, like Yossarian in Joseph Heller's *Catch-22*, with the terrible lesson that man is matter, Claude translates what he sees into the more familiar context of his agricultural past, thereby controlling his own momentary trauma. On the next page, however, as several soldiers carry the dying man to an aid station, the narrator (again presumably mirroring Claude's consciousness) now divests the doctor's suffering of any comforting comparisons: "[T]he motion started the blood again and tore away the clots that had formed over his wounds." Claude listens as the doctor "began to vomit and to strangle" (324).

From this point on in the narrative, the effects of weaponry on human bodies appear with such suddenness and repetition that no psychological defense mechanism can deny them. A French girl shot by a sniper falls forward, "blood and brains oozing out of her yellow hair" (346). Dell Able staggers back from the sniper's lair "with his jaw shattered and the blood spouting from the left side of his neck"; Gerhardt attempts "to close the artery with his finger" (347). As for the German soldier who causes this graphically described carnage, a homosexual aristocrat perhaps modeled after the title character in D. H. Lawrence's "The Prussian Officer,"[15] he dies from a "bullet in the brain," fired "straight through one of his blue eyes" (348). And by the time Claude and his men enter the Boar's Head Trench, macabre reminders of war's grisly products are everywhere—including the very walls of the fortifications they now occupy. Like a grotesque version of Barclay Owens's archaeological site, the trench offers a cutaway view of an anything but ancient burial ground: "a large fat boot stuck stiffly from the side"; "under the sand bags, a dark hand reached out; the five fingers, well apart, looked like the swollen roots of some noxious weed" (361). In his moment of glory, directing the rifle fire of his men from atop the parapet, Claude literally stands on a mass grave.

Cather's refusal in such hair-raising passages to gloss over military carnage suggests her considerable commitment to graphic realism. *One of Ours* presents a portrait of American military action that is credible in its specific details (often shockingly so) and faithful to the broadest possible outline of overseas combat experience. How, then, do we account for the seeming failures in tone and vocabulary that occasionally surface in book 5? Why does a text that for the most part so unflinchingly chronicles the physical consequences of military violence lapse at key moments into language that softens, even glamorizes, combat? In chapter 1 I suggested that Cather's novel resembles Conrad's *Lord Jim* in the way that its inconsistent point of view and multiplicity of subjective voices continually thwart the kind of thematic integrity one expects (at least through the application of formalist or structuralist critical methodologies) to discover in more conventional fiction. To borrow Ian Watt's formulation, Cather's text, like Conrad's (or any work of modernism), is centrifugal in its significance (191), spinning ever outward from one contradicted or modified set of conclusions to another, always pulling away from a coherent center of meaning. In book 5 Cather heightens this effect by modulating back and forth between two antithetical discourses of military experience, thereby creating a tension that prevents us from interpreting Claude *exclusively* as a dupe whose idealism blindly denies the horrors that surround him or *exclusively* as a hero whose grand exit truly represents an admirable sacrifice. In effect, the split nature of Cather's language in book 5 invites us to perceive both interpretations simultaneously. Once again, *One of Ours* seems more concerned with conveying the ambiguities of war and the idealism that it satisfies than with constructing a cogent celebration or parody of military valor.

The first of these discourses, characterized by an almost clinical recording of battlefield grotesquery, has its origins in the tradition of naturalistic war fiction launched by Emile Zola's rendering of the Franco-Prussian War in *La Debacle*, the first major war novel to describe candidly, even obsessively, the appearance of wounds and corpses. While other nineteenth-century writers—including Tolstoy (whose epic battle scenes in *War and Peace* are surprisingly sanitized)—honor the unspoken proprieties of war fiction and politely deflect their descriptions of gore or disfigurement, Zola plunges us directly into the kinds of hospital horrors that Dr. Sweeney later confronted: "But the most upsetting wounds were gaping stomachs, chests or heads. Some of the men's trunks were bleeding through terrible gashes, and knots of twisted entrails pushed up the skin, vital organs that had been pierced or hacked" (279). Likewise in the scenes depicting combat, Zola's soldiers (whether French or German) never euphemistically "fall." Instead, Zola details each collision between flesh and metal: "the bullet got him in the groin" (245); "a lieutenant had his body cut in two" (257); "another was hit in the throat by a bullet and reeled over to the wall where he made a continual snoring noise, with his whole body jerking in convulsions" (246). Little wonder that Tennyson, whose "Charge of the Light Brigade" unironically celebrates the glory of military folly, bemoaned English audiences' "wallowing in troughs of Zolaism" (472). Although Cather expressed reservations about *La Debacle*—in an 1894 article on Zola she bemoaned the novel's "absolute inability to recognize beauty" ("Zola" 142)—she may have turned to its model of precisely described carnage in her own rendering of front-line action.

Moreover, Cather's extensive reading of World War I narratives, which she undertook in preparation for writing book 5 of *One of Ours*, probably included Henri Barbusse's celebrated novel *Le Feu* (first translated into English as *Under Fire* in 1917). Regarded throughout most of the 1920s as the preeminent European novel of World War I combat (until Remarque's *All Quiet on the Western Front* met with worldwide acclaim), *Le Feu* follows the day-to-day experiences of a French infantry squad on the Western Front and in one horrific scene after another displays a Zolaesque refusal to spare the reader's feelings. Indeed, the chapter titled "The Doorway" details the terrible sights that greet a pair of soldiers as they cross a shell-pounded stretch of battlefield littered with cadavers and body parts. Some of Barbusse's anatomies of human debris in this chapter, which reads at times a like coroner's report, lead one to wonder how *Le Feu* evaded censorship in wartime France, let alone in Great Britain and the United States. In one passage, for example, Barbusse's poilus stumble upon a row of decomposed corpses recently unearthed from a collapsed trench: "Of several the faces are black as tar, the lips hugely distended. . . . Between two bodies, protruding uncertainly from one or the other, is a severed wrist, ending with a cluster of strings" (153). Another cadaver, reduced to a "heap," is unrecognizable except for the telltale "gape of a trouser pocket. An insect goes in and out of it" (153). Cather's nightmarish description of the Boar's Head Trench abounds in similarly macabre details. When Claude and David first inspect the position, they notice that the floor "worked and moved as if boa constrictors were wiggling down there—soft bodies, lightly covered." "Clouds of wet, buzzing flies" rise from the dead (360). "Squirting sounds," produced by "liquefying entrails," emanate from a pile of corpses in the Snout (the very spot, ironically, where Claude will cheerfully meet his own destruction). Though Cather hardly shared the scientific pretensions of naturalists or their dogmatic emphasis on socioeconomic determinism, some of her most grotesque scenes in book 5 nevertheless display a fascination with ugliness and an unwillingness to soften even the most gruesome of subject material reminiscent of naturalistic war fiction.[16]

The second style of discourse found in the battle scenes in book 5 comes from a much different source, though one equally appropriate for a novel inspired by G. P. Cather—from the rhetoric of official military citations and awards. As we have seen, through the postwar popularity of euphemisms such as "Roll of Honor" and "Unknown Soldier," Zola's or Barbusse's variety of language, which clinically describes the human wreckage of battle, has no place in the state-sanctioned vocabulary of commemoration. Nor does it belong in the linguistic world of military heroism—except when the hero's wounds are detailed and his triumph over pain applauded. The very act of defining a military action as heroic or courageous necessitates a rhetorical whitewashing: celebrating the hero's acceptance of risk and skill in killing the enemy (as in the case of Sgt. Alvin York, for example) is impossible without simultaneously denying that enemy's common humanity and, as Elaine Scarry would point out, erasing the physical consequences of one man's "heroic" action upon the body of another. Thus, in order to construct "heroism" out of the mutual butchery of war, the euphemistic and abstract language of military citations and awards must essentially argue that the hero (along with the fellow countrymen whom he saves through his actions) matters as a human being, while the bodiless opponents whom he "neutralizes," "takes out," or "mops up" do not.

To see this rhetorical dynamic at work, one need look no further than the citation that accompanied G. P. Cather's posthumously awarded Distinguished Service Cross, which Myrtle Cather received on his behalf in 1919. However, before considering the language of this document and its apparent influence on Cather's text, I should point out that at least one of its "facts" is completely erroneous— and in a way that reveals much about the interpretive urgencies underlying military awards. Reproduced in *American Decorations*, a record published in 1927 of every major military award bestowed by the U.S. Army between 1862 and 1926, the citation describes Lt. Grosvenor P. Cather's actions "near Cantigny, France" on "May 27, 1918," and reads as follows:

> During a strong enemy attack Lieutenant Cather mounted the parapet of his trench, and, although exposed to withering machine-gun fire, he so skillfully directed the fire of his automatic rifles that the attack was repulsed. In this action he fell mortally wounded. Posthumously awarded. Medal presented to widow, Mrs. Grosvenor P. Cather. (209)

Like the thousands of other World War I citations recorded in *American Decorations*, including those bestowed upon such legendary figures as Sergeant York, Eddie Rickenbacker, and members of the Lost Battalion, this account of self-sacrifice vividly evidences the survival of Civil War–style leadership and theatrics amid the mechanized and seemingly impersonal arena of the Western Front. Indeed, if skeptical reviewers such as H. L. Mencken, who found Claude's heroics preposterous, had later consulted the record of World War I valor contained in *American Decorations*, they would have encountered on almost every page acts of courage far more outlandish than Claude's. Even Lieutenant Wheeler's moment of glory pales beside that of Sgt. Harry Adams, who "captured single handed approximately 300 prisoners" (127), or that of Pvt. George Dilboy (the most celebrated Greek-American hero of the war), who continued his lone attack on a German machine-gun nest "with his right leg nearly severed above the knee and with several bullet holes in his body" (26). Cather may have strayed from the tenets of literary realism by giving Claude such an extraordinary exit, but she could have argued with good reason that such acts of heroism did happen.

In regard to the specifics of Lieutenant Cather's citation, there is, however, a problem: G.P. apparently did *not* die, as the citation claims, on 27 May or during the action described above. In fact, if we return to Sergeant Prettyman's account, which Anne Taylor supplied secondhand to Myrtle Cather, an intriguing inconsistency emerges. According to Prettyman, G.P. was killed on 28 May, the day following his courageous defeat of a German raid, and in a manner far less dramatic than what his citation describes. Like Hemingway's Frederic Henry, who is anticlimactically blown up while eating cheese, Lieutenant Cather was hit by a shell fragment shortly after "talking to some men" at a post located some distance from the front line. Granted, Prettyman's description implies that G.P. was standing rather daringly above the top of the trench when the shell struck. But no German attack was then in progress. In other words, G. P. Cather fell victim to the banal vagaries of World War I–style attrition. After surviving close-quarters combat and after coolly exposing himself to immediate danger, Lieutenant Cather was killed by an artillery projectile fired by an invisible enemy miles away. As I have pointed out elsewhere, Prettyman's testimony is itself highly questionable. But in this particular case another piece of evidence corroborates the sergeant's account. Among the G. P. Cather–related correspondence housed at the University of Nebraska–Lincoln is a letter apparently written in response to a query from Franc Cather by M. Morris Andrews, a lieutenant in the Twenty-sixth Infantry (see fig. 12). Like Anne Taylor's letter, Andrews's letter offers consolatory tribute to the deceased's "never failing interest and energy" and predictably reassures the Cather family that G.P. "died instantly." More interestingly, however, this document also contradicts the official version of G.P.'s demise. Here again we read that Lieutenant Cather died on 28 May, not 27 May, and that he warded off a German

Fig. 12. Officers of the First battalion, Twenty-sixth Infantry Regiment. Taken in Haudivillers, France, April 1918.

Lt. G. P. Cather is number four (fourth from the left).

Lt. M. Morris Andrews is number twenty.

Maj. Theodore Roosevelt, son of President Roosevelt, is number nine.

From Roosevelt, *Avenge Americans.*

raid the *day before* his death: "Lieut. Cather," Andrews wrote, "was hit by a shell about nine o'clock in the morning, while visiting his men in the trench."[17]

Whether intentionally or not, by removing the interval of time that separated Cather's heroic conduct on 27 May from his death the next day, the U.S. Army established a version of his fate that satisfied the demands of drama and perhaps propaganda, not accuracy.[18] To have admitted the truth—that death on a World War I battlefield could come just as easily while one was walking away from "some men" as it could while one was heroically defeating an enemy attack—would have resulted in a far less stirring and inspirational narrative. In short, the army could not have constructed the record of G. P. Cather's valor in any other way. The lieutenant *had* to expire at the moment of his greatest triumph, still defiant and heedless of enemy soldiers located not miles but yards away. Thus, Hemingway might more accurately have attributed the source for Cather's allegedly fanciful portrayal of military sacrifice to the U.S. Army rather than D. W. Griffith.

The style of language in G. P. Cather's citation also contributes to the document's distortions. Note, for instance, the sheer blandness of the well-worn verbs used to describe Lieutenant Cather's actions: the officer "*mounted* the parapet," "*directed* the fire of his automatic rifles," and ultimately "*fell*" (209 emphasis mine). Or the clichéd adjective used to describe the German machine-gun fire—"withering" (209). Nothing, I suspect, could be further from the actual events than the picture of smooth and deliberate action that such language creates. Connoting an image of assured motion, the word "mounted," for example, hardly suggests the movements of an officer (in his first battle no less) scrambling to an exposed position to command his men. Likewise, by reducing the soldiers in G. P. Cather's platoon to their weapons—the lieutenant, we are told, "directed" automatic-rifle *fire*, not automatic-rifle *men*—the citation conveys the impression of a purely mechanical sequence, one neatly separated from the raw human emotions of combat: Lieutenant Cather issued orders; the automatic-rifle fire reached its target; the attack was "repulsed" (209). As Elaine Scarry would observe, there are no bodies, no physical human beings (apart from G.P. himself), anywhere in this account. The lieutenant faced a "strong German attack" (as opposed to "attackers" or "enemy soldiers"), which he "repulsed" through guns that, rhetorically at least, had no operators. Also absent are the screaming and gesticulating that must have gone on as Cather communicated with his men above the roar of their weapons, to say nothing of the fear and confusion that probably surrounded the entire episode. Furthermore, if the German machine-gun fire was truly "withering" (by which I assume that anyone standing or crouching above the top of the trench risked almost certain death) Cather's men may have been reluctant to expose themselves at all. Perhaps G. P. Cather did not so much direct automatic-rifle fire as rally the terrified soldiers under his command.

Given the extent to which Claude Wheeler's final actions mimic the U.S. Army version of those of G. P. Cather, it comes as little surprise that Cather knew of her cousin's citation. In an undated letter to Franc Cather, the novelist expresses her delight over the official recognition of G.P.'s heroism.[19] As I suggested in chapter 1, in her depiction of Claude's death Cather probably borrowed several important details from Sergeant Prettyman's testimony, including G. P. Cather's supposedly painless chest wound. Other details, however, clearly have their origin in Cather's citation. For example, the narrator emphasizes that Claude (like G.P.) leaves the comparative safety of his trench to signal targets to his men: "[F]rom here [on the parapet] he could correct the range and direct the fire" (366). Claude's daring also proves decisive (just as G.P.'s supposedly did), enabling his troops to hold the Germans off just long enough for American reinforcements to arrive. And of course Cather's protagonist dies at his moment of greatest glory, thus imitating the erroneous but dramatically compelling script established for G. P. Cather's memory by the U.S. Army.

G. P. Cather's citation perhaps also inspired the military discourse that sometimes crops up in Cather's descriptions of military action. Indeed, several of the phrases in book 5 that we have already considered, such as the abstract references to rifles "recover[ing] themselves" or to "fire tak[ing] effect," might have come straight from the pages of *American Decorations*. Cather's description—or rather nondescription—of the German soldiers who attack the Snout seems especially indebted to this citation-style rhetoric. Just as the official account of G. P. Cather's courage transforms the human beings who are "repulsed" by his automatic rifles into an abstraction, into a "strong German attack," Cather at one point describes the mass of men advancing on Claude's trench as a "line": "The right of the Hun line swerved out, not more than twenty yards from the battered Snout, trying to run to shelter under that pile of debris and human bodies. A quick concentration of rifle fire depressed it, and the swell came out again toward the left" (366). This is one of the most disturbing passages in *One of Ours* (even if one views Claude's consciousness as its source)—and one of the most awkwardly written. How, for example, does one visualize "the right of the Hun line . . . trying to run to shelter"? The first part of this statement etherealizes the attackers into a truly intangible object, the "right" side of a "line," while the second contradictorily emphasizes their animation and vulnerability (as further reinforced by the passing reference to "human bodies"). The strain on Cather's prose created by the accommodation of military discourse also becomes apparent in the second sentence quoted above. A first-time reader of *One of Ours* may have to go over this sentence twice before realizing that the indefinite pronoun in the first clause refers to the "right of the Hun line," not the "pile of debris and human bodies" mentioned at the end of the preceding sentence. Such stylistic infelicities, which rarely appear elsewhere in the novel, perhaps signal Cather's discomfort with the style of language she selected for the penultimate chapter.

For Cather's contemporary male critics, Claude's theatrical death scene signaled the limits of the female imagination when confronted with the masculine subject of war. But this chauvinistic response not only fails to acknowledge the naturalistic descriptions featured elsewhere in *One of Ours*, it also overlooks the contradictory methods of narration that Cather employs. Just as Cather's vocabulary of battle changes from scene to scene—shifting from Zolaesque bluntness one moment to patriotic obfuscation the next—the text seems torn between a mode of narration that *explains* combat (through the kind of mechanical sequencing discussed above) and one that *mirrors* its essential chaos. The latter approach produces some of the finest passages in book 5. Consider, for example, the highly impressionistic scene in chapter 11 that forces the reader to share Claude's confusion as he is thrown down a ravine and half buried by a bursting shell:

> Claude, at the rear, felt the ground rise under him, and he was swept with a mountain of earth and rock down into the ravine. He never knew whether he lost consciousness or not. It seemed to him that he went on having continuous sensations. The first, that of being blown to pieces; of swelling to an enormous size under intolerable pressure, then bursting. Next he felt himself shrink and tingle, like a frost-bitten body thawing out. Then he swelled again, and burst. This was repeated, he didn't know how often. He soon realized that he was lying under a great weight of earth;—his body, not his head. He felt rain falling on his face. His left hand was free, and still attached to his arm. He moved it cautiously to his face. (322)

Unlike the panoramic, cliché-ridden account of Claude's final battle, this intensely imagined passage plunges us directly into the confusion of combat. Note, for instance, that the narrator never states explicitly that an enemy projectile has landed near Claude. Instead we experience the episode just as Claude does, as he suddenly feels "the ground rise" and glimpses a "mountain of earth and rock" surrealistically created out of thin air. Likewise Cather postpones the revelation that Claude is half-buried for several sentences, thus forcing the reader to interpret the garbled messages that Claude's shell-shocked consciousness receives from his body: "Next he felt himself shrink and tingle, like a frost-bitten body thawing out. Then he swelled again, and burst. This was repeated, he didn't know how often." Moreover, Cather's style adds beautifully to the effect, especially at the end of the passage where short declarative sentences, almost Hemingway-like in their repetition of pronouns and deadpan tone, capture Claude's tentative assessment of his wounds: "He felt rain falling on his face. His left hand was free, and still attached to his arm. He moved it cautiously to his face."

On a technical level, Cather's narration in this instance owes much to Joseph Conrad, whose practice of "delayed decoding," first identified by critic Ian Watt, replicates on a narrative level the perceptual confusion that his characters experience in moments of shock or stress (Watt 175). Just as Cather refuses to divulge Claude's condition until the reader has first shared his disorientation, Conrad's delayed decoding describes the *effects* of a sudden event before establishing their *cause*. Indeed, it is possible that in her account of Claude's near death from an explosion Cather drew upon a remarkably similar passage in Conrad's short story titled "Youth." Narrated in the first person by Marlow—a veteran sailor who also appears in Conrad's *Heart of Darkness*, *Lord Jim*, and *Chance*— "Youth" presents a series of maritime disasters, all befalling one ship, that reach their climax with a coal-dust explosion. Marlow's account of this event so thoroughly re-creates his initial sense of bewilderment that the reader remains uncertain for several sentences of exactly what is being described:

> About ten, . . . I stepped down on the main deck for a moment. The carpenter's bench stood abaft the mainmast: I leaned against it sucking my pipe, and the carpenter, a young chap, came to talk to me. He remarked, "I think we have done very well, haven't we?" and then I perceived with annoyance the fool was trying to tilt the bench. I said curtly, "Don't, Chips," and immediately became aware of a queer sensation, of an absurd delusion—I seemed somehow to be in the air. I heard all round me like a pent-up breath released—as if a thousand giants simultaneously had said Phoo!—and felt a dull concussion which made my ribs ache suddenly. No doubt about it—I was in the air and my body was describing a short parabola. (134)

While another writer might have described this event in five simple words—"the ship suddenly blew up"—Conrad's method of narration (like the stream-of-consciousness technique later employed by Richardson, Woolf, and Joyce) reminds us that "experience," the subjective product of stimuli acting upon an individual human nervous system, bears little resemblance to the rational sequence of cause and effect provided in realistic narratives. Whether Cather knew this particular passage or not, the similarities between her method of depicting trauma and Conrad's suggest, yet again, that *One of Ours* owes far more to literary modernism than one might initially assume.

As the account of Claude's half burial demonstrates, the device of delayed decoding lends itself especially well to the depiction of combat. However, Cather did not always use it. When the mine buried beneath the Snout explodes eight chapters later and signals the opening of Claude's final battle, we immediately sense that the text has shifted into a different, far less impressionistic mode of narration. Now, instead of forming an initially incoherent jumble, events unfold in a blow-by-blow manner, again consistent with the mechanical motions described by military citations, and assume the clarity of chess moves. As if on cue, the Snout erupts immediately after Claude expresses his concern that "'Fritz is acting queerly'": "While he was speaking, everything was explained. The Boar's Snout spread apart with an explosion that split the earth, and went up in a volcano of smoke and flame" (365). While the metaphorical image in the second sentence—"a volcano of smoke and flame"—briefly conveys the workings of Claude's consciousness as he struggles to assimilate the explosion, the narrator does not pause to follow the process whereby Claude's impressions settle into a conclusion. Nor is the reader invited to share the protagonist's momentary shock or confusion. Instead, the narrator quickly pulls away from Claude's perspective and, in one of the novel's many moments of inconsistency, supplies a paragraph-long, omniscient account of exactly how and when the Germans mined the trench. Then come the passages of citation language with their recovering rifles, line of Huns, and fire that takes effect.

Given the various vocabularies that Cather applies to military action and the surprising degree of sophistication displayed by her narration, enough internal evidence exists to suggest that she *chose* to describe Claude's heroism and death in the manner that she did. The question then is, why? If, once again, we assume that *One of Ours* is "centrifugal" in its analysis of idealism and war, a possible answer presents itself. Perhaps by mixing discourses in a manner guaranteed to create ambiguity Cather sought to avoid creating either an explicitly antiwar novel (which Dos Passos had already done) or an outright celebration of the Great Crusade (something the novelist's disappointment in postwar America would not have allowed). The former would have been easy enough. Cather could have sent her protagonist to France as an anonymous private (Claude's qualifications for a commission, incidentally, are curiously unclear in *One of Ours*), shattered his idealism through the kind of brutalizing military system depicted in *Three Soldiers*, and then killed him off in some pointless machine-gun massacre on the slopes of Montfaucon. Mencken, Lewis, and Hemingway would doubtless have approved. By the same token, a more patriotic and jingoistic version of Claude's tale would have required little imagination. The novel could have ended, for example, with Claude's posthumous homecoming—with the patriotic fanfare and grandiloquence of the G. P. Cather ceremony in Bladen, Nebraska. Or, as I have suggested elsewhere, Cather could have saved the last word for Mme. Olive, who, hearing of Claude's noble demise, reflects on the "men of destiny" who saved her nation from the Huns.

The modernist effect that Cather achieves by rejecting these alternatives perhaps becomes clearest if we liken the novel to a film (a comparison that Cather, who hated Hollywood, would not necessarily appreciate). In cinematic terms, book 5 juxtaposes grainy, black-and-white footage with scenes in Technicolor and cuts back and forth between close-ups of battlefield gore and wide-angle views of military spectacle. Some sections, such as the impressionistic account of Claude's wounding, have the intimate, immediate feel of a movie shot with a handheld camera. Others, such as the climactic battle scene in chapter 18, have the epic scope if not of *Birth of a Nation* then of King Vidor's *Big Parade*. The sense of instability and contradiction Cather creates through this visual and thematic montage is, to put it mildly, unsettling. As Guy Reynolds writes (primarily of book 5), "The unevenness of the text, the technical failures and clashing discourses, testify to Cather's difficulties in gauging the true 'national significance' of the war" (123). Yet this sense of confusion, which Reynolds attributes to Cather's doomed attempt to "maintain a progressive momentum against the weight of historical experience" (123), is endemic to her modernist approach and therefore does not in itself demonstrate that *One of Ours* fails as a novel. As with many modernist works, the "clashing discourses" in Cather's text uncomfortably remind us that there is always more than one way to tell a story, that all narrative, no matter how purportedly "realistic," "authentic," or "official," is constructed. The disparity between the two visions of war incongruously spliced together in *One of Ours* ultimately emphasizes the inadequacy of each. An exclusive focus on battlefield horrors, Cather seems to suggest, does not explain the ability of war to elicit "unconquerable" resolve and selflessness in its participants. By the same token, epic vistas of charging Huns and men "like rock" ignore the harm to the body inflicted by weapons and the soldiers who operate them. In *One of Ours* we experience World War I combat, by turns, through the language of naturalism and then through the glamorizing idiom of military heroics, but neither of these discourses ultimately proves authoritative or, on its own, explains the meaning of a single death drawn from the eight million inflicted by the "War to End All Wars."

2. *Claude Wheeler and the Lost Battalion*

Like the narrator's language, which shifts uneasily between the discursive world of Henri Barbusse and that of *American Decorations*, the subject material in book 5 of *One of Ours* represents a complex blend of opposites, establishing Claude Wheeler as both a military Everyman whose experiences typify those of the "average" doughboy and a larger-than-life hero who goes out, as they say, in a blaze of glory. Perhaps most telling in regard to the former is the care with which Cather rewrote the details of G. P. Cather's military career, providing her hero with a more typical and therefore more seemingly authentic tour of duty. Ironically, the sequence of military events described by Cather's sometimes jarring and distracting language in book 5 reveals a careful avoidance of anything exceptional or even uncommon in Claude's overseas experiences — at least until his heroic demise. Contrary to the assumptions of many readers, for example, Lt. Claude Wheeler meets his fate not in the battle of Cantigny, where fewer than twenty thousand Americans saw action, but in the opening phase of the Meuse-Argonne Offensive four months later, a campaign that ultimately involved more than one million members of the AEF. The only reference to Cantigny in *One of Ours* appears in chapter 2 of book 5 when Claude learns, on his second day in France, that the lost American was wounded in that very battle. Cather makes the general location of Claude's death clear in chapter 15. After Claude and David bid farewell to the Fleurys and rejoin their company "on the 20th of September," they travel by rail then by foot "into the Argonne" (340), a name that referred specifically to the dense forest on the left flank of the U.S. Army and more generally to the enormous Meuse-Argonne Offensive that opened along a twenty-mile front on 26 September 1918 and lasted until the armistice.

In addition, Claude Wheeler arrives in France much later than G. P. Cather did. Several pieces of evidence point to this significant alteration. While aboard the *Anchises*, for example, Claude mentions to Albert Usher that he has just spent a year or so as an instructor in stateside training camps; add to this interval the three or four months Claude spends in training following his enlistment in April 1917, and we can calculate the month of his arrival in France as roughly July or August 1918, an estimate further supported by references in the opening of book 5 to men recently wounded at the battle of Belleau Wood, which ended on 25 June 1918. Unlike G. P. Cather, who had the distinction of serving in the first American division to land overseas and who died in the first American battle of the war, Claude crosses the Atlantic at a time when American mobilization had reached its peak, when ten thousand soldiers embarked a day.

But most American soldiers who saw combat in the First World War reached France at least two months earlier than Claude does, typically in April or May 1918. According to statistics compiled after the war, most of the hundreds of thousands who landed in July or August missed the fighting (Ayres 33). Nevertheless, for those who arrived in the spring of 1918, Claude's experience of steadily mounting danger, beginning with his initiation into trench warfare and culminating in his participation in the Meuse-Argonne Offensive (where approximately 120,000 Americans were killed or wounded [Braim 151]), would have seemed familiar and credible— regardless of the relatively minor implausibilities created by Claude's summertime arrival. The reason for this is that Pershing, fearful of sending his troops into battle unprepared (and perhaps even more fearful that the British and French Armies would claim them once he declared their readiness), required that each of his divisions complete an additional two months of training in France, followed by several weeks of duty in a relatively quiet sector of trenches. Thus, very few of the American divisions available during the summer of 1918 fought in an important campaign prior to the fall. Even though Claude reaches France relatively late in 1918, the essential outline of his combat experience, ending with the one battle that almost every American combatant witnessed, would have rung true with the vast majority of veterans who read *One of Ours*.

In order to time Claude's death with the opening phase of the Meuse-Argonne Offensive, Cather packs five months' worth of military experience into approximately eight weeks. For example, the months of overseas training that American troops typically received becomes for Claude's unit two weeks. By the same token, the period of time that Claude's battalion subsequently spends in a quiet sector "east of the Somme" (289), approximately twenty days, is considerably shorter than what most doughboys actually experienced. The result of this creative telescoping is an account of AEF service that offers an historically faithful sequence of events but in an abbreviated and intensified manner. Claude's infatuation with France and contrasting rebirth as an American, his growing sense of solidarity with his fellow soldiers, and his fulfilling friendship with David Gerhardt all required, Cather apparently concluded, a *sustained* treatment by the narrator, one that follows Claude's responses to his new environment on an almost day-to-day basis. Thus, had Cather transported Claude to France earlier in 1918 and adopted the same generally seamless approach, book 5 would have added unnecessarily to the novel's length. In addition, the sense of symmetry that Cather achieves by breaking book 5 into the same number of chapters as book 1 and by dividing the novel almost evenly between Claude's downward spiral in Nebraska and his rejuvenation within the U.S. Army would have been lost. Scrutiny of the time line in book 5 reveals a sophisticated balancing of historical accuracy on the one hand and artistic integrity on the other.

Like her adherence to common experiential denominators, Cather's refusal to disclose the name of Claude's regiment or division also broadens the appeal of her narrative. Clearly tied to no particular unit, Claude becomes for much of book 5 a military Everyman. The only place where Cather even hints at her protagonist's regimental affiliation (misleadingly, as it turns out) occurs at the end of the macabre scene in which Claude, innocently bathing in a shell crater, disturbs a hidden corpse. The comic sign that Claude and his companions subsequently erect (an example of battlefield humor akin to Bruce Bairnsfather's famous World War I cartoons) reads, "No Public Bathing! Private Beach! C. Wheeler, Co. B. *2-th Inf'try*" (296 emphasis mine). The unit designation that Cather half disguises here subtly acknowledges the principal inspiration for Claude Wheeler: Lt. G. P. Cather served in the Twenty-sixth Infantry, though in Company A, not B. To family members and fellow Nebraskans familiar with G.P.'s story, Cather makes a barely perceptible nod. As an indicator of Claude Wheeler's affiliation, however, the passage is a red herring. As we have already seen, Claude reaches the front line months after the First Division went into action. Nor is there any indication that Claude joins that unit as a replacement officer. On the contrary, Claude serves in France with the same group of enlisted men that he oversees aboard the *Anchises*. For example, Corp. Bert Fuller, the soldier who "misconducts himself" in chapter 6 of book 4, reappears throughout book 5 still under Lieutenant Wheeler's command. While the sign posted beside Claude's gruesome swimming hole teasingly implies that he serves in the same regiment as Cather's cousin, everything else in the depiction of his wartime experience, from the month of his arrival in France to the description of the soldiers in his platoon, contradicts this conclusion. Thus, in a narrative that stresses the protagonist's discovery of America (while he serves overseas), Claude's military status remains, appropriately enough, uncomplicated by state affiliation or by the organizational pecking order that in the First World War placed so-called Regular Army units (such as G. P. Cather's First Division) above National Guard units, which in turn ranked higher than organizations assembled out of conscripts. Claude is, quite simply, an American soldier, one whose subordinates might just as easily be draftees as volunteers or National Guardsmen and whose combat experiences might be anyone's—at least until he scales the parapet.

Moreover, the obscured place-names Cather uses make it impossible to locate correspondences between the specific movements of Claude's unit and those of some real-life organization, thus adding to the universal quality of the protagonist's experiences. In chapter 5, for example, Cather informs us that Claude's company has "reached the training camp at S——"; several chapters later Claude is "sent back to Division Headquarters at Q——" (301). As for the trench titles Cather uses, they too are appropriately generic (though far from lacking, as I will argue later, metaphorical significance). "Rupprecht Trench" and "Moltke Trench," for example, acknowledge the German Army's widespread practice of naming fortifications after famous military leaders (in these instances, Crown Prince Rupprecht of Bavaria and Count Helmut Von Moltke of Prussia) and so could be located anywhere on the Meuse-Argonne front. Indeed, the period trench map reproduced in Martin Gilbert's *Atlas of the First World War*, which depicts perhaps a mile or so of trenches from a typical sector on the Western Front, features a "Tirpitz Trench." Trenches named after animals, such as the "Boar's Head Trench" that Claude dies defending, were likewise ubiquitous: Gilbert's sample map again confirms Cather's fidelity to the military usages of the Great War by including a "Goat Trench."

In short, rather than adhere to the specific record of overseas service presented in G. P. Cather's letters, Cather provides her protagonist with a more typical—and therefore more seemingly realistic—set of wartime experiences. Anything that would directly link Lieutenant Wheeler to Lieutenant Cather and thus shatter the illusion of universality created in book 5 was carefully excised from the text.[20] When it came to Claude's death, however, Cather had little choice but to move beyond the realm of "ordinary" military action. The logic of her narrative demanded that Claude expire in a fashion that would dramatically emphasize the depth of his wartime fulfillment (in contrast with his peacetime misery) and the extent of his solidarity with other American soldiers. In addition, as Sharon O'Brien observes, Cather's inspiration for *One of Ours* was rooted in the startling contrast between G.P.'s seemingly certain destiny as a farmer (the future that Cather's cousin so dourly described for her in 1914) and his unexpectedly exotic and noteworthy fate on the battlefields of France (189).[21] While Cather apparently found G.P.'s personality less than compelling, his *story*, with its prosaic beginning and poetic end, illuminated the tantalizing possibilities of American life in the twentieth century and, at the same time, its many ironies.

As we have seen, in her account of Claude's final actions Cather drew many significant details from G. P. Cather's Distinguished Service Cross citation. Like Cather's cousin, Claude climbs to an exposed position, directs the fire of his men, successfully defeats a German attack, and then falls "mortally wounded." But a closer examination of chapter 18 reveals that Cather heightened the drama and thus further separated her account of Claude's death from the predominantly realistic narrative that precedes it by borrowing several key features from the most popular American legend of the First World War—the story of the Lost Battalion.

On 2 October 1918, while advancing into the dense undergrowth of the Argonne Forest, four companies of draftees in the Seventy-seventh (New York) Division became separated from the main body of the American army and were subsequently encircled by the enemy. Trapped in a ravine known as the "Pocket," the men held on for five days without food and with very little water, withstanding numerous German attacks as well as a lethal barrage accidentally fired at them by distant American artillery (the latter halted only through the assistance of "Cher Ami," the most decorated carrier pigeon of the Great War). Four days into the siege, the Germans gave the Americans the opportunity to surrender. The commander of the battalion, Maj. Charles W. Whittlesey, refused, and when help finally arrived on 7 October fewer than 200 of the 554 men who entered the Pocket were still alive. But the story does not end there. On 26 November 1921, just two weeks after attending the Unknown Soldier ceremony at Arlington, Whittlesey provided a disturbing coda to this dramatic tale of American military doggedness by disappearing over the side of a Havana-bound steamer. Letters of farewell discovered in his cabin contained little in the way of explanation. However, four of the friends who received Whittlesey's final communication subsequently issued a joint statement that concluded, "His was a battle casualty" (qtd. in Coffman, Introduction viii).

As former World War I correspondents Thomas M. Johnson and Fletcher Pratt demonstrate in their definitive account of the Lost Battalion, the ferocious determination displayed by Whittlesey and his men, combined with the haunting story of the major's suicide, quickly grew into a legend, spawning innumerable embellishments and outright fictions. For example, the name "Lost Battalion" was a misnomer created by journalists anxious to locate some romance in the otherwise monotonous attrition that characterized the Meuse-Argonne campaign. The men trapped in the Pocket did not, in fact, constitute a single battalion but elements from four different battalions mixed together. Nor, for that matter, did the word "lost" fit their situation. Almost from the beginning of the siege, the commander of the Seventy-seventh Division knew Whittlesey's general location (based on coordinates supplied by Whittlesey himself via carrier pigeon). Likewise, Whittlesey's indignant response to the German surrender plea, the climax of the tale (at least as constructed in popular imagination), was apocryphal. As Johnson and Pratt point out, he never said, "Go to Hell!" And finally, the widespread belief that Whittlesey committed suicide out of a sense of personal responsibility for the Lost Battalion's casualties as opposed to the lingering effects of shell shock (what we would today call post-traumatic stress syndrome) appears questionable in light of the evidence. In actuality, Whittlesey advanced into the Pocket under protest and, once outflanked, refused to retreat chiefly because his orders prohibited him from doing so. An understandable sense of guilt may have driven Whittlesey to leap into the Caribbean, but the real responsibility for the Lost Battalion's suffering rested with his superiors and with the confusion endemic to waging war in a dense forest.

Recently reprinted by the University of Nebraska Press, Johnson and Pratt's account now includes a blurb on the back cover that summarizes the attractions of the legend: "Until World War II pushed the Lost Battalion out of the national memory with its own scenes of horror and heroism, mention of the unit's name summoned up what America admired in its soldiers: unpretentious courage, dogged resistance, and good cheer and adaption under adversity" (a description that also, as we will see, fits the fictional defenders of the

Snout). But other factors explain the legend's popularity as well. For example, the humble nature of the men involved (Whittlesey, unlike G. P. Cather, commanded conscripts, not volunteers) combined with their eclectic race and ethnicity (a Chinese-American and a Native American as well as numerous first-generation European immigrants served in the Pocket) also added to the incident's appeal. The military and civilian Progressives who shaped the culture of the AEF could not have asked for a better illustration of their great theme, American solidarity. In addition, the story's rapid transferal into cultural myth points to the American public's hunger, both during the war and in the years immediately following it, for drama and superhuman heroics in the midst of combat conditions that usually fostered little of either. The Meuse-Argonne Offensive, of which the Lost Battalion's adventures made up a tiny fraction, is recorded in some of the dullest maps ever to appear in military atlases. There were no dramatic flanking movements or sudden breakthroughs. Lined up, side by side, the American divisions that fought there pushed straight into the German lines—sometimes gaining only a few yards at a time. In the midst of this sluggish enterprise, the Lost Battalion, with its inspiring display of unbreakable American spirit, hearkened back to other dramatic moments in American military history when a hopelessly outnumbered or surrounded force decided to fight to the death. The Pocket might have been Bunker Hill, Little Round Top, or, for that matter, the Alamo.

In *One of Ours* Cather signals her familiarity with the legend of the Lost Battalion, or at least its haunting final chapter, when she includes a reference to former heroes who "slip over a vessel's side and disappear into the sea" (370) in Mrs. Wheeler's closing reflections. Spectacled, Harvard-educated, and employed as a Manhattan attorney prior to the war, Whittlesey bore more resemblance to David Gerhardt than to Claude Wheeler. Nevertheless, Whittlesey serves in this passage as a tragic double for Cather's protagonist, his suicide dramatically symbolizing, at least for Mrs. Wheeler, the incompatibility between idealism as exemplified by military valor and the postwar world with its renewed emphasis on competition and greed. It is also likely that Cather knew the military details of the Lost Battalion's story. As a resident of New York City, which proudly claimed the men of the Seventy-seventh Division as its own, she could hardly have avoided knowing about them. Whittlesey and the other survivors received a hero's welcome when they returned to Manhattan in 1919, and every detail of the story—including the extraordinary number of Congressional Medals of Honor and Distinguished Service Crosses conferred upon the living and the dead—received extensive coverage by the New York press. Despite her contempt for movies, Cather may also have been acquainted with the then celebrated film titled *The Lost Battalion* (1919), which reenacted the episode with supposedly scrupulous authenticity and featured many of its real-life participants. And finally, in her survey of World War I narratives, the novelist perhaps encountered "Buck Private" McCollum's *History and Rhymes of the Lost Battalion* (first published in 1919), a popular volume written by one of the Lost Battalion survivors. Containing one of the most detailed narratives of the legend then available, supplemented with doggerel verse and commemorative artwork (including images of the Statue of Liberty at sunrise), McCollum's book blended horror and humor in a fashion that established the citizen soldiers of the Lost Battalion as zealous warriors who, at the same time, remained capable of laughing at the absurdities of army life. As a former member of Whittlesey's regiment wrote in a letter of endorsement added to the book in its 1923 edition, the "entertaining poems" in *History and Rhymes* were "characteristic of that humor which always applied to the true American spirit" (140). Cather may have discovered in McCollum's often jocular account details useful in enhancing the drama of Claude's demise, and at the same time she perhaps received yet another indication that Dos Passos's brutalized doughboys in *Three Soldiers* were not representative of American servicemen (a conclusion she expressed to Dorothy Canfield Fisher [Lee 169]).

It is hardly surprising, then, that beyond Cather's fairly explicit allusion to Whittlesey's suicide, the Lost Battalion legend informs much of the military action in chapter 18. Note, for example, the massive German attack that Claude repulses. Rather than depict the presumably small-scale "raid" that G. P. Cather confronted, Cather presents a force comparable in strength to the Germans who surrounded Whittlesey's command—a force capable, in other words, of annihilating Lieutenant Wheeler's similarly outnumbered troops. Like the Lost Battalion, the Americans besieged in the Snout (a place-name reminiscent of the Pocket in its terseness and banality) fight a seemingly hopeless battle and are kept from collapsing (just as the men of Lost Battalion were) by the inspirational leadership of their commander. By exposing himself to enemy fire at the critical moment, Claude galvanizes the previously wavering troops under his command. He instantly realizes that he has them "in hand" (366). In the same way Whittlesey's personal conduct, marked from the beginning of the siege by a complete absence of panic or concern for his own safety, created an infectious sense of confidence in his soldiers. Previously nicknamed "Galloping Charlie" because of his awkwardly long legs and tyrannical disposition, Whittlesey blossomed under stress, displaying an almost maternal, Claude-like concern for his men (albeit while refusing to save their lives through surrender) and an indifference to personal danger akin to Claude's parapet-mounted heroics. As Johnson and Pratt write, while most members of the Lost Battalion clung to whatever cover they could find, the "crane-like figure" of their commander could always be seen "striding about the position . . . like the worried president of a corporation, perfectly oblivious of the noise and death all around him" (131). In addition, Cather further evokes the Lost Battalion legend by cutting Claude and his men off from the rest of the American army by means of a German artillery barrage and by leaving them open to attack on three sides, circumstances again reminiscent of the New Yorkers' predicament. Indeed, she even goes so far as to make the fate of Claude's company rest on two runners, Sergeant Hicks and David Gerhardt, who undertake the seemingly suicidal task of crossing the barrage and locating American reinforcements. The same desperate action occurred repeatedly during the Lost Battalion's ordeal as numerous volunteers, most of whom were killed or captured, attempted to slip through the ring of Germans surrounding the Pocket and to reconnect with the rest of the Seventy-seventh Division. In essence, Cather creates a miniature and once again abbreviated version of a widely known event, establishing within the span of a few minutes rather than days the same sense of esprit de corps and robust determination associated with the Lost Battalion legend.

Perhaps the most significant evocation of the Lost Battalion, however, appears at the conclusion of the paragraph describing Claude's final battle. Here the narrator presents the protagonist's ecstatic realization that he commands "wonderful men," the climax of his journey from cultural outsider to patriotic junior officer, in language that would have instantly reminded readers in 1922 of Whittlesey and his dogged New Yorkers: "When David came up with the supports he might find them dead, but he would find them all there. They were to stay until they were carried out to be buried. They were mortal, but they were unconquerable" (366). Like Whittlesey, Claude rejects the notion of surrender and would rather see his force annihilated than yield its position to the Germans. On one level, this suicidal determination simply reflects U.S. Army doctrine. As Johnson and Pratt explain in their analysis of the Lost Battalion's similar tenacity, "[I]t had been unceasingly drummed into Charles W. Whittlesey, as into every other officer of the AEF . . . that any retreat, even local, would include a loss of the ascendancy in morale which the Allied Armies, and especially the Americans, had gained . . . at the price of so much blood" (91). In other words, the leadership of the AEF expected its men to stand and fight regardless of losses. Warned by Colonel Scott that a retreat from the Boar's Head Trench would "'let down the whole line'" (359), Claude accepts the hypothetical massacre of his men as a military necessity and acts in a manner consistent with AEF policy.

A more romantic and less rational motive also influences his decision making, however, one that takes on an especially disturbing significance when we read the battle for the Snout as a condensed version of the best-known American legend of the war. Claude's cathartic sense of communion with his subordinates, whose "eyes never [leave] him" as he stands on the parapet, seems in a perverse way to depend on their imminent death. One notes, for instance, that central to the protagonist's climactic vision of his "unconquerable" troops is the image of their shared destruction—of the community of defiant corpses that David will discover when he returns with reinforcements. In other words, Claude's rapture during the seconds preceding his mortal wounding represents more than the culmination of his overseas Americanization: in his final reflections,

Cather's protagonist unconsciously reveals a death wish—not just for himself but for his entire command. Just as Claude associates the sexual fulfillment achieved by the lost American and his lover with the conditions of the grave—the couple's embrace is "so long and still that it was like death" (271)—his conception of military brotherhood defines mass annihilation (à la the Sacred Band) as the ultimate expression of solidarity. Only through their mutual destruction will he and his Chosen Corps continue to stand together "like rock."

By weaving this disturbing theme into a situation that seems on the surface to exemplify the same soldierly virtues that the American public located in the Lost Battalion legend, Cather once again achieves a distinctly modernist ambiguity. On the one hand, the subtle parallels between Claude's beleaguered force and Whittlesey's famous New Yorkers serve to ennoble the protagonist's demise. Even more than G. P. Cather—whose death, a day too late, required revision by the U.S. Army—Claude becomes the apotheosis of the self-sacrificing doughboy and in the final moments of his life inspires his men to enact their own miniature version of a celebrated military incident. For many (perhaps even most) of Cather's readers in 1922, the story of the Lost Battalion, then a powerful presence in the American cultural memory of the Great War, may have shaped their interpretation of the penultimate chapter. Intuiting the connections between Lieutenant Wheeler and Major Whittlesey, between the Snout and the Pocket, such readers perhaps concluded that Claude's military idyll ends with a flourish unqualified by any misgivings over the human loss that military glory demands. In a sense, the story of the Lost Battalion lends, through its mythic stature, a kind of respectability to Claude's final actions (regardless of his arguably irrational motives). Isn't America best served, after all, by soldiers who (in the words that now appear on the back cover of Johnson and Pratt's account) display "unpretentious courage, dogged resistance, and good cheer" in the face of overwhelming adversity? Shouldn't we all be proud of men who put the welfare of others above their own lives, who vow to die where they stand rather than yield a single inch (or clod) of soil to the enemy? If Cather intended to write a sincere homage to martial heroism as inspired by her cousin, then she could not have devised a more effective strategy than invoking the one World War I legend that all Americans knew.

At the same time, however, chapter 18 displays, like so much of *One of Ours*, an unnerving ability to accommodate diametrically opposed readings. Like the swimming hole where Claude and comrades so happily frolic (until Claude retrieves a rusty memento mori from the bottom), the climax of the novel reveals, when examined more closely, a host of submerged horrors: beneath the patriotic resolve that Claude manifests lurks an unrecognized death wish; beneath the parapet that he heroically mounts lie the "complaining" corpses of others who have died defending the same viscera-filled tract of ground; and beneath the lines and arrows that a military cartographer would use to represent the American and German forces are place-names that ominously mark the battlefield as the domain not of heroes but of beasts. Indeed, one of the most disturbing features of chapter 18 is the contrast between the military discourse that Cather employs, with its comfortingly technical jargon, and the animalistic titles of the positions that Claude and his men occupy. The former displays the human need to make war "rational." A military expert, for example, might summarize the desperate firefight presented in chapter 18 as a magnificent "holding action." The latter points to the primitive brutality concealed by just such usages. Reflecting on one level Cather's research on Western Front usages, trench titles such as the "Snout" or the "Boar's Head" also have a symbolic resonance (one cannot help thinking of Golding's *Lord of the Flies* in this connection), linking Claude and his subordinates to wild animals—and to the demonized enemy they oppose (the French, after all, often referred to their German adversaries as "swine" or "pigs").[22] This disturbing connection opens the text once again to questions that Cather, in typical fashion, leaves unanswered. Does chapter 18 present the power of war to bring out the best in its participants, to transform ordinary human beings into "wonderful," "unconquerable" supermen? Is war, for all its horrors, finally the only solution for sensitive dreamers who want more out of life than the banality and crass materialism offered by a frontierless world? Or is Cather suggesting, through the dark implication that Claude *wants* his position to be overrun, *wants* everyone to die, that all military heroics, including the exceptionally inspiring story of the Lost Battalion, have their basis in bestial irrationality—in an ultimately libidinous desire for destruction? Does war represent an ennobling escape from the modern wasteland, or an atavistic descent into something worse?

Cather further complicates our response to the climax of *One of Ours* by suddenly enacting a timeless military myth. When male reviewers in 1922 complained of the artificial, Hollywood-like quality of Claude's death scene, they failed to recognize the appropriateness of such explicit contrivance. The scene seems clichéd precisely because Cather has tapped deep into the American mythology of war, creating a situation that parallels not only the story of the Lost Battalion but that of every other outnumbered, outgunned force celebrated in American history—from the ragtag army assembled at the Alamo to (in a war that Cather lived to see) the beleaguered defenders of Wake Island and Bastogne. Thus we already know when Colonel Scott warns Claude of the vital importance of the Boar's Head Trench that the Germans will launch a massive assault and that Claude's leadership will receive the ultimate test. Nor does it take very long to figure out that Claude will need messengers to brave the German barrage and that his closest friend will, of course, volunteer. The plot in chapter 18 unfolds with such predictability because the war story that Cather tells in this section is, as they say, as old as America. Inspired partly by the circumstances of G. P. Cather's demise and partly by the legend of the Lost Battalion, the final battle scenes in *One of Ours* also invoke what one might call the Myth of the Last Stand, a scenario played out over and over again in American war novels and films.

For a lesson in the structure of this myth and to see just how thoroughly Cather understood it one need only compare the penultimate chapter of her 1922 novel with the closing battle scenes in Steven Spielberg's *Saving Private Ryan*. The similarities are striking. Like Claude and his company, Spielberg's band of American Rangers led by Captain Miller (Tom Hanks) prove "unconquerable" when they decide to fight to the last man while defending a strategically crucial position (à la the Boar's Head Trench) from a German tank column. Outnumbered and outgunned, Miller and his handful of men eventually become trapped in a fall-back position (suggestively nicknamed "the Alamo"), and at the film's climax Miller is mortally wounded while bravely exposing himself, in a Claude-like gesture, to the enemy's guns. All appears to be lost, but then, like Cather's Missourians who pour out of the communication trench in the nick of time, ensuring that Claude's sacrifice has not been in vain, an American airplane swoops over the expiring Captain Miller and demolishes the Panzers. Almost simultaneously, a column of American tanks also comes to the rescue, the World War II equivalent of the cavalry who save the settlers at the end of a western. Hailed as the most realistic war film ever made, *Saving Private Ryan* demonstrates that the romantic appeal of fighting to the last man is alive and well.

Indeed, as with Oliver Stone's *Platoon*, which concludes with essentially the same larger-than-life scenario, Spielberg's enactment of the Myth the Last Stand, albeit with more graphic gore than usual, plays havoc with his realism in a fashion reminiscent of chapter 18 of *One of Ours*. As critic Milton A. Cohen observes in a wry assessment of the movie's contradictions, the Germans who possess such lethal accuracy in the first reel as they mow down the American landing force on Omaha Beach mysteriously lose their aim when it comes time to wrest the "Alamo" from five or six Americans. Scores of Germans die for every G.I. who is hit. By the same token, the Germans in *One of Ours*, who manage in chapter 6 to pinpoint the exact location of the doctor's flashlight and to drop a shell precisely on its coordinates, suddenly become inept when confronted with Claude's defiance. They even fail to capitalize on the mine (yet another subterranean horror) that explodes beneath the Americans' feet. Renowned for its so-called infiltration tactics—these involved attacking positions such as Claude's with small bands of men, armed primarily with grenades, and systematically probing the enemy's defenses for weak spots—the German Army had, by 1918, abandoned the kind of mass frontal assault that Cather presents. An advance "eight deep . . . in long, waving lines" (364) sounds more like a description of the legendary British forces at Bunker Hill or New Orleans—precisely the kind of cultural connection Cather wants us to make. And how does Claude keep his attackers, who form such a convenient shooting gallery, at bay? By entrusting the Snout's defense to the individual American marksman: "It was up to the rifles" (365). Significantly,

Claude's machine guns, the most technologically advanced weapons at his disposal (and the only ones that could plausibly hold off such a superior force), are blown to pieces by the mine. Thus, everything depends on a World War I version of the Minutemen with their Kentucky rifles. One half expects Claude to deliver the classic order, "Don't fire until you see the whites of their eyes."

· · · · · · · · · ·

As Mencken, Lewis, and Hemingway so eagerly observed, as a literally faithful depiction of combat *One of Ours* falls short of the mark—but no more so, I would contend, than *Saving Private Ryan*, a war story that, unlike Cather's novel, has received numerous accolades for its supposed realism. Moreover, the sense of exaggeration and unreality surrounding the climax of the novel, which proceeds a largely convincing account of fairly typical AEF experiences, is appropriate in ways that eluded Cather's earliest male critics. Whether intentional or not, the text's sudden (and, given the critical climate in 1922, highly risky) invocation of American military mythology fits the modernist texture of Cather's narrative with its "clashing discourses," inconsistent point of view, and disturbing juxtapositions. And it takes Cather's theme of Americanization to another level. If, as Joseph Urgo suggests, *One of Ours* focuses on the process through which American culture "harvests" (160) its warriors, Claude's final battle, a miniaturized version of the most popular American legend of the First World War and a variation on a deeply embedded cultural myth, both completes and renews a perverse growing cycle. Destined to receive the kind of acclaim afforded Whittlesey and his men, Claude's larger-than-life heroics will serve as an example for other young Americans—for other Claude Wheelers seeking fulfillment in war (or the death that war provides). Thus, as a result of Cather's conflicted language and ambivalence toward the dictates of literary realism, her novel charts a journey more complex and compelling than that featured in any other American novel of the First World War. We see Claude transformed from alienated Nebraskan into exuberant common soldier, then finally into a figure of American myth who will represent the dubious satisfactions of battle for future generations.

4

THE FIRST WORLD WAR
AS "THE THING NOT NAMED"

In *One of Ours* Cather created a soldier of the Great War who could only have hailed, as the title that Cather finally adopted suggests, from the United States. Claude Wheeler's journey from Nebraska to the Argonne reverberates with American themes at the time — the closing of the West (and the corresponding search for a new frontier) and the formulation, amid the dawn of the mass-media age, of a truly monolithic national culture, one capable of uniting even a New York violinist with a Nebraska "hayseed." Claude's story, we never forget, is an American story redolent of American martial mythology (particularly our culture's continuing fascination with Alamo-like last stands) and the commemorative iconography that adorned unit histories and war memorials from the 1920s. As I have demonstrated, the novel's notorious ambiguity in its second half does not spring from any avoidance of culturally pervasive myths or national preoc-cupations. Rather, the absence of clear-cut meaning in *One of Ours*, the source of a nearly eighty-year-old debate over the novel's basic strengths and weaknesses, stems from the essentially modernist mix-ture of contradictory discourses, jarring thematic juxtapositions, and conflicting perspectives that Cather applies to *America's* first world war. We read the novel with the knowledge, reinforced on every page, that despite his quest (ultimately abandoned) for an alternative cultural orientation, Claude truly is one of *ours*, a distinctly American product whose story enables Cather to explore the cultural constructs through which Americans "made sense" of the First World War.

In her 1925 novel *The Professor's House*, Cather returns to the subject of the Great War but abandons the focus on American cultural formulations that so dominates *One of Ours*. She also rejects the distinctly Midwestern settings and characters, drawn largely from her formative experiences in Webster County, that link her novels from *O Pioneers!* through *A Lost Lady*. In *The Professor's House* the agricultural landscape of south-central Nebraska, intimately and often beautifully evoked in *One of Ours*, gives way to one of the least tangible of Cather's American settings — the shadowy university town of Hamilton, located on the shores of Lake Michigan. Likewise, the thoroughly provincial Claude Wheeler, a character shaped (despite his protestations) by his Nebraska environment, is replaced by the internationally sophisticated Napoleon Godfrey St. Peter, a man whose life and consciousness are split, like his scholarship, between Europe and America. Indeed, the Europeanized St. Peter remains effortlessly detached from his American background in a way that Claude, a "Hamlet of the Plains" (as Sinclair Lewis called him), would have found impossible. Though raised in Kansas at the center of the so-called American heartland, St. Peter is in this sense the least American of Cather's American protagonists, and he appears within a text that displays, at least in books 1 and 3, virtually none of the meticulous attention to local color (try visualizing the professor's campus or the town of Hamilton) that characterizes Cather's earlier novels. Only "Tom Outland's Story," the most conventionally furnished section of the novel, places us within a truly tangible American setting.

Yet Outland himself, the "fallen soldier" at the center of *The Professor's House*, occupies a cultural position no less liminal than St. Peter's: once a railroad "call boy" (159) and cowpuncher, the orphan from the Wild West meets his fate on a battlefield in Europe — but *not*, significantly, as a member of the progressive American melting pot known as the AEF. Unlike Claude, who undergoes a subtle process of Americanization while paradoxically experiencing Europe for the first and last time, Outland dies defending a conception of civilization, however vague, that is greater than his own country. He leaves for the Western Front apparently at the instigation of his childhood teacher, a Belgian priest, and presumably with the approval of his academic mentor, a devout Francophile. Moreover, unlike Claude's death in 1918, which one can easily imagine attracting the kind of patriotic ritual that defined G. P. Cather's death, Outland's obscure demise in 1915, two years before the American declaration of war, remains detached from the culture of American military commemoration. The one enduring memorial to Outland, the Marselluses' bizarre residential museum (named in the inventor's honor), is designed to appeal, as Louie puts it, to Outland's "brother scientists" (31) — to members, that is, of an international clientele. As we see when Sir Edgar reveals his familiarity with the Outland engine, the inventor transcends his nationality, at least posthumously, in a way that Claude (whose story ends on "the banks of Lovely Creek, where it began" [369]) does not. By the same token, in the one passage where St. Peter's thoughts turn directly to the "great catastrophe" that has "swept away" (236) his protégé, he imagines Outland not in connection with an American setting but amid the Luxembourg Gardens of Paris. St. Peter is saddened less by Outland's absence in Hamilton — indeed, the professor even envies Outland's "escape" (237) from the world-weariness of middle age — than by the lost opportunity to rediscover Europe in the young man's company.

Shifting from Frankfort to Hamilton, from the world of American agriculture (and its discontents) to the internationalized milieu of academia, enabled Cather to address subject material far more sweeping in its significance than the already formidable topic she explored in *One of Ours*. While *One of Ours* offers a disturbingly inconclusive study of American martial idealism (especially its origins and ambiguities), *The Professor's House* examines the terrifying "vacuum" left behind for intellectuals on both sides of the Atlantic by an incomprehensible world war. Indeed, the blandness of the novel's university setting, a location both literally and metaphorically remote from the Nebraska Catherland, suddenly makes sense when we consider that Cather is no longer interested in *America's* first world war—or, more specifically, in the sense of optimism and solidarity that thousands of Claude Wheelers, contrary to the mythos of the lost generation, felt as they helped defeat Imperial Germany in the summer and fall of 1918. Instead, *The Professor's House* addresses a truly daunting international theme: the impact of the Great War, with its unprecedented scale and destructiveness, on the intellectual foundations of Western Civilization. In the background of the novel lurk not Cantigny or the Argonne but "battles" like the Somme and Verdun, unthinkable bloodbaths (more than a million deaths combined) that shocked observers in Europe and North America alike. And it is the implications of such colossal horrors for the study of history and the development of applied science that Cather develops as her chief war-related theme.

Critics have long acknowledged that the "great catastrophe" (236) into which Tom Outland disappears plays an integral if somewhat elusive function in the meaning of this cryptic text. With its "unfurnished" style, fragmentary structure, and thematic bleakness, *The Professor's House* has frequently been characterized as Cather's novel of the modern wasteland, her portrait of a broken age left reeling by the industrialized depravity of 1914 to 1918. Yet the novel rarely refers directly to the Great War, a fact that perhaps explains why few commentators have examined the text alongside kindred works such as Virginia Woolf's *Mrs. Dalloway* and Rebecca West's *Return of the Soldier*, studies of Armageddon that likewise focus not on battlefield horrors but on the shattered inner lives left in the war's wake. Ironically, after offending reviewers such as Mencken and Lewis by presenting combat directly and by substituting her unique variety of modernism for the insistent naturalism that such critics expected of "truthful" war literature, Cather managed to create in *The Professor's House* one of the darkest assessments of the Great War ever written—but in a way that again confounds all expectations. As a result, the recent wave of critical studies devoted to World War I literature, especially to works by women writers, has largely ignored the novel, thus omitting from the cultural history of the war a major text by a leading American writer.[1]

In this chapter, then, I contend that the First World War inhabits (or haunts) *The Professor's House* in ways that only become clear once we engage in the kind of intuitive interpretation that Cather herself encourages in "The Novel Démeublé." Insisting on a definition of literary achievement that holds subtlety and suggestion over "mere verisimilitude" (40), Cather maintains that the value of fiction as art derives less from its documentary content—less, that is, from the *things* (or furnishings) it borrows from real life—than from the ineffable "mood" or "emotional aura" (41) that the artist creates around this mere matter. "High quality" in fiction, asserts Cather in her most famous critical dictum, comes from "the inexplicable presence of the thing not named" (41). Though this statement appears within the context of Cather's attack on "over-furnished" fiction—on the inventory-laden works of Sinclair Lewis, for example—it does not quite fit the main theme of her admittedly diffuse essay. How, exactly, do we move from the argument that "material objects" matter less than a narrative's "consistent mood" to the assertion that "the thing not named," an amorphous entity somehow removed from the actual words on the page, defines the "quality" of a novel? What does Cather *mean* by "the thing not named"? Is this phrase synonymous with the "verbal mood" and "emotional aura" (41–42) mentioned, in parallel clauses, in the same sentence? Or does Cather intend a broader meaning? For the sake of my own analysis, I assume that Cather has more in mind here than simply the emotional atmosphere that, ideally at least, envelops a novel's physical "furnishings." In my view, Cather suggests that we read with a kind of double vision, focusing simultaneously on what the narrative names and leaves unnamed. In other words, she encourages us to consider how the text's silence— or, to shift metaphors, its negative space—contributes to its overall significance.

Thus, in the first part of the following discussion I will consider how the meaning of *The Professor's House* changes and intensifies once we conceive of the First World War as a kind of thematic phantom, one whose ghostly presence, "felt upon the page without being specifically named there" (41), pervades even those scenes that do not contain a single reference to the event itself. In particular, I will focus on the novel's treatment of St. Peter's academic discipline, which suffered a crisis of confidence in the 1920s (due largely to the war), and on its presentation of science and technology, forces in modern history that adopt the orphan Outland for their ultimately destructive and commercial purposes. In both of these areas, the First World War often lurks just beyond the immediate reach of Cather's language, a palpable but invisible specter whose presence the reader ascertains through only the sparsest of clues. In the second part of the chapter I return to the subject with which I opened this study, the First World War and the culture of American military commemoration, and contend that the various memorials constructed (or contemplated) in Tom Outland's honor reveal the ultimate failure of America's first world war to form a coherent body of myth.

1. History, Science, and the "Great Catastrophe"

Filled with images of mutability and annihilation, *The Professor's House* is Cather's book of the dead, and at its heart stand two interrelated studies of vanished human beings. A would-be archaeologist (like Barclay Owens in *One of Ours*), Tom Outland examines and catalogs the artifacts of the mesa dwellers and speculates on the warfare that presumably caused their disappearance. Years later, Professor Godfrey St. Peter, who mourns his protégé's death in the First World War, devotes his own scholarly attention to the record kept by Outland during his excavations. The latter project—or, more specifically, the change in St. Peter's scholarly aspirations that it represents—provides a useful starting point for our consideration of the First World War as "the thing not named." The professor's goal is "to edit and annotate" (150) Outland's technical diary, and for much of book 3 he uses this project as means of reconnecting with his lost friend and with his own, long dormant, "original ego" (241). But this editorial endeavor raises some interesting questions that Cather, in characteristic fashion, leaves unanswered. Given the academic indifference toward Native American history that Outland encounters in Washington DC, we wonder, for example, just who will publish the scholarly edition of his diary or read it? Is there really an audience for a book devoted to ancient American treasures that have already been hauled off to Germany? Moreover, the absence of references to other publications by St. Peter, apart from his Oxford Prize–winning *Spanish Adventurers in North America*, poses a still more intriguing question: is the professor's editing of the Outland diary (a cathartic but from a professional standpoint rather esoteric activity) the only scholarly project that St. Peter has undertaken with any seriousness since Outland's death in 1915? The answer, I believe, is yes.

Such an assertion, I realize, appears to fly in the face of overwhelming evidence to the contrary. For example, vague references to other manuscripts in progress, usually described simply as "papers" (85), appear throughout book 1. St. Peter is constantly slipping away to his study to "work" (even before he begins the task of editing Outland's diary), and during his conversation with Augusta in chapter 1 he rationalizes his attachment to familiar surroundings in terms of professional, not personal, necessity: "'I can't have this room changed if I'm going to *work* here,'" he tells her (12 emphasis mine). In addition, St. Peter makes it clear at the beginning of the novel that the "papers" we occasionally glimpse on his desk are not student essays, presumably part of the university-related tasks he completes on campus. "'I'm staying on,'" he announces to Augusta, "'until I finish a piece of writing'" (11)—*something*, that is, other than the introduction and notes for Outland's diary, which he does not begin to compose until chapter 17. And then there are the many sections of book 1 that depict St. Peter toiling with great effort. For instance, he even spends the daylight hours of Christmas in his study, delighted at having "the whole day" (82) set aside for his ambiguous labors. And by lunchtime, he finds that he has created an appetite though his intense activity: "He had been working hard, he judged, because he was so hungry" (85).

Despite St. Peter's compulsive attachment to his professional "centre of operations" (16) and despite the myriad references in book 1 to his mysterious "work," nothing significant seems to come from his apparent industriousness, at least nothing comparable to the acclaimed volumes of Spanish colonial history that established his reputation years before. Cather's narrator is oddly silent on the subject of St. Peter's *recent* publications (if indeed there are any), thus implying that both his personal *and* professional life have never recovered from Tom Outland's death. Likewise, the narrator says nothing about the quality or content of St. Peter's current projects (whatever they are) — a silence that, like so many in this cryptic novel, arguably speaks volumes. Although at the opening of the novel St. Peter has recently won the "Oxford prize" for the final two volumes of his *Spanish Adventurers in North America,* this honor, presumably bestowed upon the professor in 1919, is misleading. The awarding of such a prize would probably have been postponed for the duration of the Great War, and I see nothing to indicate that St. Peter completed his "great work" any later than 1914 (the year he travels to Mexico). Thus, if one accepts Klaus P. Stich's persuasive assertion that *The Professor's House* opens in the year 1920 (240), St. Peter's greatest honor perhaps recognizes an achievement already five years old.[2] Nor has St. Peter recently embarked on any of the scholarly travel essential for an historian working out of an isolated land-grant institution. His journey through "Old Mexico" with Outland in the summer of 1914, shortly before the young man departs for the Foreign Legion, is the last such professional excursion mentioned by the narrator. When St. Peter travels to Chicago with Lillian, Rosamund, and Louie in chapter 8, he does so not to work in the University of Chicago Library but to deliver "lectures" (75) — excerpts, perhaps, from what he has already published. Nor do St. Peter's waning labors in book 3 suggest the level of scholarly engagement that he displayed prior to 1915. I have already noted the esoteric nature of the one writing project, apart from the *Spanish Adventurers,* that Cather specifies — St. Peter's editing of the Outland diary. Just as revealing is the halting progress St. Peter makes with this task. Cather notes that he works on it in a "desultory way" and that he discovers, at midsummer, that he had "pleasantly trifled away nearly two months at a task which should have taken little more than a week" (238–39).

In short, although renowned for his eight-volume masterpiece, St. Peter is now (in terms of genuine historical research) apparently inactive. Unable to move on to something new — whether the thoroughly modern house that he can finally afford or a fresh research project that will truly engage his talents as an historian — St. Peter clings to his old study more for the sake of daydreaming than scholarly productivity and uses his current project as an excuse for imaginatively circling and recircling his days with Tom Outland. No longer a "creative sanctuary" (Harrell 199) where the professor once wove archival data into compelling historical narrative, St. Peter's study has now become his private enchanted mesa, a hideaway for solipsistic reflection.[3] In other words, the only history the professor now studies with any intensity is his personal history. He has apparently abandoned, as the members of a university tenure or promotion committee might say, his "scholarly agenda," his "engagement with his discipline." With the Great War, with Outland's death in Flanders, history in the academic sense has, for St. Peter, lost its attractiveness—and perhaps its meaning. The world has broken in two.

I emphasize the ambiguous nature of St. Peter's scholarly pursuits in book 1 because his apparent disengagement from the study of history mirrors a larger crisis within his academic discipline. Indeed, to register, albeit in a characteristically indirect fashion, the traumatic impact of the Great War on the intellectual consciousness of Europe and the United States, Cather could not have selected a more appropriate figure than a professor of history—especially one with such a multinational background and cosmopolitan set of interests. Among the fields of study shaken by such unimaginable bloodshed, history, the discipline expected to explain how the unthinkable had happened, was the hardest hit of all—especially in Europe. As Modris Eksteins observes, the sheer horror and vastness of the First World War suggested to many European historians in the 1920s and '30s that history had come to an end, that human events had reached such a level of monstrousness that their analysis, in terms of cause and effect, was no longer possible or perhaps even relevant. How could historians even begin to "explain" a cataclysm that killed eight million people and opened the way for a global pandemic that killed twenty-one million more? How could the historical imagination, so accustomed to envisioning the past as a rational progression, accommodate the grotesque processes that led the scientific advances of the Enlightenment and a century and a half of industrial progress to culminate in howitzers, mustard gas, and a corridor of graves and shell-churned earth stretching from Switzerland to the North Sea? How were historians to study a world that, as Fitzgerald's Dick Diver puts it, "blew itself up" (68)? Belonging more properly "to an age of rationalism, to the eighteenth and particularly the nineteenth century," the study of the past now struck many of its practitioners as a decrepit discipline, one out of step with a terrifying new age that required psychologists for its explanation, not historians (Eksteins 291). In the preface to his 1934 *History of Europe* (published one year after Hitler became chancellor of Germany), the English historian H. A. L. Fisher expressed skepticism about the presence of an ultimate meaning in history and displayed a world-weariness reminiscent of St. Peter's despondency: "Men wiser and more learned than I have discerned in history a plot, a rhythm, a predetermined pattern. These harmonies are concealed from me. I can see only one emergency following upon another as wave follows upon wave" (qtd. in Eksteins 291). For Fisher, too, the world had broken in two.

Among historians in the United States, the Great War left a similarly disorienting legacy, opening intellectual fissures that would ultimately threaten to topple the entire discipline. Chief among these, as Peter Novick demonstrates in his study of the "objectivity question" and the American historical profession, was the postwar battle between American historians of the "old school," who continued to advocate the disciplined pursuit of scholarly objectivity, and the growing number of "historical relativists," who argued that the version of "truth" offered by historians would always remain just that—a *version*, an inevitably subjective construct. On one side of St. Peter's discipline stood scholars who still clung to the "noble dream" of reconstructing past events *as they actually happened*; on the other stood those who perceived that "historical interpretation always had been, and for various technical reasons always would be, 'relative' to the historian's time, place, values, and purposes" (Novick 166). While this debate would, as Novick observes, probably have occurred without the First World War (its intellectual seeds were planted well before Sarajevo), the generally embarrassing conduct of the history professorate in 1917 and 1918 gave it a special urgency.

Few in the discipline could take much pride in their wartime "achievements." Among their patriotic activities during the war, American historians assembled pseudoscholarly monographs devoted to the origins and history of Teutonic brutality, harangued Chautauqua crowds on the correspondingly saintly historical record of England and France, and lent their talents to such academically dubious endeavors as the *War Cyclopedia* published in 1918 by the Orwellian Committee for Public Information. Edited by historical luminaries from the University of Wisconsin, Princeton University, and the University of Indiana and outfitted with all the rhetorical trappings of a supposedly factual reference work, the book includes anti-German entries for such carefully selected terms as "Atrocities," "Frightfulness," and "Forbidden Methods of Warfare." The entry for "Blockade," on the other hand, opens with the predictable phrase, "a right long recognized in international law" (Paxson, Corwn, and Harding 39). As for potentially damning topics like "Bertrand Russell" or "the Boer War," the editors of the *Cyclopedia* apparently found it prudent to omit them altogether (Novick 127). Academics from noted history departments also contributed to the committee's *German War Practices* and its companion volume *German Treatment of Conquered Territory*. Part of the "Red, White, and Blue" pamphlet series, which Woodrow Wilson (a former history professor) personally endorsed, both of these supposedly scholarly monographs resemble the eighteenth-century novels of Daniel Defoe or the twentieth-century writings of Robert Graves in their use of invented documents and disingenuous techniques for establishing authority. In short, the hair-raising ease with which American historians put away their objectivity for the duration, like recruits changing into uniform, helped create the atmosphere of contentiousness and self-doubt that surrounded American history departments in the 1920s—and that we see reflected in *The Professor's House*. For nearly two years Uncle Sam, not the pursuit of truth, dictated the professional responsibilities of American historians. As a result, few historians in the postwar years escaped the mood of unease and soul-searching that settled on their profession.

Beyond offering the bitter spectacle of historical writing transmogrified into propaganda, the Great War also confronted American historians with the same queasy sense of global madness—of a new dark ages—that so haunted European intellectuals. Though historians generally backed the war effort with a zealousness they would later regret, many could not help but conclude that reason, the cornerstone of nineteenth-century social science, no longer seemed to rule the world. Nor did Western Civilization (or what was left of it) still inhabit the positivistic universe of inevitable progress and ever-expanding human benevolence. The war, as Robert Graves put it, had said "good-bye to all that." A deeply Eurocentric discipline in 1920, history was filled with American academics who felt the disorienting effects of the war as keenly as if they had been citizens of France, Great Britain, or Germany, nations that lost millions, rather than thousands, of men. In 1925, the year that *The Professor's House* was published, one such historian, Clifford W. Alford, bemoaned the incompatibility between historians who came of age before 1914 and the host of modern horrors and nettlesome epistemological issues that historical scholarship now had to accommodate. A self-confessed member of the "old school," who once "walked the straight and narrow road of approved scholarship [and] learned to babble the words of Von Ranke," Alford now felt betrayed by his discipline's misguided trust in human reason and scholarly objectivity. History no longer mattered when "all the spawn of hell roamed at will over the world and made of it a shambles. . . . The pretty edifice . . . of history which had been designed and built by my contemporaries was rent asunder. . . . The meaning we historians had read into events was false, cruelly false" (qtd. in Novick 132). In despair, Alford even suggested that Henry Ford was right: the First World War (the title that historian Charles A. Beard pessimistically used for conflict from 1919 onward) had demonstrated that history really was just "bunk" (130).

Such, then, is the turbulent academic background against which St. Peter's individual crisis unfolds. And lest the reader conclude that Hamilton is far from Verdun, Cather makes her professor precisely the kind of American academic who would have felt the nihilistic implications of the Great War with special keenness. Godfrey's various ties to Europe, both personal and professional, give him, like the expatriate protagonists in Hemingway's *The Sun Also Rises* and Fitzgerald's *Tender Is the Night*, a special appreciation for the essentially *European* disaster represented by the First World War, an event most American eyewitnesses passed through (in the final months of the fighting) as optimistic tourists. Indeed, one hardly thinks of Napoleon Godfrey St. Peter as an *American* at all. Descended from a member of the Grande Armée and named after the French emperor, the professor looks "like a Spaniard" (4) (or, more precisely, like a figure from El Greco); sports a European-style goatee or "Van Dyke" (4) (unfashionable even for an academic in the clean-shaven America of the 1920s); sips Spanish sherry (smuggled duty-free through Mexico); swims while wearing a French-made "rubber visor" (57) (likened to a Greek warrior's helmet); wins an English prize for history (awarded in pounds rather than dollars); and constructs an enclosed, French-style garden (complete with "French marigolds and dahlias" [6]).⁴ Likewise, St. Peter's linguistic accomplishments set him well apart from his notoriously monolingual homeland. Fluent in Latin, French, and Spanish, St. Peter also presumably knows German, a language most turn-of-the-century American historians acquired regardless of their specialty in order to study Von Ranke and other Teutonic theoreticians. Moreover, St. Peter's dialogue in the novel, laced with sophisticated wit, contains hardly any Americanisms or traces of Midwestern slang. Like the foreign languages he so effortlessly speaks, St. Peter's *English* never once betrays his humble upbringing in Michigan and rural Kansas. On the contrary, St. Peter sometimes treats his native tongue as if he has just learned it. In chapter 1, for example, he requests that Augusta keep his eccentric attachment to the old house "'confidential,'" otherwise "'people might begin to say that Mrs. Peter and I had—how do they put it, parted, separated?'" (11).

In addition to emphasizing St. Peter's Iberian appearance, Frenchified habits and tastes, and mastery of romance languages, Cather also establishes the professor's house (or, rather, houses) as a point of interchange between Europe and America. St. Peter's research, devoted to Spanish exploration and colonial conquest, links the old world and the new. So too do the various visitors who pass through the St. Peter home. The Belgian priest, Father Duchene, for example, leaves his parish in New Mexico and stays with the St. Peters for four days in August 1914 before whisking Tom Outland off to the Western Front. And of course Outland himself adds to this sense of hemispheric intermingling by introducing his Pueblo pottery into the St. Peter household, a domestic environment more typically characterized by French flowers and Spanish wines. For Outland, St. Peter's domicile is a kind of way station, a halfway point between the supposedly unsophisticated American frontier, where Outland has dug deeper into his nation's past than most history professors, and the distant battlefields of Europe, where this devotee of indigenous American culture ironically dies in the name of a foreign country, an *outland*. Another visitor, the knighted English historian Sir Edgar Spilling, humorously adds to the St. Peters' transatlantic prestige by journeying all the way to Hamilton via Canada to consult with the professor on "manuscripts" located half a world away—"in certain mouldering monasteries in Spain" (31). Like St. Peter's Europeanized appearance and Eurocentric academic training, all this longitudinal coming and going—in book 3, St. Peter awaits the return of his family from (where else?) Europe—reinforces the notion that the professor has observed the monstrous spectacle of 1914 to 1918 from a more intimate and informed vantage point than that of most Americans.

Where, then, does Cather connect St. Peter's inner "misfortunes" (250) with the epistemological crisis that the Great War has precipitated within his discipline? And how does Tom Outland's shadowy destiny as a scientist turned soldier affect both St. Peter's view of modern history (especially his scorn for technological progress) and the reader's intuitive conception of "the thing not named"? At first sight, such questions appear simply to bounce off of Cather's sphinx-like text. We know that Tom Outland died on the Western Front while serving in the French Foreign Legion and that his demise *must* have occasioned discussion of the Great War and its meaning among the St. Peters who loved him. But such discussion has been hauled off with the rest of the furnishings. One searches in vain in *The Professor's House* for the kind of extended analysis of wartime loss that dominates the final chapter of *One of Ours*, as Mrs. Wheeler broods over the "desolating disappointment" (370) that followed the Great Crusade. Indeed, even St. Peter, a Francophile who presumably applauded Outland's enlistment (even as he regretting losing the younger man's companionship), remains curiously circumspect on the subject, never speaking directly of the most significant historical event of his life. As we will see, the professor's personal indignation over the war directly enters the text only once—in a highly metaphorical passage, whose full significance many readers may miss. In short, for the critic who seeks (as I do) to place *The Professor's House* squarely within the category of fiction devoted to the aftereffects of the Great War—in the company, that is, of novels such as Virginia Woolf's *Mrs. Dalloway* and Ernest Hemingway's *The Sun Also Rises*— Cather has prepared interpretive obstacles no less daunting than those confronting Tom Outland in his study of a vanished people who left no written records.

Nevertheless, if we read *The Professor's House* with the assumption that the silence surrounding the Great War points to its very significance, the text suddenly reveals surprising new levels of meanings. To illustrate this approach, I will examine three sections in particular, two of which *seem* to ignore the war entirely: first, the encounter between Professors St. Peter and Langtry, which subtly establishes the rise of historical relativism as one of St. Peter's chief professional frustrations; second, St. Peter's classroom lecture on scientific progress as a component of modern history, the full significance of which only becomes clear when we reexamine Tom Outland's ironic journey from the mesa to the Western Front; and third, the professor's terse characterization of the First World War as the "great catastrophe," a climactic passage that openly addresses several war-related themes established almost invisibly elsewhere.

St. Peter's encounter with his longtime adversary, Professor Horace Langtry, proves far less removed from the battlefields of France and from the resulting crisis in historical epistemology than one might assume. Revealingly, the effeminate Langtry irritates St. Peter for reasons that go beyond his political connections (Langtry owes his professorship to an influential uncle), his opposition to nonutilitarian scholarship (Langtry contends that St. Peter should be writing textbooks), and his Victor Morse–like affectation of English dress and manner (in a rare comic moment, the narrator notes Langtry's absurd "bowler hat" and "horn-handled walking stick" [41]). What St. Peter finds *most* offensive about his "professional rival and enemy" (41) are the younger historian's "lax methods" (43), his indifference toward the rules of evidence. The version of history that Langtry accepts from his students, for example, has nothing to do with archival research—or even with learning essential names and dates. In "Lily Langtry's" course, "A student could read almost anything that had ever been written in the United States and get credit for it in

American history. He could charge up the time spent in perusing 'The Scarlet Letter' to Colonial history, and 'Tom Sawyer' to the Missouri Compromise" (43). While this equating of literature and history represents on one level Langtry's unscrupulous effort "to make his courses popular" (43), it also has theoretical implications that would have been especially irksome to a defender of nineteenth-century rationalist definitions of historical inquiry. Of course, St. Peter's own historical practice, as revealed when he nostalgically recollects the process of writing the *Spanish Adventurers*, hardly resembles the dispassionate, scientific ideal promoted by late nineteenth-century history graduate programs. On the contrary, romantic rhetoric and imagery suffuse his fondest memories as an historian. St. Peter commences his eight-volume masterpiece with a Beethovenesque flourish—"I will do this dazzling, this beautiful, this utterly impossible thing!" (16)—and conceives of the "design of his book" in a scene straight from the romantic sublime: while gazing at the Sierra Nevadas, at "snow peak after snow peak, high beyond the flight of fancy, gleaming like crystal and topaz" (89). But St. Peter is also a meticulous researcher who brings more to the writing of history than just his own imagination. He spends two of his sabbatical years "in Spain studying records" (16), and as we have seen, his exhaustive knowledge of certain "sources" attracts the attention of Sir Edgar, who travels all the way "from his cousin's place in Saskatchewan" (26) in order to benefit from St. Peter's archival expertise.

Langtry's historical pedagogy is offensive, then, not because it utilizes fiction but because it flippantly equates the version of truth achieved by the artist's imagination, which freely invents, with that offered by the historian's painstaking, albeit subjective, evaluation of tangible sources. Instead of viewing the two as complementary (a position with which St. Peter would likely agree), Langtry treats them as interchangeable. In other words, historical relativism has arrived at Hamilton. Langtry's almost postmodern scrambling of fact and fiction, of historical discourse and literature, suggests that he has abandoned the pursuit of an "objective," verifiable version of the past and that the past, exploded by an incomprehensible world war, no longer matters as a subject independent of its manipulation in the present. Into the rivalry between these two academics, one a disciplined student of the archives (who appears, however, to have lost his passion for research), the other an advocate of "history" as a subjective free-for-all, Cather reproduces in microcosm the philosophical debate that fractured so many American history departments after 1918. Professors St. Peter and Langtry represent the two halves of a discipline that by 1920 was breaking in two.

Likewise, the scene in which St. Peter lectures his class on "'science as a phase of human development'" (54), a subject he views with understandable skepticism, takes on added profundity when read against the backdrop of a war that saw so many horrific technological "advances." As David Stouck observes, St. Peter's contention that modern science has simply "'given us a lot of ingenious toys'" without matching the richer pleasures provided by "'art and religion'" (54–55) reflects his longing for a "more deeply meaningful and morally coherent world" and his "profound conservatism" (Stouck 206). But St. Peter's dismissive characterization of science as a producer of frivolous playthings that "'take our attention away from the real problems'" also carries a terrible irony. As St. Peter is bitterly aware, the war that killed his protégé introduced more than its share of "ingenious toys." As H. G. Wells accurately forecast in his 1903 short story "The Land Ironclads," scientists and engineers, not generals, dictated both the course of the First World War and the nature of its peculiar horrors. Nineteen fifteen, the year that Cather specifies for Outland's death, saw the introduction of poison gas, carefully formulated by leading German chemists, at the First Battle of Ypres. Also in that year the French Army, including its Foreign Legion, hurled itself against the German trenches in a series of pointless and infamously bloody campaigns.[5] The reason for their failure: the modern machine gun, a device whose internal mechanism, introduced by American inventor Hiram Maxim in 1884, applied principles of physics by utilizing the recoil energy released by one round to position the next inside the firing chamber, thus producing a continuous stream of bullets. It is precisely this weapon, the creation of a fellow American, that presumably kills Tom Outland, an inventor whose own scientific discoveries inevitably spawn military hardware. In the wake of the First World War, neither St. Peter nor the "'fat-faced boys'" (56) in his senior class (who have barely missed witnessing modern warfare firsthand) can escape the grim truth that science, as a force in human history, has not stopped at merely providing superficial "amazements" or "distraction" (54–55). At the end of his lecture, the professor turns to the one bright student in his class and gives him an assignment: "'You might tell me next week, Miller, what you think science has done for us, besides making us very comfortable'" (56). We never hear Miller's response, but Cather's text implicitly offers one of its own. What else has science done for mankind? It has provided the knowledge necessary for the refinement of military aircraft, zeppelins, flamethrowers, U-boats, fragmentation grenades, modern high explosives, mustard gas, and all the other Frankenstein monsters brought to life during the Great War for Civilization.[6]

By naming "the thing not named" in this fashion, I may appear to be taking interpretive liberties with Cather's novel. However, Tom Outland's metamorphosis following his arrival in Hamilton beautifully illustrates this very linkage between science and war, discovery and destruction, and thus encourages us to discern unspoken horrors lurking within the professor's dismissive but restrained assessment of scientific "progress." David Stouck argues that in becoming a scientist and engineer Outland betrays the contemplative reverence for antiquity and nature that he displays on the Blue Mesa. Unable to sustain a vision of human beings existing in harmony with their surroundings, as the mesa dwellers did, Outland joins the ranks of progressive industrialists bent on controlling and exploiting the environment. He "takes his place in the modern world," a world that St. Peter comes to regard as almost unendurable, and is subsequently "killed in a war that is the product of modern technology and dubious morality" (Stouck 209). All true enough. But Cather makes Outland's fate at the hands of machinery (specifically, the *machine* gun) doubly ironic by revealing that the young man's chief scientific contribution, "the principle of the Outland vacuum" (30), eventually follows him onto the battlefield. Both the scientist and his discovery are sucked into the vortex—the "vacuum"—of war.

The details of this disturbing twist emerge during the dinner scene in chapter 2 when Louie excitedly explains to Sir Edgar that his newly constructed home, done in the style of a "'Norwegian manor house,'" will be called "Outland," in honor of the "'brilliant young American scientist and inventor'" (30). Surprisingly, Sir Edgar recognizes Outland's name but not in connection with the young man's extraordinary archaeological discoveries. Presumably a specialist, like his host, in Spanish colonization (a subject not entirely unrelated to the study of Pueblo culture), the Englishman's obliviousness to Outland's *historical* contribution reinforces our suspicion that St. Peter's pet project, the scholarly edition of his protégé's archaeological diary, has very little marketability. Ironically, the one achievement of Outland's with which Sir Edgar *is* familiar turns out to be the "Outland engine," a piece of military machinery the English historian encountered during the war while working in the "construction department" of the "Air Service" (31). Cather wisely omits any technical details when it comes to this engine, the Outland vacuum, or the mysterious (and apparently related) "gas" (126) that Professor Crane claims, in a later scene, to have assisted Outland in creating.[7] The connection with the "Air Service," however, is disturbing. Outland's scientific "principle" becomes, through Louie's pragmatic entrepreneurship, a revolutionary (and remunerative) component in the development of military aviation. Thus, the scientist's disinterested quest for knowledge has in this case indirectly produced a link in the technological chain stretching from the crude biplanes of the First World War, which were limited primarily to the skies above the Western Front, to the sophisticated aircraft of the Second World War, which managed to reach and flatten cities such as Coventry, Dresden, and Hiroshima. What have Outland's specific scientific accomplishments done for mankind? They have helped facilitate the emergence of "total war," a coldly accurate term for the systematic destruction of enemy soldiers *and* (via air power) enemy cities and civilian populations. Equally ominous are the titles of Outland's discoveries and inventions. "Vacuum" carries the associations of nothingness or oblivion, death. By the same token, "Outland engine" has a sinister ring, reminding one of the medieval "siege engine," a contraption designed expressly for destruction, and of nineteenth- or early twentieth-century metaphors for industrialism run amuck—Thomas Carlyle's "steam engine" and Henry Adams's "Dynamo." And of course the unsettling connotations of the word "gas" in a World War I context speak for themselves.

Outland's ironic fate as a scientist turned cannon fodder (whose discoveries then facilitate the destruction of others) takes on still more significance when we consider that the two sides of the deceased inventor's personality, his love of the past and his passion for science and technology, reflect the same dangerous mixture of nostalgia and modernity that characterized European armies as they entered battle in the summer of 1914. Lillian's reference to Outland's "chivalry of the cinema" (151) captures his dual nature perfectly. Outland expresses his antiquated sense of "chivalry," his penchant for knightly quests, through his trip to Washington, where he seeks to slay the dragons of governmental apathy and cultural Eurocentrism, and through his no less idealistic (and foolish) entry into the Great War for Civilization. Though a "clear-sighted and hard-headed" researcher, Outland is "quixotic" (151) when it comes to human affairs, and he probably bases his decision to enlist on the kinds of atrocity stories that inundated the American press in August 1914 via British propagandists. No doubt Father Duchene discusses the "rape of Belgium" with the young scientist during their four days together in Hamilton. The word "cinema," on the other hand, reminds us that Outland—part cowboy, part knight-errant—is also very much a man of early twentieth-century America with its moving pictures, automobiles, and fledgling aeronautical technology. The word also suggests that Outland's chivalrous impulses do not always stem, as they did on the Blue Mesa, from tangible circumstances that he observes directly. Like Claude Wheeler, Tom Outland is a child of the mass-media age and thus susceptible to manipulation— his selfless entry into the Great War perhaps an "exaggerated" (151) imitation of something he has seen on a screen or read about in a newspaper.

Swept into battle by the same chivalrous ideals that brought disaster to the mesa and the same melodramatic fantasies of "self-sacrificing friendship and disinterested love" (151), Outland cannot survive the killing fields in Flanders because the science he so adores with the other half of his divided personality has turned malevolent and is lying in wait for him. The discoverer of the "Outland Vacuum" discovers in the Great War a moral vacuum where chivalrous gestures like the Christmas truce of 1914 have given way to the use of chemical agents. The scientist who paves the way for the "Outland engine" meets the Maxim machine gun—the ultimate engine of death. Yet Outland's internal contradictions simply mirror those of the European nations who poured their armies onto, and *into*, the moonscape of the Western Front. Indeed, bizarre juxtapositions of the chivalric and the technological, the medieval and the modern, are everywhere in the First World War. In the midst of a conflict that introduced modern submarines and tanks, France, for example, cultivated the heroic legend of Joan of Arc (subsequently embraced by America), whose armored form appears on innumerable propaganda posters. Likewise in Germany, the nation most eager to exploit new forms of military technology, crowds at fund-raising rallies purchased iron nails, which they then drove into gigantic statues of Hindenburg and other German commanders, thereby creating a symbolic suit of armor for their armies in the field. And in England, the birthplace of the industrial revolution, thousands of young men volunteered to avenge "poor little Belgium" with a sense of outraged morality more in tune with *Ivanhoe* than with the geopolitical realities of early twentieth-century Europe. Arthur Machen's 1914 short story "The Bowmen" played on such chivalric idealism by imagining the archers of Agincourt returning from the dead to help slay the Hun. Quickly transposed from fiction into folklore, the tale helped inspire the legendary Angels of Mons, whose celestial "holding action" during the British Army's retreat across Flanders was widely regarded as an actual event (Winter 67–68).

Regardless of nationality, soldiers in the First World War quickly found their knightly aspirations at odds with the impersonal, mechanized style of carnage that more than a century of industrialization now facilitated. Indeed, once the positions held by the two sides stabilized, the Western Front, which propagandists such as Machen painted as an arena for chivalric action (and divine intervention), resembled nothing so much as a vast industrial complex. For example, light railways, normally associated with mining operations, were used to carry supplies and ammunition to the front lines. Between 1914 and 1918, engineers on both sides laid literally thousands of miles of narrow-gauge track to serve trench systems, subterranean cities in effect, that remained as fixed in their location as industrial facilities in the north of England or the Ruhr Valley. Likewise, the demand for ever more destructive artillery resulted in the creation of guns (such as the famous howitzer "Big Bertha") so immense that they resembled individual factories—each with steel platforms, catwalks, and gigantic cranes (used to lift the six-foot-tall projectiles that such weapons fired). The day-to-day routine followed by soldiers on the Western Front further added to the war's industrial atmosphere. They performed tasks such as wiring or trench repair in shifts and rotated in and out of front-line positions according to set schedules.

However, even amid this mechanistic environment, a product of applied science, medieval associations never completely disappeared. The forward thrust of modernity had a way of turning back upon itself. For example, the ultramodern "Air Service," the beneficiary of Outland's scientific inquiry, retained a chivalric aura for much of the war, as the "knights of the air" reintroduced man-to-man combat, albeit in a form entirely dependent on twentieth-century technology. By far the strangest juxtaposition of the medieval and the modern, however, came when the body armor metaphorically created during German home-front rallies became a battlefield reality. In 1917 the German Army issued steel breastplates to machine gunners and snipers as a (rather ineffective) defense against high-velocity bullets and shell fragments. American soldiers often made trophies of such armor (typically found riddled with holes), and several period photographs depict the doughboys' bemused fascination with a military implement that appeared to have wandered into the trenches from a European castle or museum.[8] In short, Outland's mixture of anachronism and modernity, his conflicting aspirations as idealistic crusader and hardheaded scientist, points to the contradictory impulses imbedded deep within the war that destroys him. In the end, the orphan who forsakes the mesa for the modern world fulfills the same obscure destiny as the millions of other would-be crusaders whom the engines of industrialized warfare consigned to the outland of the dead. If we think of Outland's ironic journey as a central (albeit unstated) component in St. Peter's rejection of science and technology, the First World War, "the thing not named," moves closer to the center of Cather's text.

The two themes we have considered so far—the shattering impact of the First World War on St. Peter's academic discipline and the conflict's disturbing implications for scientific and technological "progress"—come together in the only passage in the novel where the professor's thoughts turn directly to the event that has killed his protégé, demolished the epistemological foundations of his discipline, and reinforced his sense of personal and professional alienation. In the first chapter of book 3, St. Peter regrets that he never had the opportunity to visit the Luxembourg Gardens with Tom Outland and to behold once more the Delacroix monument, with its depiction of a youth struggling to snatch a palm from Time. Or perhaps, St. Peter reflects, the youth was trying to "lay a palm. Not that it mattered. It might have mattered to Tom, had not chance, in one great catastrophe, swept away all youth and all palms, and almost Time itself" (236). Significantly, St. Peter attributes the "great catastrophe" of the First World War entirely to "chance," thus imagining history as a product of terrifying randomness—of chaos. Like H. A. L. Fisher, he can no longer perceive within past events any plot, rhythm, or predetermined pattern. Once a master of historical narrative, of understanding the past through a combination of art and scholarly discipline, St. Peter now seems to agree with Clifford W. Alford that "the meaning we historians [once] read into events was false, cruelly false" (qtd. in Novick 132).

In addition, the professor defines the Great War not as an outgrowth of preceding events—that is, as a subject open to analysis in terms of cause and effect—but as an obliteration of everything that came before it. Cather's repetition of the word "all" emphasizes the conflict's awful finality. The war swept away "all youth" not just by killing or scarring an entire generation of young men and women but by robbing Western culture of its innocence, its naive faith in the inevitability of progress and improvement. No one, this passage implies, will ever be young again. Likewise, the reference to "palms" (symbols of heroism featured on military medals such as the Croix de Guerre) signals the end of martial romanticism and parallels Hemingway's assertion in *A Farewell to Arms* that "words such as glory, honor, [and] courage" (196) had become obscene in light of the machine gun and the high-explosive projectile. Fueled by the "gas" that researchers such as Tom Outland provide, industrialized warfare has left the notion of military glory as riddled as the bodies in no-man's-land. And then comes the curious reference to "Time itself." Here again St. Peter seems to touch on the crisis in his own discipline. Time has "almost" been "swept away" because the study of history—that is, the study of the relationship between humanity and time—no longer matters in a world where "all the spawn of hell [roam] at will" (qtd. in Novick 132). Relativism now reigns.

Offering little more than an intimation of St. Peter's deepest feelings about the war, this cryptic sentence will probably pass unnoticed by the first- or even second-time reader of *The Professor's House*. But its implications are devastating, especially when considered in light of earlier scenes. St. Peter fondly recalls a nineteenth-century tribute to art, located in an orderly garden (like his own) at the heart of Europe, but then suddenly realizes that everything contained in this sunlit memory of high culture—order, beauty, and aspiration—has vanished into the nihilistic "vacuum" of the First World War. St. Peter's terse summation of the conflict does nothing less than consign all of Western Civilization to oblivion.

It is hardly a coincidence then that Cather's increasingly listless and apathetic professor finds himself, near the end of the novel, at the point of near suffocation from "gas" (251). Here Cather echoes the World War I horrors that have broken St. Peter's world in two and makes yet another reference to Tom Outland's misapplied science. Indeed, Cather's description of the "long anticipated coincidence" (252) that nearly kills St. Peter in his sleep subtly evokes the distant battlefields in Europe. Half-stupefied by fumes, St. Peter becomes drowsily aware of the wind "increasing in *violence*," then of artillery-like "noises—things *banging* and *slamming* about" (251 emphasis mine). When he finally awakes, St. Peter finds himself in a room "pitch-black and full of gas" (251). At the chilling climax of *The Professor's House*, "the thing not named" reveals its terrible reach, invading St. Peter's intellectual refuge as if to transform it, momentarily, into a dugout on the Western Front. As this scene intimates, the ghost haunting *The Professor's House* is the Great War, a phantom whose presence, simultaneously ubiquitous and invisible, can perhaps best be described through the almost spiritualistic language that Cather offers in "The Novel Démeublé"—as an "overtone divined by the ear but not heard by it" (41).

2. "A Sort of Memorial"

Throughout the preceding section I related the sinister connotations of the term "Outland vacuum" to the vast and, for many postwar historians, incomprehensible cataclysm of 1914–18. But there is another metaphorical vacuum in *The Professor's House*. Throughout the novel we see various characters attempt, without success, to fill in the interpretive vacuum presented by Outland's shadowy death. How, this novel asks, do we make sense of the war dead—those removed to the ultimate outland—in a world without fixed values, a world of relativism? In *One of Ours* Cather appropriates imagery from American war memorials as a way of linking Claude Wheeler's idealism to the Progressive vision of the Great Crusade, a vision that public shrines such as the Liberty Memorial attempted (with considerable aesthetic and ideological clumsiness) to carry into the 1920s. *The Professor's House*, on the other hand, examines the desire for meaning, for closure, that prompts such memorials. Beginning in a sense where *One of Ours* leaves off, the novel explores the cultural forms created to dignify military sacrifice and, ultimately, reveals the inability of these forms to accommodate the ambiguities of the First World War.

The impulse to memorialize Outland is everywhere in the novel. We see it first in the various relics, lovingly preserved by Outland's survivors, that mark his impact on the St. Peter family and the academic community of Hamilton. Despite her love of ostentation, Rosamund, for example, still treasures the relatively crude silver and turquoise bracelet—"'one of Tom's trinkets,'" Kathleen remarks (92)—that Outland gave her during their engagement. Likewise, St. Peter keeps Outland's "Mexican blanket" (111) in his study as a functional but cherished reminder of his lost pupil. When examined carefully, however, even such seemingly trivial keepsakes reveal a breakdown in the correspondence between commemorative ges-

tures and the absent individual they ostensibly signify. Neither relic
fits its context. Neither is understood in a way that truly connects
the living to the dead.

Rosamund clings to her bracelet, for instance, while ignoring the
meaning of its sacred stone. Years earlier when Outland presents
a pair of turquoises to the professor's daughters, he stresses the
superiority of indigenous beauty, however modest, over imported
flashiness. The stones, he explains, are "'just the way they come out
of the mine, before the jewelers have *tampered* with them and made
them look green. The Indians like them this way'" (102 emphasis
mine). Outland's contemptuous use of the word "tampered" reveals
his bitterness, born in Washington DC, over the arrogance his culture
displays toward all things Native American. In its natural shade of
"soft blue," turquoise resembles "robins' eggs" or "the sea on halcyon
days of summer" (102). But of course "jewelers" can do better,
turning this innately beautiful stone "green," the color of Kathleen's
jealous complexion. As it turns out, the significance Outland attaches
to turquoise, a symbol (like the Cliff City) of aesthetics defined
by nature and locality, is lost on his "'virtual widow'" (34). Now
adorned not with native stones but with diamonds and imported
furs, Rosamund fills her preposterous "Norwegian manor house"
with Old World antiques. European bric-a-brac has buried the simple
"'turquoise set in dull silver'" (90). In other words, Rosamund
retains the memento but understands nothing of its meaning.

Likewise, although in keeping with the intermingling of Europe and America that characterizes the professor's life in general,
Outland's Mexican blanket carries associations that are antithetical
to St. Peter's increasingly claustrophobic, even literally suffocating,
hideaway. "Faded in streaks to amethyst," this simple but beautiful
piece of fabric evokes the open spaces of the American Southwest
and, through its "horsey" (111) smell, brings to mind the kind of ar-
duous but meaningful journeys undertaken by Archbishop Latour or
Father Vaillant in *Death Comes for the Archbishop*. However, although
St. Peter adores this relic—"'Nothing,'" he tells Kathleen, "'could
part me from that blanket'" (111)—he has renounced the life of action
and engagement that it represents. No longer interested in travel
or new experiences, St. Peter slips during the course of the novel

into a nearly comatose state, and it is Outland's blanket, ironically enough, that he uses to cover himself during his ever more frequent and death-like afternoon naps. Ironically, this memento signifying a lost American, one swallowed up long ago by the Western Front, seems far less deathly than the professor's study, "a shadowy crypt" (94), or St. Peter's other belongings. Once associated with creativity and ambition, the professor's desk has become a grave, a "hole one could crawl into" (141). St. Peter's "old couch" reminds him of the "sham upholstery . . . put in coffins" (248). Here again the object used to memorialize Outland is at odds with its surroundings, its true meaning ignored.

This sense of disconnection between the living and the dead also pervades Scott McGregor's account of the memorial luncheon organized by Louie Marsellus for the "Association of Electrical Engineers" (94). Called upon to provide "personal recollections" of Outland, Scott finds himself unable to fit the dead man into the interpretive context created by Louie's well-intentioned ceremony. "'I didn't express myself very well,'" Scott tells the professor. "'I'm not much of a speaker, anyhow, and this time I seemed to be talking uphill. You know, Tom isn't very real to me any more. Sometimes I think he was just a—a glittering idea'" (94).

Scott's poignant sense of the inscrutability of the dead stands in marked contrast to Louie's ultraconfident "understanding" of Outland and his incessant (perhaps guilt-driven) attempts to pay homage to the deceased inventor. When Louie first meets Sir Edgar, for example, he provides the kind of summative obituary for Outland that no one else in the novel seems capable of constructing: "'We have named our place for Tom Outland, a brilliant young American scientist and inventor, who was killed in Flanders, fighting with the Foreign Legion, the second year of the war, when he was barely thirty years of age. Before he dashed off to the front, this youngster had discovered the principle of the Outland vacuum, worked out the construction of the Outland engine that is revolutionizing aviation'" (30). Louie's effortless encapsulation of Outland might have come straight from a World War I–period newspaper or from one of the innumerable memorial volumes—books with titles like *Tulsa County in the World War*, *Reno's Response*, and *Our Part in the Great War*—

that small-town presses across the United States proudly published in 1919 or 1920. Note, for instance, the cliché-ridden vocabulary Louie employs (Outland was a "*'brilliant* young American scientist and inventor'" who "*'dashed off* to the front'" [30 emphasis mine]) and the standardized, journalistic details he uses to establish the time and place of Outland's death ("'in Flanders, fighting with the Foreign Legion, the second year of the war'"). Nor can Louie resist concluding this capsule biography with a subtle salesman's pitch. Outland's greatest achievement: the highly profitable engine (marketed by none other than Marsellus himself) that is "'revolutionizing aviation'" (30). Ironically, Louie's generous but subtly self-serving description of Outland omits virtually all the personality traits and achievements that the professor and his family found so attractive in the young man. Indeed, the scientist and soldier Louie describes is a mere shadow compared with the amateur archaeologist and crusading advocate of historical preservation that we meet in "Tom Outland's Story." In Louie's world of engineering and entrepreneurial speculation, only Outland's connection to gadgetry and to war, the ultimate stimulus to technology markets, really matters.

It is ironic, then, that of all the characters who in some fashion memorialize Outland, Louie Marsellus (who never met him) creates the most lavish monuments to his memory. We learn, for example, that Louie has used the fortune generated by the Outland engine to endow various scholarships at St. Peter's university, academic honors that almost certainly bear Outland's name. Then there is the informational luncheon, which Scott attends, an opulent affair devoted almost entirely to the demonstration of Outland's technical genius. However, the most "outlandish" (to use Scott's pun) of these commemorative gestures is Louie's decision not only to christen his new home "Outland" but to make it a shrine to the dead inventor, "'a sort of memorial.'" As Louie explains to Sir Edgar, when negotiations with the university are completed, Outland will contain "'all the apparatus'" that the young man used in his experiments, together with his "'library and pictures.'" "'When brother scientists come to Hamilton,'" Louie proudly declares, "'at Outland they will find his books and instruments, all the sources of his inspiration'" (31).

As a memorial, the Marselluses' new home abounds in grotesque ironies. To begin with, Louie presumably expects to acquire the contents of Outland's laboratory, materials that St. Peter's university might use for its own purposes, in exchange for the scholarships that he has endowed. Academics reading *The Professor's House* will have little difficulty detecting in Cather's shadowy details the kind of bargaining that all too often takes place when public universities court wealthy donors. If such a transaction has indeed been agreed upon, and I see nothing in the text that directly contradicts this reading, Louie's residential museum, the future home of exhibits essentially *bought* from a state-funded institution, symbolizes the erosion of higher education by the forces of commercialism and privatization—the very forces that St. Peter, a beleaguered defender of noncommercial scholarship and the liberal arts, has staunchly opposed. Ironically, Outland's "apparatus" will be removed from its academic context, hauled off from the modest institution that Outland chose over Johns Hopkins, in order to serve an advertisement masquerading as a memorial. Moreover, this transferal of artifacts from the public sector to the private echoes Fechtig's raid on the treasures of the Blue Mesa. History, the professor might observe, has repeated itself. Only vaguely interested in profit (Dr. Crane concedes that Outland spoke of the "'commercial value'" of his gas "'not more than half a dozen times'" [126] in three years), Outland would likely respond with horror to the capitalistic underpinnings of his most prominent monument.

Likewise, the incongruity between the Marsellus home, an imitation of a "Norwegian manor house," and its location amid "'primeval forest'" (28) on the shores of Lake Michigan runs completely contrary to the aesthetic preferences of its namesake, who prized the indigenous over the imported. Unlike the Cliff City, which is *part* of the mesa and completely at one with its surroundings, "Outland" essentially represents the imposition of a European aesthetic on an American landscape. Indeed, while Louie insists that "Outland" is "'very harmonious with its setting, just the right thing for rugged pine woods and high headlands'" (28), the entire project betrays the Eurocentric tastes of its owners as well as their indifference toward a true fusion of design and setting. The Marselluses' architect, for example, is himself an import, "'a young Norwegian, trained in Paris'" (28), and although Cather describes the Norwegian's design only sketchily, one might broadly characterize its style as "twentieth-century feudal." Ironically, Louie the American entrepreneur cannot resist the "manor house," a title brimming with Old World aristocratic associations that fit neither the Marselluses, who exemplify the nouveau riche, nor Outland, the quintessential self-made man. The opulent fixtures and furnishings the Marselluses select for this structure also display the couple's rejection of American design. During the dinner scene in chapter 2, for example, Louie refers to the "'wonderful wrought-iron door fittings'" that he and Rosamund have had "copied" (29) from presumably European originals. "'None of your Colonial glass knobs for us!'" he jokes, without realizing that the McGregors (consistently the more provincial of the two couples) have just "glass-knobbed their new bungalow throughout" (29). And when St. Peter returns home from Chicago in chapter 14 after witnessing Rosamund's "'orgy of acquisition,'" Lillian inquires whether he helped his daughter obtain a "'painted Spanish bedroom set'" (135).

Such extravagance in the service of comfort *and* commercial self-promotion (one imagines potential investors in Outland engines enjoying Rosamund's regally decorated guest rooms) stands in marked contrast with the ramshackle physics buildings from which Outland's scientific equipment will soon be removed. In a notable illustration of public parsimony (juxtaposed with Louie's private lavishness), Cather describes the physics laboratory as a once-promising structure, originally designed along the lines of the "old Smithsonian building in Washington," that the state legislature eventually "spoiled" by "grinding down the contractor to cheap execution" (124). St. Peter and Dr. Crane, we are told, both fought for the "integrity" of this structure years before the novel opens. As with most of their political efforts, however, "nothing came of their pains" (124). Nor, one suspects, would anyone in 1920 succeed in convincing St. Peter's university, which has compromised its "integrity" in ways that go beyond the merely architectural, of a simple fact—that the appellation "Outland" belongs most properly not to Louie's absurd manor house, where the inventor will be falsely summed up at endless public relations gatherings, but to the dilapidated physics building, where his light "used to burn so far into the night" (74). Though an oddity in the case of a private residence, the practice of naming buildings after war heroes was common enough on American university campuses in the 1920s. The Outland Memorial Physics Building, however, is not to be. St. Peter's university has, in effect, already sold the rights to the Outland name and entrusted the memory of its most distinguished student to the wisdom of big business.

Informing Cather's wry treatment of "Outland" and adding to its myriad ironies is the lively debate, which reached its climax around 1920, over the appropriateness of so-called living memorials. As G. Kurt Piehler explains in *Remembering War the American Way,* as soon as the First World War ended a number of American political Progressives, aligned with "professional recreation workers" (108), called for an end to the impractical style of memorializing that in the previous century left battlefields cluttered with unsightly monuments. The "War to End All Wars," they argued, demanded a new, more meaningful form of commemoration, one that would link the memory of the fallen not to useless stone monoliths or statues (of the kind that Lyon Hartwell creates) but to "bridges, parks, libraries, playgrounds, and community centers" (108). The impulse to memorialize, in other words, could be translated into the improvement of public facilities. The dead would be honored through structures that benefit the living. The hundreds, if not thousands, of memorial halls, memorial auditoriums, and memorial stadiums constructed in the 1920s that endure to this day in American cities and on American university campuses testify to the success of such reformers. Indeed, a pamphlet produced in the early 1920s by Cather's alma mater, the University of Nebraska, illustrates the kind of persuasive appeals that advocates of "living memorials" employed. Titled "We Will Build the Nebraska Stadium in 1923," the pamphlet subtly implies that a football stadium, a structure guaranteed to attract a regular audience, will serve as a more efficacious reminder of the dead than statues or courthouse murals, objects obviously less tied to the public's timeless need for sports and entertainment. Nebraska Stadium, the pamphlet declares, "will be a living memorial for Nebraska's heroic dead. Thousands and thousands of Nebraskans will pass through the stadium's gates year after year—and before the eyes of each will be bronze tablets bearing the names of the University of Nebraska students killed in the World War" (2). As the pamphlet promised, the ground-breaking ceremony for this "living memorial" (subsequently renamed "Memorial Stadium") took place in 1923, two years before Cather published *The Professor's House*.

But the call for functional commemoration also met with resistance. Organizations such as the American Federation of Arts, the National Sculpture Society, and the U.S. Commission of Fine Arts asserted that art, not engineering, best represented the fallen and denounced the notion of *useful* memorials as an insult to the war dead (Piehler, *Remembering War the American Way* 111). Trade journals from the period, such as the cleverly titled *Monumental News*, demonstrate that beneath the outrage expressed by opponents of "living memorials" lurked a fear that the nation's practical materialists—its Louis Marselluses—might exploit commemoration for their own commercial purposes. One such opponent, for example, declared that every advance made by America in its history was a response "to the call of [the] ideal, the spiritual, [and] the poetic," "every fall backward" a result of "the worship of the crassly material" (qtd. in Piehler 109). Another contrasted the stability of commemorative artwork (however lacking in aesthetics) with the impermanence of memorial buildings and funds. Interestingly, this writer singles out science and commerce, the two forces Louie brings together in "Outland," as the enemies of immutable meaning. Builders of memorials, he suggests, should oppose modernity not cooperate with it: "The monument in our park or square is PERMANENT. Neither fire nor the progress of science will destroy it! Commerce dares not hope to banish it! . . . It may be a poor piece of art, but on Memorial day, we gather there with bared heads and pay tribute to the glorious men of another day! We cannot gather about some pile of money which is left as a Memorial fund. . . . Our old Memorial Hall will not accommodate us!" (qtd. in Piehler 109). Even more relevant to Cather's novel was a cartoon featured in the February 1919 issue of *Monumental News*. Titled "If the 'Useful Memorial' Cranks Had Built Them," the cartoon imagines several famous monuments—including the Great Pyramid, the Arc de Triomphe, and the Statue of Liberty—transformed into ridiculously utilitarian structures. The Great Pyramid, for example, becomes an enormous billboard with "'Ad' Space to Let." Across its face in gigantic letters is a huckster's slogan: "Eat Pharaoh's Sawdusto, the Great Breakfast Food." By the same token, the Arc de Triomphe becomes "Triumph Apartments"; the Statue of Liberty becomes the headquarters of a construction company. A sandblasting hose replaces Lady Liberty's torch (Piehler 110). Although readers of the *Monumental Times* had their own "crassly material" stake in the "living memorial" debate—sculptors and monument manufactures obviously feared losing business to the "recreation workers"—the cartoon warned that profit, not patriotism, lay behind the postwar challenges to traditional commemoration.

One can easily imagine what critics of functional memorializing would have thought of "Outland," a monument both to the deceased inventor (or at least to the reductive version of "Tom Outland" that Louie and Rosamund place on display) and to Jazz Age conspicuous consumption. Nor would advocates of "living memorials" find much to admire in the Marselluses' bizarre home. Supporters of the memorial halls and stadiums that soon dotted the nation wanted the memory of the war dead transported from courthouse lawns and cemeteries, tranquil settings where that memory might easily be ignored or forgotten, to public spaces where vital activities took place. Within the functional structures created in their honor, the dead would live on by remaining in intimate contact with the living. Even in the midst of their pleasure, concert-goers and football fans would be forced to recollect the fallen and to pay the proper respect. As we have seen, however, Outland does not live on through the building that bears his name any more than he does through Rosamund's turquoise bracelet, whose aesthetic lessons she has forgotten, or St. Peter's Mexican blanket, whose significance he now ignores. Nowhere in the novel do commemorative gestures truly connect the living to the dead. As an especially misguided "living memorial," "Outland" does more, however, than simply stress the disjuncture between acts of remembrance and their object. The Marselluses' shrine unintentionally symbolizes the way that the couple *lives off* Outland—in a sense, feeding on the dead.

Arguing for the presence of such a ghoulish theme may seem like a stretch until one realizes that Cather's text often conflates commemoration and consumption. When Scott describes the meeting ("some lunch!") of the Association of Electrical Engineers, for example, he remarks that "'we had poor Tom served up again'" (94). "Poor Tom" and dining seem to go hand in hand. Indeed, if we return to the dinner scene where Louie first offers his simplistic encapsulation of Outland as soldier and scientist, we can see that the narrator juxtaposes the physical act of *eating* with Louie's rhetorical cannibalizing of Outland's identity (only bits and pieces of which fit with the entrepreneur's commercial purposes). Louie pauses from his purely relativistic history of Outland's accomplishments just "long enough to have some intercourse with the roast before it was taken away" (31). And the next day St. Peter remarks to Lillian that he wishes the Marselluses would "'not convert [Outland's] very bones into a personal asset'" (36). This macabre imagery underscores the monstrousness of what Louie and Rosamund have done. Less the honoree than the victim of his opulent memorial, Outland has been reduced to a mere commodity, something to be passed out (or "served up") at promotional luncheons—like an item on the menu or the bundle of cigars that Scott receives while covering the meeting. Thus the "living memorial" ostensibly constructed in Outland's honor bears an unsettling resemblance to the degraded monuments imagined by the cartoonist in *Monumental Times*. "Outland," the place, negates Outland, the person, by literally showcasing only those elements of his "many-sided mind" that will help sell engines. Louie might as well decorate his own "useful memorial" with the kind of advertising placards that the cartoonist imagined for the Great Pyramid.

The referential confusion caused by the title "Outland" further underscores the speed and effectiveness with which business interests *consume* the inventor's identity and determine the ultimately superficial nature of his public commemoration. The morning after Louie announces the name of his new home, St. Peter realizes to his chagrin that now there are *two* Outlands. When Lillian criticizes his unspoken disapproval of Louie, the professor replies, "'I admit I can't bear it when he talks about Outland as his affair. (*I mean Tom, of course, not their confounded place!*) This calling it after him passes my comprehension'" (36 emphasis mine). The very fact that St. Peter must offer this parenthetical clarification points to the insidious linguistic implications of the Marselluses' gesture. By appropriating the inventor's name, they have severed the sign from its original referent and in redirecting its meaning, laid claim to an authority they do not rightfully possess. Solidified by its title, which suggests a one-to-one correspondence between the memorial and the man, and backed by the Marselluses' vast wealth and public-relations acumen, "Outland" presents a monolithic public image of the inventor, one with which private memories, already fading, cannot compete. In a later scene Kathleen remarks to her father, "'[O]ur Tom is much nicer than *theirs*'" (113). But "*our* Tom," a tenuous construct that Kathleen herself has difficulty describing ("'Always very different from the other college boys,'" she vaguely recounts, "'[a]lways had something in his voice, in his eyes'" [112]), has little chance of overturning the Marselluses' literally concretized version of Outland the soldier and scientist. Nor can Scott's similarly amorphous conception of Outland as a "glittering idea" stand up to the far more tangible image of the inventor conveyed by his enshrined "apparatus" and "library." When Louie confidently describes Outland to Sir Edgar, Scott wrestles with "a desire to shout to the Britisher that Marsellus had never so much as seen Tom Outland, while he, McGregor, had been his classmate and friend" (31). However, although Scott is tempted to denounce the self-appointed architect of Outland's public memory, it is unclear what kind of memorial he himself would erect.

Now that the word "Outland" is securely tied to their own handpicked and commercially self-serving set of referents, Louie and Rosamund set about ensuring its adoption into common currency. Louie mentions, for example, that he has "'already ordered the house stationery'" (29). In other words, every piece of outgoing mail from the Marselluses' residence will reinforce the couple's dominion over Outland's memory and perpetuate their equating of the building with the complex individual it supposedly commemorates. Likewise, the journalists, including Scott McGregor, whom Louie carefully includes at functions held in his home will carry the new "Outland" into the newspapers, thus spreading the usage still further. Indeed, by chapter 10 of book 1, which contains Scott's account of the luncheon, even Cather's third-person narrator can no longer resist referring to the Marselluses' residence by its "outlandishly" inappropriate title: Louie, we read, "gave a luncheon for the visiting engineers at the Country Club, and then motored them to *Outland*" (94 emphasis mine). Even within the narrative itself, "Outland" proves an unavoidable "engine" of meaning.

The only memorial mentioned in *The Professor's House* that might counterbalance the Marselluses' reductive but increasingly privileged model of "Tom Outland" is the professor's scholarly edition of the Outland diary—ironically, a project he seems unlikely to finish. Although Outland's disillusioning experience at the Smithsonian Institute may suggest that his archaeological journal (as opposed to his later scientific formulas) has only the smallest of potential markets, the book St. Peter hopes to create nevertheless falls within a familiar World War I genre. Indeed, diaries, collections of letters, and "complete" editions of poems by individuals killed overseas— invariably introduced and edited by close friends, relatives, or former teachers—dominated publishers' lists in 1917 and 1918 and continued to appear well into the 1920s. *Victor Chapman's Letters from France* (1917), a text Cather owned and read, falls into this category, as do a number of best-selling literary titles (many by writers whom critic James J. Kirschke has identified as possible inspirations for Tom Outland) that the novelist likely encountered during the war years. In 1916, for example, Scribner and Sons published a popular and, as it turned out, influential collection of war poetry by Alan Seeger, an American killed in 1915 while serving (like Tom Outland) with the French Foreign Legion. The book's introduction by William Archer might have eulogized Cather's character: "This book contains the undesigned, but all the more spontaneous and authentic biography of a very rare spirit. It contains the record of a short life, into which was crowded far more of keen experience and high aspiration . . . than is given to most men, even of high vitality, to extract from a life of twice the length" (xi). Cather was probably also familiar with *The Collected Poems of Rupert Brooke* (1915), which exposed thousands of Americans to England's quintessential happy warrior, who literally died from a mosquito bite on his way to Gallipoli; *Poems, Essays, and Letters* by Joyce Kilmer (1918), a two-volume work that immortalized the one notable literary casualty suffered by the famous New York regiment, the "Fighting 69th"; and *In Flanders Fields and Other Poems* (1919), a tribute to Lt. Col. John McCrae, the Canadian soldier who authored the single most frequently quoted poem of the First World War. Such volumes, textual memorials in effect, follow a number of funereal conventions. The introduction to these texts, for example, is usually titled "Memoir" or "An Essay in Character." Here the editor provides personal recollections of the author, together with testimony from other friends or family members; offers a narrative of the deceased's military service (overtly propagandistic in the case of wartime publications); and, if possible, includes documents such as telegrams, final orders, or manuscript facsimiles to add an air of tangibility and authority. The photograph featured as the frontispiece usually shows the author in uniform.

Though standard for posthumously published writings by "fallen" soldiers, such rhetorical trappings may at first sight seem irrelevant to Outland's painstaking account of archaeological excavation, his "minute description of each tool . . . of every piece of cloth and pottery" (238). Outland's "plain account" is not, after all, a combat narrative or a collection of poems but a highly specialized text likely to interest only a handful of professional archaeologists and aficionados of pre-Columbian art. But St. Peter's editorial apparatus could hardly ignore the war or fail to adopt at least some of the conventions described above—especially in the introduction, which the professor regards as the most difficult part of his task, its chief "bother" (150). "To mean anything," St. Peter realizes, the diary "must be prefaced by a sketch of Outland, and some account of his later life and achievements. To write of his scientific work would be comparatively easy. But that was not all the story; his was a many-sided mind, though a simple and straightforward personality" (150). The potential value of St. Peter's scholarly project as a corrective to the overly simplified version of Outland symbolized by the Marselluses' home immediately becomes clear in this passage. The professor realizes, as Louie and Rosamund do not, that Outland's posthumous contribution to American free enterprise does not represent the sum of his achievements. No amount of conspicuous consumption can truly *digest* Outland's "many-sided mind." Moreover, as an historian and as Outland's closest friend and confidant, St. Peter seems eminently qualified to reverse the alchemical process whereby his protégé has been translated into "'chemicals and dollars and cents'" (112). The professor alone, it would seem, has the ability to create a true "living memorial," one that will reanimate the lost inventor through its fidelity to the truth.

Or does he? If we assume that St. Peter's introduction must in some fashion address Outland's death on the Western Front, perhaps even setting the inventor's fate within its historical context, then the professor's editorial task suddenly appears daunting—especially for an academic whose discipline has broken in two as a result of the war. How can the professor tell "all the story" when his subject has disappeared into a nihilistic "vacuum"? How, in other words, can St. Peter reconcile his desire to memorialize Outland with his realization that the "great catastrophe" has destroyed "even Time itself"?

The difficulty St. Peter faces in this regard becomes especially clear when we return to the textual memorials described above and consider their rhetorical consistency. In the various types of introductions that serve to mediate between the dead author and his posthumous audience, one invariably senses a rhetorical demand for uplifting interpretation—even when the editor must confront the kind of senseless demise that Claude Wheeler, a martyr to military necessity, manages to escape (at least in his own mind). Archer's introduction to Alan Seeger's *Poems*, for example, even musters enough self-delusion to offer an ennobling account of an obviously pointless machine-gun massacre: "Seeger had barely passed his twenty-eighth birthday, when, charging up to the German trenches on the field of Belloy-en-Santerre, his 'escouade' of the Foreign Legion was caught in a deadly flurry of machine-gun fire, and he fell, with most of his comrades, on the blood-stained but reconquered soil" (xi). Although the content of this passage unintentionally conveys the absurdity of Western Front combat—Seeger and his "escouade" clearly never had a chance—its vocabulary comes straight from the nineteenth century. The "charging" poet dies "on the field of Belloy-en-Santerre" (as opposed to no-man's-land), the victim of a connotatively harmless "flurry" of machine-gun fire. Just how the "blood-stained . . . soil," another nineteenth-century martial cliché, qualifies for the adjective "reconquered" is unclear given Archer's disclosure that "most" of Seeger's companions "fell" beside him. Likewise, Margaret Lavington's biographical note in *The Collected Poems of Rupert Brooke* attempts to establish an aura of patriotism and romance around Brooke's anticlimactic demise from blood poisoning: Brooke died, Lavington writes, "for England on the day of St. Michael and Saint George. He was buried [on the island of Scyros] at night, by torchlight, in an olive grove about a mile inland" (172). And in "An Essay in Character," which appends *In Flanders Fields and Other Poems*, Sir Andrew Macphail lavishes so much attention (nearly four pages) on the military pomp and circumstance displayed at John McCrae's funeral that one nearly forgets the cruel irony represented by the poet's fate: the author of the most widely quoted lines of the Great War died not while fighting the German "foe" amid "Flanders fields" but while fighting pneumonia in a British base hospital.

In short, the style of discourse used to frame posthumously published works by soldiers seems far more in tune with Louie Marsellus's conception of Outland than with St. Peter's. Indeed, the professor's disapproval of Louie's "'florid style'" of expression (36) with its facile references to "'death and glory'" (31) leaves little question whether he would find the conventions of textual memorials palatable.[9] St. Peter's awareness that four years of assembly-line carnage have swept away the "palms" of war, its seductive romance and pageantry, leaves little room for consolatory or sentimental imagery—for flurries of machine-gun fire, torch-lit services amid olive groves, or "a hundred nursing Sisters" (Macphail 137) lining the route to a French cemetery. To treat Outland's wartime death in the way that 1920s-era publishers and readers expected would, in effect, require the professor to betray his deepest insights into the obliterating absurdity of the "War to End All Wars." At the same time, however, it is difficult if not impossible to imagine a way around the rhetorical demand for uplift. Could Cather's historian really bring himself to admit in writing and within the context of his professional scholarship that the Great War ultimately meant nothing? And how does the editor of a posthumously published diary announce the unthinkable—that the diary's author was in the end nothing more than cannon fodder? Perhaps St. Peter's reticence on the subject of the Great War—note that he never shares his thoughts on the "great catastrophe" with anyone—suggests that he finds his bleak but honest assessment of the conflict just as difficult to bear as Louie's shallow and self-serving talk of "death and glory." A kind of paralysis brought on by the sheer horror of what St. Peter beholds freezes his speech. The historian who understands that the Great War has ended history can neither give utterance to this terrible truth nor mouth the patriotic clichés and military euphemisms used by others to console themselves.

Cather's narrator never states directly whether St. Peter completes his textual memorial. However, if I am correct in my assertion that St. Peter's nihilistic vision of the "great catastrophe" would inevitably come into conflict with the conventions upon which editors of books by dead soldiers relied, it would seem that the Great War finally brings the professor's project to a creative impasse. When we last hear of the Outland diary, in chapter 2 of book 3, the narrator conveys St. Peter's renewed delight with the Hemingwayesque sparseness of Outland's prose: "To St. Peter this plain account was almost beautiful, because of the stupidities it avoided and the things it did not say. If words had cost money, Tom couldn't have used them more sparingly" (238). The professor finds a welcome relief from the "florid" exuberance of Louie Marsellus in Outland's pared-down narrative. But of St. Peter's progress with the introduction and annotations we learn almost nothing except that he begins his work in a "desultory way" and then "trifl[es] away nearly two months on a task which should have taken little more than a week" (238–39). By the second paragraph of chapter 2, St. Peter has uncharacteristically lapsed into "day-dreams" (239), an indication that his process of "falling out" (250) has begun, and from this point on the narrative races toward the professor's appointment with poison gas. Tom Outland's diary is never mentioned again.

In the end, then, the "fallen soldier" at the center of *The Professor's House* eludes a genuinely meaningful form of commemoration and remains consigned to an interpretive "vacuum." Although "Tom Outland's Story" provides a vivid rendering of the young man's "straightforward" personality, if not his "many-sided mind," his memory within the community of Hamilton is ultimately fragmented and *relative*, broken up among the misunderstood relics, misguided or unfinished memorials, and fading recollections that ostensibly signify this lost American but never quite match up with their referent. Though named, Outland is finally an Unknown Soldier—an enigma constructed, by turns, as a "glittering idea," a boy with "'something in his voice [and] eyes,'" and a "brilliant young American scientist and inventor." Of these subjective constructs, Louie and Rosamund's brick-and-mortar version of "Outland" will almost certainly prevail, but only because it is backed by cash and deeply tied to American values that lie hidden beneath the couple's European furnishings.

In *Sapphira and the Slave Girl*, published fifteen years after *The Professor's House*, Cather provides a sardonic corollary to her romantic treatment of military commemoration in "The Namesake." While Cather's 1907 short story presents war memorials as visionary art—as the product of a cathartic confrontation with "race and blood and kindred" (146)—her final novel underscores the disjuncture between public memory and truth. Now war memorials lie. In the closing chapter, for example, we learn that Martin Colbert, the odious would-be rapist of Nancy, does not survive the Civil War and that his family "'made a great to-do about him after he was dead, and put up a monument'" (290). At the close of her career, years after the world had broken in two, Cather could no longer envision the kind of idealized correspondence between a memorial and its subject that Lyon Hartwell achieves with "The Color Sergeant." Colbert the Confederate Cavalryman receives his shrine, but as Mrs. Blake observes, the "'neighborhood was relieved'" (290) to be rid of the dissolute rake who wore the uniform. As we have seen, *The Professor's House* anticipates this ironic treatment of commemoration by juxtaposing Outland's animated personality as established through his own language in book 2 with the Marselluses' lifeless "living memorial," a structure that through its cavalier assumption of authority metaphorically kills (and consumes) *its* namesake. Like the mummified bodies that Fechtig purchases from Roddy Blake, Outland's memory takes its place in the "orgy of acquisition." By the close of this grim novel, the passionate student of the past who once claimed the former denizens of the Blue Mesa as his "ancestors" (219) has been quietly buried, along with his turquoise and Mexican blanket. No one, not even St. Peter, can restore him to life. But the scientist and soldier lives on, preserved within the residential headquarters of Louie's company as a youthful patriarch of American productivity, the father of an economic engine.

At the same time, however, the posthumous section of Tom Outland's story ultimately represents more than a study of commercialized remembrance—more than a sardonic attack on Jazz Age "outlandishness." Broader themes relating to American culture in general and to the Great War also emerge. The Marselluses achieve their takeover of Outland's identity primarily through their capital, ironically generated by the dead man's discoveries, but also through their embrace (masked by their European decor) of quintessential American values. Indeed, the couple's deification of Outland the inventor, as opposed to Outland the archaeologist and quixotic defender of a vanished people, succeeds because it taps directly into the American passion for practicality and application—the cultural forces Claude found so suffocating in Nebraska and St. Peter has resisted for decades. In a sense, to mean something in America, to connect with our national myths, Outland's identity *must* be moved from the university, that place of notorious impracticality (note Dr. Crane's anything but applicable inquiry into "the extent of space" [122]), to the home of an aspiring business tycoon. Anti-intellectualism indirectly fuels the posthumous editing of Outland's diverse interests and experiences. Hamilton, as it turns out, is perhaps *not* so removed from Frankfort.

Moreover, the ambiguous nature of the conflict in which Outland dies—or rather the lack of consensus, in Hamilton or anywhere else, over its true meaning—prevents any real alternative to the Marselluses' monument from emerging. Louie Marsellus, a generous and likable character whose wartime actions can nevertheless be described as outright profiteering, speaks without irony of "death and glory." Nowhere in the effusions of Outland's self-appointed promoter do we sense any misgivings about the war itself. As evidenced by the dinnertime obituary that St. Peter's son-in-law "serves up" in chapter 2, Outland's life and death make effortless sense to Louie because, for him at least, the war that terminates the inventor's brilliant career poses no serious epistemological challenges. Along with the millions of other Americans who continued during the interwar decades to uphold the Myth of the Great Crusade, Louie still imagines heroes who "dashed off to the front" and to whom his country is "terribly indebted" (31). The historian St. Peter, on the other hand, has looked too deeply into the heart of twentieth-century darkness and therefore becomes incapable of constructing a truly authoritative monument to his protégé's multifaceted genius. Ultimately, then, the ghost haunting *The Professor's House* produces its own obscurity within the text. The "great catastrophe" becomes "the thing not named" because silence, Cather suggests, is finally the only language that fits an unthinkable world war.

· · · · · · · · · ·

Without question *The Professor's House*, which stands among the finest American novels of the 1920s, is a far more satisfying work than *One of Ours*. But it would be a mistake to view these texts as stages in a developmental progression—to argue, for instance, that Cather first had to blunder her way through *One of Ours* before reaching the level of insight into the First World War and its international ramifications that she displays in *The Professor's House*. Lacking the precision and elegance of Cather's best work, *One of Ours* has yet to recover fully from the jaundiced reading it received initially from influential reviewers such as Mencken and Lewis, who essentially argued that the novel addressed the wrong war in the wrong way (and from the perspective of the wrong gender). Published on the heels of Dos Passos's *Three Soldiers*, a work that set the naturalistic agenda for many American war novels to come (including James Jones's *From Here to Eternity* and Norman Mailer's *Naked and the Dead*), Cather's disturbing study of personal liberation through military violence not only dared to enter the masculine domain of the trenches but refused to denounce unequivocally American participation in the fraud-laden Great War for Civilization. Expecting a tale of wartime brutalization, full of *explicit* irony and the overt debunking of military myths, such reviewers confronted instead an exquisitely subtle novel whose chief success resides less in its achievement of a unified thematic structure than in the questions it "centrifugally" poses—and leaves unanswered.

As evidenced by the polarized interpretations the novel instantly attracted, few readers at the time of its publication, just four years after the armistice, were prepared for such an intensely modernist treatment of the Great Crusade. Thus, few could see that the novel's contradictions and ambiguities, especially in book 5, reflect not muddled thinking (or, worse, a descent into patriotic blather) but an effort to render simultaneously the attractions and repulsions of war. True to the paradoxes at the heart of its subject, this difficult novel asks its audience to confront and even identify with the desires (not ignoble in themselves) that find fulfillment in the ultimately anything but noble activity of killing. Like Frederic Manning's *Middle Parts of Fortune*, a text that similarly falls outside the categories of explicitly pro- or antiwar literature, *One of Ours* refuses to simplify its complex subject, preferring instead to depict war as "a peculiarly human activity," one shaped "not by beasts, or by Gods," but by "men" (Manning n.p.). Eighty years after the chorus of male disapproval first rose, like a critical "holding action," to refuse Cather entry into the front lines of literary commentary on warfare, it is long past time to recognize her 1922 novel as a major work of twentieth-century American war literature.

By the same token *The Professor's House*, an even more important text, does not in the end constitute an artistic reworking or refinement of *One of Ours*. Though *The Professor's House* moves beyond Claude Wheeler's story in the sense that it focuses on the absence rather than the creation of an ill-fated American warrior, radically different preoccupations animate these two novels. Presented paradoxically in *One of Ours* as an arena for Claude's long-thwarted idealism *and* as the domain of bestial irrationality, the Great War emerges (or rather remains *submerged*) in Cather's 1925 novel as an evil so terrible that numbed silence becomes its chief description— and its only history. No one, apart from the Marselluses, whose monument displays the power of commerce in a world without meaning, can articulate the significance of Outland's death in Flanders fields. Through its enormity and horror, the war has swept away the intellectual assumptions required for its translation into narrative. Poison gas—and by extension all the other "ingenious toys" deployed in industrialized warfare—drives the historian into an interpretive then literal stupor. Only the reader seeking "the thing not named" will discover the traces of this terrible collapse, which lie hidden like the pottery shards and mummies that Tom Outland unearths in his study of an ancient disaster.

For decades cultural historians have largely ignored Cather's contribution to the literature of the First World War for two main reasons. First, the neglect stems from Cather's idiosyncratic methods of analyzing the conflict and its aftermath. Filled with paradox and ambiguity, *One of Ours* eludes the kind of theme-based classification that war-literature scholars typically employ. The book represents neither an expression of 1917-vintage jingoism (as some of its least sympathetic Vietnam-era critics allege) nor a clear-cut instance of postwar disenchantment (the view most widely accepted since the 1980s). In *The Professor's House*, an even more problematic response to war, the "great catastrophe" of 1914–18 is central—but nearly invisible. Revealing its unnamed presence requires the most painstaking of textual archaeology. Second, the achievements for which Cather is most widely known, her groundbreaking depiction of Nebraska pioneers and her virtual reinvention of the historical novel in *Death Comes for the Archbishop* and *Shadows on the Rock*, have overshadowed her compulsive examination of the international cataclysm that coincided with the arrival of her artistic maturity. The First World War, an episode now almost as faint within American cultural memory as the Spanish-American War (or, for that matter, the War of 1812), is hardly the first thing non-Cather specialists think of when they hear the writer's name. As I have tried to demonstrate throughout this study, however, Cather's now secure reputation as a major American writer will remain incomplete until her treatment of the First World War, in novels of disturbing insight and haunting beauty, is understood and appreciated.

NOTES

Introduction

1. According to Bennett, Cather became so "aroused and interested" by G. P. Cather's letters that she remarked to friends, "I never knew he was that kind of fellow. He revealed himself to me in his letters, and let me tell you, he's going to be my next book" (15). The forthcoming Willa Cather scholarly edition of *One of Ours*, edited by Richard Harris, contains an extensive discussion of G. P. Cather's wartime correspondence, a collection of materials never before made available. All serious Cather scholars will wish to consult this edition.

2. For the most complete survey of criticism on *One of Ours* for 1922–70, see Prendergast, "*One of Ours*: Willa Cather's Successful Failure."

3. Other notable articles written or published in the 1980s are Gelfant, "'What Was It . . . ?'"; S. O'Brien, "Combat Envy and Survivor Guilt"; Ryan, "No Woman's Land"; and Yongue, "For Better and For Worse." All of these analyses (except O'Brien's) essentially advocate an ironic reading of the novel.

4. Of the now numerous articles and book chapters devoted to *One of Ours*, Stout's discussion of the novel in *Willa Cather: The Writer and Her World* comes closest to offering the kind of reading I have in mind. Stout writes, "Claude is fooled in his

entire attitude toward the war. But the diffuse irony of Cather's writing does not allow us to say what a correct attitude would be. Clarity is exposed as reductive. Unwilling as she was to adopt the view of modernists who wrote of a world lacking all meaning, she instead created a succession of limited and illusory meanings, false floors that keep dropping us, if not into the nihilism of a Hemingway ('Our nada who art in nada . . .'), at least into radical uncertainty. A single meaning may be there somewhere at the bottom, but we cannot detect what it is. And so the irony that surrounds Claude's more general misconceptions is less crisp, less clear in its import, than the limited ironies of his 'foolings'" (176). While I do not agree that Claude's *entire* view of the war is delusional—too much of Cather herself finds its way into Claude's romanticizing of wartime France and into his seductive vision of military comradery—I do concur with the assertion that "Clarity is exposed as reductive" in *One of Ours* and that the text offers no "single meaning."

1. Americans Lost

1. As a void, however, the monument embodied an essential instability, attracting not only cathartic identification on the part of veterans and grieving families but ironic treatment from writers disenchanted with commemorative rhetoric. Indeed, for such writers the tomb proved an irresistible target, the perfect illustration—because it "honored" a body so shattered by modern weaponry that even its identity was obliterated—of the gap between battlefield reality and the American public's limited imagination. Stallings's 1924 novel *Plumes*, for example, concludes with a chilling scene in which a young child learns, while visiting the tomb with his father (a crippled former Marine), to ignore the euphemistic language of memorials and to see that a general is nothing more than "'a man who makes little boys sleep in graves'" (348). Likewise, in *1919*, the second volume of the *U.S.A.* trilogy, Dos Passos mocks the ethnocentrism lurking behind the nation's commemorative efforts, even behind the seemingly inclusive tomb: "'Make sure he ain't a dinge, boys, make sure

he ain't a guinea or a kike,'" remarks a graves registration man as he presumably sorts through the sets of remains from which Sergeant Younger will choose: "'[H]ow can you tell when a guy's a hundredpercent when all you've got's a gunnysack full of bones, bronze buttons stamped with the screaming eagle and a pair of roll puttees?'" (540). And in an even bitterer twist, March presents the Unknown Soldier as a disillusioned Marine in his 1933 novel *Company K*: eviscerated by a German shell and impaled on barbed wire, the dying Marine flings away his dog tags in the hope, ironically, that his remains will never be used as a patriotic symbol (181).

2. Franc Cather, letter to E. H. Prettyman, 27 December 1919, Archives and Special Collections, University of Nebraska–Lincoln Libraries. Franc Cather's comments were prompted by a query contained in E. H. Prettyman's 3 September 1919 letter: "[A]re you going to have G.P.['s] body brought back or not[?]."

3. Anne Taylor, letter to Myrtle Cather, 18 October 1918, Nebraska State Historical Society, Willa Cather Pioneer Memorial Collection, Red Cloud. All quotations used in this study are true to the original sources and include any and all idiosyncrasies in spelling and diction.

4. Housed in the Archives and Special Collections Department of the University of Nebraska–Lincoln Libraries, the letters sent to Franc Cather by E. H. Prettyman and his mother, Alice Prettyman, offer a heartbreaking glimpse of the suffering inflicted by World War I weaponry. Severely wounded in France, Sergeant Prettyman conducted his correspondence while confined to a bed in U.S. General Hospital No. 3 in Rahway, N.J. In a letter dated 2 October 1919, he reveals that his injured leg is still "not very well" and that he anticipates having it "operated on again for the 10th time." After visiting her son in the hospital, Alice Prettyman remarks in a letter dated 10 January 1919 that "he is only 21 but looks 30, poor boy."

5. E. H. Prettyman, letter to Franc Cather, 24 November 1918, Archives and Special Collections, University of Nebraska–Lincoln Libraries.

6. Coombs's ultrathorough *Before Endeavours Fade* contains no

mention of the First Division memorial at Cantigny. Hundreds, if not thousands, of memorials erected on World War I battlefields were removed in later years by farmers seeking additional arable land.

7. Two excellent studies of European World War I memorials as well as other forms of remembrance are Mosse, *Fallen Soldiers,* and Winter, *Sites of Memory, Sites of Mourning.*

8. Willa Cather, letter to Charles Cather, 7 July 1921, Archives and Special Collections, University of Nebraska–Lincoln Libraries. G. P. Cather's name apparently attracted error. In Roosevelt's *Average Americans,* an account of Roosevelt's service in the First Division, G.P. appears first as "Grover P. Cather," then as Lt. "Cathers" (145).

9. Paraphrase of Willa Cather's letter to Dorothy Canfield Fisher, 8 March 1922, Archives and Special Collections, University of Nebraska–Lincoln Libraries.

10. *One of Ours* resembles *Sons and Lovers* chiefly through its emphasis on an intense and in many respects paralyzing mother-son relationship. In addition, Enid recalls Miriam, the similarly spiritual and frigid love interest of Paul Morel.

11. For an insightful comparison of Cather's World War I fiction with Woolf's, see Schaefer, "The Great War and 'This Late Age of World's Experience' in Cather and Woolf."

12. In a fascinating article titled "Willa Cather's *One of Ours*: In Distant Effigy," McComas convincingly examines "the way in which the war provides Claude the displaced means to counter his own long-endured victimization by his father" (95).

13. For a detailed treatment of Alvin York's involvement in the film *Sergeant York,* see Perry, *Sgt. York,* 235–75.

2. Americans Found

1. For an interesting discussion of Claude as a "linguistic cripple, semantically and rhetorically," see Nelson, *Willa Cather and France,* 31–32.

2. West's novel focuses on a shell-shocked soldier's rejection of his wife, whom he no longer remembers (and never loved), and his

renewed pursuit of a childhood sweetheart. In the end, he suffers the fate that Claude fears for the lost American: he is "cured" and once again conforms to the passion-denying conventions of his culture.

3. In his otherwise excellent essay titled "Claude's Case," Cramer makes no mention of the lost American and his lover, an omission that distorts one of Cramer's key examples. When offering support for his claim that among the soldiers aboard the *Anchises* Claude is "the least interested in women" (157–58), Cramer mentions the Nebraskan's refusal to accompany Victor Morse to a brothel and then moves immediately into his next example. However, Claude's fastidiousness during his dinner with Victor takes on a different meaning when placed in context, for it is just after this scene that the protagonist has his sexually charged encounter with the lost American and his lover. In other words, Claude's refusal is immediately followed by an explicit display of his *heterosexual* desire. Though I agree completely that homoerotic feeling partially defines Claude's military experiences, the protagonist's actions in this *specific* instance simply do not add up to a clear-cut illustration of sexual preference. An even more misleading manipulation of the text occurs in Boxwell, "In Formation." Arguing that Claude's erotic gaze seeks out the lost American, rather than his French lover, Boxwell concludes his discussion of the connection between the two men with the following quotation: "'All day, as Claude came and went, he looked among the crowds for that young face, so compassionate and tender'" (301). Perhaps unintentionally, Boxwell implies that the "young face" in this passage is that of the lost American. In reality, the narrator is referring to the soldier's female companion, whose features Claude finds sexually arousing.

4. For a discussion of "Soldier's Home" as a depiction of the cultural conditions that would have greeted Claude Wheeler and Victor Morse had they survived the war and returned to the United States, see my essay, "'Where Do We Go from Here?'"

5. Frederick Sweeney, personal diary, Nebraska State Historical Society, Willa Cather Pioneer Memorial Collection, Red Cloud.

6. For a thoughtful treatment of wartime constructs of masculinity

within the context of English culture, see Caesar, *Taking It Like a Man*.

7. As Ryder astutely observes in "Sinclair Lewis and Willa Cather," the doughboys' technological plans for their home away from home would "ostensibly . . . convert Beaufort into Frankfort" (152).

3. Cather and Combat

1. I would include in this category Brittain's *Testament of Youth;* Canfield Fisher's *Home Fires in France;* Rathbone's *We That Were Young;* Smith's *Not So Quiet . . . ;* Wharton's *The Marne* and *A Son at the Front;* West's *Return of the Soldier;* and Woolf's *Jacob's Room*, *Mrs. Dalloway*, and *To the Lighthouse*.

2. Ironically, according to Miller in "Anti-Heroic Theme and Structure," Hemingway perhaps learned a great deal about war writing from the author whom he ridiculed in his "snide, patronizing, and sexist attack" (103): "A useful structural principle he may have learned from Cather and eventually applied in *A Farewell to Arms* was the principle of sustained contrast developed in *One of Ours* between Claude's peacetime existence and marriage in Nebraska, associated with spiritual death, and his wartime experience in France, associated with rebirth and resurrection" (104). For another comparison between Cather's World War I writing and Hemingway's, see Rohrkemper, "The Great War, the Midwest, and Modernism."

3. For a discussion of *One of Ours* and the Pulitzer Prize, see Stuckey, *Pulitzer Prize Novels*. According to Stuckey, the novel won over its competitors, including Lewis's *Babbitt*, because of its celebration of conformity: "In spite of . . . the fact that it is more sensitively written than Pulitzer Prize books usually are, *One of Ours* is similar in one important way to a number of other prize winners. Its 'happy' ending (like that of *Alice Adams* and, many years later, of Herman Wouk's *The Caine Mutiny*) depends upon bending the rebellious individual to the collective will. Claude Wheeler leads his troops into the fire of German guns. For 'individualism' in Pulitzer Prize fiction means merely the liberty to succeed in

ways popularly subscribed to in American society, not the right to be oneself" (45).

4. Falls's entry for *One of Ours* reads in full: "A woman's War novel may seem to be a contradiction in terms, but Miss Willa Cather has wisely made the War only a culminating episode in hers. She has drawn a remarkable picture of her hero in the midst of his family on the Nebraska farm, his childhood and adolescence, before taking him across the Atlantic and plunging him into the experiences which end with his death at the age of twenty-five. The scenes in France are as good as a non-combatant could make them, and a good deal better than those which appear in the pages of many a combatant; but perhaps that was only to be expected, for the imagination of a writer of the standard of Miss Cather, with plenty of material to assist it, is much more valuable than the direct reporting of those with commonplace minds and visions" (268–69).

5. For a more in-depth discussion of the critical practices of Norton Cru and Falls, see my essay, "Telling the Truth—Nearly," 177–79.

6. Hal Waldo, letter to Willa Cather, 3 April 1923, Archives and Special Collections, University of Nebraska–Lincoln Libraries.

7. Charles Bayly, Jr., letter to Willa Cather, 30 September 1922, Nebraska State Historical Society, Willa Cather Pioneer Memorial Collection, Red Cloud.

8. Elmer M. Ellsworth, letter to Willa Cather, 11 November 1922, Nebraska State Historical Society, Willa Cather Pioneer Memorial Collection, Red Cloud.

9. Kirk Bryan, letter to Willa Cather, 24 December 1922, Nebraska State Historical Society, Willa Cather Pioneer Memorial Collection, Red Cloud.

10. Caroline H. Walker, letter to Willa Cather, 10 October 1922, Nebraska State Historical Society, Willa Cather Pioneer Memorial Collection, Red Cloud.

11. Emily Colt, letter to Willa Cather, 9 February 1923, Nebraska State Historical Society, Willa Cather Pioneer Memorial Collection, Red Cloud.

12. For White's most lucid and concise presentation of this theoretical position, see "Historical Text as Literary Artifact."

13. In "The Experience of War in American Patriotic Literature," Quinn suggests that Cather may also have drawn from Empey's absurdly propagandistic guide to trench warfare, *First Call*. Though no hard evidence exists to support this claim, Cather may indeed have consulted Empey's work, perhaps borrowing the layout of her "Boar's Head Trench" from the fortifications diagram that Empey provides. This two-page drawing features sandbagged trenches and a forward machine-gun position that closely resembles the Snout. In addition, Cather likely studied Roosevelt's *Average Americans*, an account of First Division service by the commander of G. P. Cather's regiment. Interestingly, Roosevelt writes that Joan of Arc symbolizes France for him (39), and he includes a detailed description of an "old roman camp" (83), a possible source of Barclay Owens's archaeological discovery.

14. Stout provides a convincing account of Canfield Fisher's contribution to *One of Ours* in "The Making of Willa Cather's *One of Ours*." For a detailed treatment of the complex relationship between Cather and Canfield Fisher, see Madigan, "Willa Cather and Dorothy Canfield Fisher."

15. Lawrence's officer, like Cather's sniper who picks off children, combines feverishly suppressed homosexuality with sadism. The story focuses on his torture of a heterosexual orderly to whom he is attracted. In addition, Lawrence's character physically resembles Cather's. Both have close-cropped hair and icy blue eyes.

16. For the argument that in *One of Ours* Cather "explored character controlled by external forces and success and failure as results of circumstances more than of character" (234), see Murphy, "*One of Ours* as American Naturalism."

17. M. Morris Andrews, letter to Franc Cather, 5 July 1918, Archives and Special Collections, University of Nebraska–Lincoln Libraries.

18. Unfortunately G. P. Cather's grieving family was fully aware of the discrepancy and presumably bewildered by its implications. In a letter to Sergeant Prettyman, dated 27 December 1919, Franc Cather writes, "The gov't says the 27th of May 1918. It came to us as the 28th of May—you ought to know—as it was at night—it may be either."

19. Willa Cather, letter to Franc Cather, undated, Archives and Special Collections, University of Nebraska–Lincoln Libraries.

20. Of course Cather may also have feared that an overly faithful rendering of G. P. Cather's wartime experience would bring unnecessary pain to her Aunt Franc. An overly literal account of G.P.'s service might have struck many in the Cather family as an act of artistic exploitation.

21. G. P. Cather's escape from the ordinary attracted Cather's imagination even before she read his wartime correspondence. In her initial letter of condolence to Franc Cather, dated 12 June 1918, the novelist described her reaction to G.P.'s death after learning of it in the *New York Times*. Her cousin, she felt, had long been dissatisfied as a farmer. He had found his true destiny in war; he had risen through action. This letter is held in the Archives and Special Collections Department, University of Nebraska–Lincoln Libraries.

22. For an extended discussion of atavism in World War I narratives, see Bonadeo, *Mark of the Beast*, 1–49.

4. The First World War as "The Thing Not Named"

1. For an example of the invisibility of Cather's World War I writing to cultural historians, see Higonnet, *Lines of Fire*. There is not a single reference to Cather anywhere in this 656-page volume.

2. Harrell's ordinarily helpful chronology of Cather's novel in *From Mesa Verde to* The Professor's House does not indicate the year St. Peter completed *The Spanish Adventurers* (215–21). It would seem that Cather leaves this matter open for conjecture.

3. For a more positive interpretation of the professor's attachment to his study, see the excellent article by Price, "Epicurus in Hamilton."

4. Cather's textual revisions suggest her interest in keeping St. Peter separate from his American background. In the typescript of *The Professor's House*, now held in the Archives and Special Collections Department of the University of Nebraska–Lincoln, the passage describing St. Peter's vigorous swimming concludes with an image, ultimately omitted, that would have clashed with

the emphasis on the professor's Europeanized appearance and sensibility: "The old man looked like a red Indian, Scott observed to himself as he plunged in after him" (48).

5. According to Hart, *The Real War*, French offensives in Champagne and Artois during the autumn of 1915 resulted in 191,797 French losses (198). In general, 1915 was a year of pointless butchery and deadlock. However, as Ferro observes in *The Great War*, both sides regarded their casualties as "costs of victory. Orthodoxies favoured this view: Joffre, who after the Marne was Father of the country, said, 'Let us attack and attack . . . no peace or rest for the enemy'" (75).

6. For a contrasting interpretation of Cather's treatment of science in *The Professor's House*, see the fine article by Ryder, "*Ars Scientiae.*" Ryder convincingly argues that "[w]hat Cather decries in *The Professor's House* is not science itself but the materialism and commercialism that too often result from it" (14). My own reading of the novel is bleaker. In my view, Cather demonstrates that in twentieth-century America the scientific has all but become synonymous with the material and the commercial.

7. The typescript of *The Professor's House* contains evidence that Cather agonized over her description of Outland's discoveries, only to leave it in the end as vague as possible. Louie's dinnertime summary of the inventor's accomplishments, for example, contains several details that did not survive into the final text. In this earlier version, Louie explains that Outland "'worked out the construction of the bulkheaded vacuum,—that is, a vacuum protected by a gas that does not fill it'" (26). The material following the dash is scratched out, presumably by Cather. The reference to the "bulkheaded vacuum" disappeared later in the revision process.

8. Though the only nation to issue body armor on a large scale, Germany was hardly alone in its efforts to shield soldiers from modern weapons by reintroducing medieval forms of protection. The U.S. Army, for example, experimented with such anachronistic equipment as chain-mail eye protectors, medieval-looking steel visors, metal shin guards, and breastplates. For a fascinating study of World War I armor, see Dean, *Helmets and Body Armor*

in Modern Warfare. In an ironic twist that Tom Outland might have appreciated, Dean, the curator of the Department of Arms and Armor in the Metropolitan Museum of Art, actually worked with the U.S. Army in developing the medieval costume that America's modern crusaders would supposedly wear in France. The urgencies of wartime, however, led the army to purchase most of its helmets from the British and to scrap Dean's plans for additional protective clothing.

9. Patriotism and naïveté only partially explain Louie's "florid" descriptions of Tom Outland. Lurking in the background is Louie's need to surround the Outland legend with an attractive, sales-generating halo of romance. Indeed, Louie's buoyant language places him squarely within the world of Lewis's *Babbitt*, a novel filled with characters who believe that the right rhetoric will win them success. In the motivational parlance of the 1920s, the language used by St. Peter's son-in-law demonstrates that he is a true "go-getter," full of "pep."

WORKS CITED

Acocella, Joan. *Willa Cather and the Politics of Criticism*. Lincoln: U of Nebraska P, 2000.

American Decorations: A List of Awards for the Congressional Medal of Honor, the Distinguished Service Cross, and the Distinguished Service Medal, 1862–1926. Washington, D.C.: GPO, 1927.

Anders, John P. *Willa Cather's Sexual Aesthetics and the Male Homosexual Tradition*. Lincoln: U of Nebraska P, 1999.

Andrews, M. Morris. "Details of Lieutenant G. P. Cather's Death." *Bladen Enterprise* 6 May 1921: 1.

Archer, William. Introduction. *Poems*. By Alan Seeger. New York: Scribner's, 1917. xi–xlvi.

Ayres, Leonard P. *The War with Germany: A Statistical Summary*. Washington, D.C.: GPO, 1919.

Barbusse, Henri. *Under Fire: The Story of a Squad*. Trans. Fitzwater Wray. New York: Dutton, 1917.

Barker, Pat. *The Eye in the Door*. New York: Plume, 1995.

———. *The Ghost Road*. New York: Plume, 1996.

———. *Regeneration*. New York: Plume, 1993.

Bennett, Mildred R. *The World of Willa Cather*. Lincoln: U of Nebraska P, 1961.

Bonadeo, Alfredo. *Mark of the Beast: Death and Degradation in the Literature of the Great War*. Lexington: UP of Kentucky, 1989.

Boxwell, D. A. "In Formation: Male Homosexual Desire in Willa Cather's *One of Ours.*" *Eroticism and Containment: Notes from the Flood Plain*. Ed. Carol Siegel and Ann Kibbey. New York: New York UP, 1994. 285–310.

Braim, Paul F. *The Test of Battle: The American Expeditionary Forces in the Meuse-Argonne Campaign*. Shippensburg, Pa.: White Mane, 1998.

Brittain, Vera. *Testament of Youth*. New York: Macmillan, 1933.

Britten, Thomas A. *American Indians in World War I: At Home and at War*. Albuquerque: U of New Mexico P, 1997.

Brooke, Rupert. *The Collected Poems of Rupert Brooke*. New York: Dodd, Mead, 1915.

Browne, Charles H., and J. W. McManigal. *Our Part in the Great War: What the Horton Community Did*. Horton, Kans.: Headlight, 1919.

Caesar, Adrian. *Taking It Like a Man: Suffering, Sexuality and the War Poets*. Manchester: U of Manchester P, 1993.

Canfield Fisher, Dorothy. *Home Fires in France*. New York: Holt, 1918.

Cather, Willa. *Death Comes for the Archbishop*. 1927. New York: Vintage, 1971.

———. *A Lost Lady*. 1923. New York: Vintage, 1990.

———. *Lucy Gayheart*. 1935. New York: Vintage, 1995.

———. *My Ántonia*. 1918. Boston: Houghton, 1988.

———. "The Namesake." 1903. *April Twilights*. Lincoln: U of Nebraska P, 1962. 25–26.

———. "The Namesake." 1907. *Willa Cather's Collected Short Fiction, 1892–1912*. Ed. Virginia Faulkner. Lincoln: U of Nebraska P, 1965. 137–46.

———. "The Novel Démeublé." 1936. *Willa Cather on Writing: Critical Studies on Writing as an Art*. Lincoln: U of Nebraska P, 1988. 35–43.

———. *One of Ours*. 1922. New York: Vintage, 1991.

———. *O Pioneers!* 1913. New York: Vintage, 1990.

———. "Paul's Case." 1920. *Collected Stories*. New York: Vintage, 1992. 170–89.

———. *The Professor's House*. 1925. New York: Vintage, 1990.

———. "Roll Call on the Prairies." *Red Cross Magazine*. July 1919: 27–30.

———. *Sapphira and the Slave Girl*. 1940. New York: Vintage, 1975.

———. *Shadows on the Rock*. 1931. New York: Vintage, 1995.

———. *The Song of the Lark*. 1937. Boston: Houghton, 1943.

———. "Zola: 'Like Caliban.'" *The World and the Parish: Willa Cather's Articles and Reviews, 1893–1902*. Ed. William M. Curtin. Lincoln: U of Nebraska P, 1970. 139–42.

Chapman, John Jay, ed. *Victor Chapman's Letters from France*. New York: Macmillan, 1917.

Coffman, Edward M. Introduction. *The Lost Battalion*. By Thomas M. Johnson and Fletcher Pratt. Lincoln: U of Nebraska P, 2000. v–x.

———. *The War to End All Wars: The American Military Experience in World War I*. New York: Oxford UP, 1968.

Cohen, Milton A. Rev. of *Saving Private Ryan*, dir. Steven Spielberg. *War, Literature, and the Arts* 11.1 (1999): 321–28.

Conrad, Joseph. *Heart of Darkness*. 1898. *The Portable Conrad*. Ed. Morton Dauwen Zabel. New York: Viking, 1975. 490–603.

———. *Lord Jim*. 1900. New York: Penguin, 1989.

———. "Youth." 1898. *The Portable Conrad*. Ed. Morton Dauwen Zabel. New York: Viking, 1975. 115–54.

Cooke, James J. "The American Soldier in France, 1917–1919." *Facing Armageddon: The First World War Experienced*. Ed. Hugh Cecil and Peter H. Little. London: Leo Cooper, 1996. 242–55.

———. *The Rainbow Division in the Great War, 1917–1919*. London: Praeger, 1994.

Coombs, Rose E. B. *Before Endeavours Fade: A Guide to the Battlefields of the First World War*. London: After the Battle, 1990.

Cooperman, Stanley. *World War I and the American Novel*. Baltimore: Johns Hopkins UP, 1967.

Cramer, Timothy R. "Claude's Case: A Study of Homosexual Temperament in Willa Cather's *One of Ours*." *South Dakota Review* 31.3 (1993): 147–60.

Cummings, E. E. *The Enormous Room*. 1922. New York: Liveright, 1978.

Dean, Brashford. *Helmets and Body Armor in Modern Warfare.* 1930. Tuckahoe, N.Y.: Pugliese, 1977.

"Dedication of the War Memorial." [Red Cloud, Nebr.]: n.p., 1951.

Dienst, Charles F., et al. *History of the 353rd Infantry Regiment.* N.p.: 353rd Infantry Soc., 1921.

Dos Passos, John. *1919.* 1931. Boston: Houghton, 1946.

———. *Three Soldiers.* New York: Doran, 1921.

The 88th Division in the World War. New York: Wynkoop Hallenbeck Crawford, 1919.

Eksteins, Modris. *Rites of Spring: The Great War and the Birth of the Modern Age.* New York: Doubleday, 1989.

Empey, Arthur Guy. *First Call: Guide Posts to Berlin.* New York: Putnam's, 1918.

Faber, Rebecca J. "'All the World Seemed Touched with Gold': Willa Cather and *One of Ours.*" Diss. U of Nebraska–Lincoln, 1995.

———. "Some of His: Cather's Use of Dr. Sweeney's Diary in *One of Ours.*" *Willa Cather Pioneer Memorial Newsletter* 37.1 (1993): 5–9.

Falls, Cyril. *War Books: An Annotated Bibliography of Books about the Great War.* London: Davies, 1930.

Faulks, Sebastian. *Birdsong.* New York: Random, 1993.

Ferro, Marc. *The Great War, 1914–1918.* 1969. New York: Military Heritage, 1989.

Findley, Timothy. *The Wars.* New York: Penguin, 1978.

Fitzgerald, F. Scott. *Tender Is the Night.* New York: Scribner's, 1933.

Fussell, Paul. *The Great War and Modern Memory.* London: Oxford UP, 1975.

Gelfant, Blanche H. "'What Was It . . . ?': The Secret of Family Accord in *One of Ours.*" *Willa Cather: Family, Community, and History.* Ed. John J. Murphy, Linda Hunter Adams, and Paul Rawlins. Provo: Brigham Young U Humanities, 1990. 85–102.

Gilbert, Martin. *Atlas of the First World War.* London: Dorset, 1984.

Graves, Robert. *Good-bye to All That.* London: Cape, 1929.

Griffiths, Frederick T. "The Woman Warrior: Willa Cather and *One of Ours.*" *Women's Studies* 11 (1984): 261–85.

Harrell, David. *From Mesa Verde to* The Professor's House. Albuquerque: U of New Mexico P, 1992.

Hart, B. H. Liddell. *The Real War, 1914–1918*. 1930. Boston: Little, 1964.

Haterius, Carl E. *Reminiscences of the 137th Infantry*. Topeka, Kans.: Crane, 1919.

Heller, Joseph. *Catch-22*. 1955. New York: Dell, 1994.

Helprin, Mark. *A Soldier of the Great War*. San Diego: Harcourt, 1991.

Hemingway, Ernest. *Ernest Hemingway: Selected Letters, 1917–1961*. Ed. Carlos Baker. New York: Scribner's, 1981.

———. *A Farewell to Arms*. New York: Scribner's, 1929.

———, ed. *Men at War: The Best War Stories of All Time*. 1942. New York: Berkley, 1960.

———. "Soldier's Home." *In Our Time*. 1925. New York: Simon, 1996. 69–77.

Henny, Fred. *Reno's Response: Reno County in the World War*. [Kansas]: n.p., n.d.

Higgonet, Margaret R., ed. *Lines of Fire: Women Writers of World War I*. New York: Plume, 1999.

Historical Sketch of German Area Occupied by the 89th Division. Trier: Lintz, 1919.

Holden, Frank. *War Memories*. Athens, Ga.: Athens Book Company, 1922.

Howard, Sidney. "Miss Cather Goes to War." Rev. of *One of Ours*, by Willa Cather. *Bookman* 56 (Oct. 1922): 217–18.

"Impressive Military Funeral Conducted by Legion Boys in Honor of the Late Lieut. G. P. Cather Jr." *Bladen Examiner* 6 May 1921: 1.

Johnson, Thomas M., and Fletcher Pratt. *The Lost Battalion*. 1938. Lincoln: U of Nebraska P, 2000.

Jones, James. *From Here to Eternity*. New York: Scribner's. 1951.

Kennedy, David M. *Over Here: The First World War and American Society*. New York: Oxford UP, 1980.

Kilmer, Joyce. *Poems, Essays, and Letters*. Ed. Robert Cortes Holliday. New York: Doran, 1918.

Kirschke, James J. *Willa Cather and Six Writers from the Great War*. Lanham, Md.: UP of America, 1991.

Lampe, William T. *Tulsa County in the World War*. Tulsa, Okla.: Tulsa County Historical Soc., 1919.

Laqueur, Thomas W. "Memory and Naming in the Great War." *Commemorations: The Politics of National Identity*. Ed. John R. Gillis. Princeton: Princeton UP, 1994. 150–67.

Lavington, Margaret. "Biographical Note." *The Collected Poems of Rupert Brooke*. New York: Dodd, Mead, 1917. 167–76.

Lawrence, D. H. "The Prussian Officer." 1914. *The Prussian Officer and Other Stories*. New York: Penguin, 1984. 1–34.

———. *Sons and Lovers*. 1913. New York: Penguin, 1994.

Lee, Hermione. *Willa Cather: Double Lives*. New York: Vintage, 1989.

Lewis, Edith. *Willa Cather Living*. New York: Knopf, 1953.

Lewis, Sinclair. *Babbitt*. 1922. *Lewis at Zenith: A Three-Novel Omnibus*. New York: Harcourt, 1961. 339–583.

———. "A Hamlet of the Plains." Rev. of *One of Ours*, by Willa Cather. *Literary Review* 3 (16 Sept. 1922): 23–24.

Macphail, Andrew. "John McCrae: An Essay in Character." *In Flanders Fields and Other Poems*. By John McCrae. New York: Putnam's, 1919.

Madigan, Mark. "Willa Cather and Dorothy Canfield Fisher: Rift, Reconciliation, and *One of Ours*." *Cather Studies 1*. Ed. Susan J. Rosowski. Lincoln: U of Nebraska P, 1990. 115–29.

Magonigle, H. Van Buren. "Description of the Memorial." *The Liberty Memorial in Kansas City, Missouri*. Kansas City: Liberty Memorial Assn., 1929. 25–37.

Mailer, Norman. *The Naked and the Dead*. 1948. New York: Holt, 1981.

Manning, Frederic. *The Middle Parts of Fortune*. 1929. New York: St. Martin's, 1977.

March, William. *Company K*. New York: Smith, 1933.

McCollum, "Buck Private." *History and Rhymes of the Lost Battalion*. 1919. Columbus, Ohio: McCollum, 1929.

McComas, Dix. "Willa Cather's *One of Ours*: In Distant Effigy." *Legacy* 14.2 (1997): 93–109.

McCrae, John. *In Flanders Fields and Other Poems*. New York: Putnam's, 1919.

McPherson, J. E. "Historical Sketch of the Memorial." *The Liberty Memorial in Kansas City, Missouri*. Kansas City: Liberty Memorial Assn., 1929. 5–24.

————. *The Story of the Great Frieze*. Kansas City: Liberty Memorial Assn., 1935.

Meigs, Mark. *Optimism at Armageddon: Voices of American Participants in the First World War*. New York: New York UP, 1997.

Mencken, H. L. "Portrait of an American Citizen." Rev. of *One of Ours*, by Willa Cather. *Smart Set* 69 (Oct. 1922): 140–42.

Miller, Paul W. "Anti-Heroic Theme and Structure in Midwestern World War I Novels from Cather to Hemingway." *Midamerica* 23 (1996): 99–108.

Mosse, George L. *Fallen Soldiers: Reshaping the Memory of the World Wars*. New York: Oxford UP, 1990.

Mother's Day 1918. Pamphlet. [France]: American YMCA, 1918.

Munro, Dana C., George C. Sellery, and August C. Krey, eds. *German Treatment of Conquered Territory*. Washington, D.C.: GPO, 1918.

————. *German War Practices*. Washington, D.C.: GPO, 1918.

Murphy, John J. "*One of Ours* as American Naturalism." *Great Plains Quarterly* 2.4 (1982): 232–38.

"Nebraska Authoress Wins $1,000." *The Omaha Bee*. N.d. Newspaper clipping. Nebraska State Historical Society, Willa Cather Pioneer Memorial Collection, Red Cloud.

Nelson, Robert J. *Willa Cather and France: In Search of the Lost Language*. Urbana: U of Illinois P, 1988.

Norton Cru, Jean. *War Books: A Study in Historical Criticism*. San Diego: San Diego UP, 1976.

Novick, Peter. *That Noble Dream: The "Objectivity Question" and the American Historical Profession*. Cambridge: Cambridge UP, 1988.

O'Brien, Sharon. "Combat Envy and Survivor Guilt: Willa Cather's 'Manly Battle Yarn.'" *Arms and the Woman: War, Gender, and Literary Representation*. Ed. Helen M. Cooper, Adrienne Auslander Munich, and Susan Merrill Squier. Chapel Hill: U of North Carolina P, 1989. 184–204.

O'Brien, Tim. "How to Tell a True War Story." *The Things They Carried*. New York: Penguin, 1990. 73–91.

Paxson, Frederic L., Edward S. Corwn, and Samuel B. Harding, eds. *War Cyclopedia: A Handbook for Ready Reference on the Great War*. Washington, D.C.: GPO, 1918.

Perry, John. *Sgt. York: His Life, Legend and Legacy*. Nashville: Broadman, 1997.

Piehler, G. Kurt. *Remembering War the American Way*. Washington, D.C.: Smithsonian Institute, 1995.

———. "The War Dead and the Gold Star: American Commemoration of the First World War." *Commemorations: The Politics of National Identity*. Ed. John R. Gillis. Princeton: Princeton UP, 1994. 168–85.

Prendergast, Arline Frances. "*One of Ours*: Willa Cather's Successful Failure." Diss. U of Pittsburgh, 1971.

Price, Michael W. "Epicurus in Hamilton: St. Peter's Contemplative Retirement to the Attic Study and Garden in *The Professor's House*." *Cather Studies 4: Willa Cather's Canadian and Old World Connections*. Ed. Robert Thacker and Michael A. Peterman. Lincoln: U of Nebraska P, 1999. 264–83.

"Program of the Dedication of the Liberty Memorial." Kansas City: Liberty Memorial Assn., 1926.

Quinn, Patrick J. "The Experience of War in American Patriotic Literature." *Facing Armageddon: The First World War Experienced*. Ed. Hugh Cecil and Peter H. Liddle. London: Cooper, 1996. 752–66.

Randall, John H. III. *The Landscape and the Looking Glass: Willa Cather's Search for Value*. Boston: Houghton, 1960.

Rankin, Edward P., Jr. *The Sante Fe Trail Leads to France: A Narrative of Battle Service of the 110th Engineers (35th Division) in the Meuse-Argonne Offensive*. Kansas City: Richardson, 1933.

Rathbone, Irene. *We That Were Young*. 1932. New York: Feminist, 1989.

Remarque, Erich Maria. *All Quiet on the Western Front*. Boston: Little, 1929.

Reynolds, Guy. *Willa Cather in Context: Progress, Race, Empire*. New York: St. Martin's, 1996.

Richmond, Robert W. "The Victory Highway: Transcontinental Memorial." *The Home Front: Shawnee County during World War I*. Ed. Daniel Fitzgerald. Topeka, Kans.: Shawnee Co. Historical Soc., 1992. 204–10.

Rohrkemper, John. "The Great War, the Midwest, and Modernism:

Cather, Dos Passos, and Hemingway." *Midwestern Miscellany* 16 (1988): 19–29.

Roosevelt, Theodore. *Average Americans*. New York: Putnam's, 1919.

Rosowski, Susan J. *The Voyage Perilous: Willa Cather's Romanticism*. Lincoln: U of Nebraska P, 1986.

Ryan, Maureen. "No Woman's Land: Gender in Willa Cather's *One of Ours*." 18.1 (1990): 65–76.

Ryder, Mary R. "*Ars Scientiae*: Willa Cather and the Mission of Science." *Willa Cather Pioneer Memorial Newsletter* 55.1 (2001): 11–16.

———. "Sinclair Lewis and Willa Cather: The Intersection of *Main Street* with *One of Ours*." *Sinclair Lewis: New Essays in Criticism*. Ed. James M. Hutchisson. Troy, N.Y.: Whitson, 1997. 147–61.

Scarry, Elaine. *The Body in Pain: The Making and Unmaking of the World*. New York: Oxford UP, 1985.

Schaefer, Josephine O'Brien. "The Great War and 'This Late Age of World's Experience' in Cather and Woolf." *Virginia Woolf and War: Fiction, Reality, and Myth*. Ed. Mark Hussey. Syracuse: Syracuse UP, 1991. 134–50.

Schwind, Jean. "The 'Beautiful' War in *One of Ours*." *Modern Fiction Studies* 30.1 (1984): 53–71.

Sergeant, Elizabeth Shepley. *Willa Cather: A Memoir*. Lincoln: U of Nebraska P, 1967.

77th Division Association. *History of the 77th Division*. New York: 77th Division Assn., 1919.

Severo, Richard, and Lewis Milford. *The Wages of War: When America's Soldiers Came Home—From Valley Forge to Vietnam*. New York: Simon, 1989.

Sherriff, R. C. *Journey's End*. 1928. New York: Penguin, 1993.

Showalter, Dennis. "America's Great War." *The Poppy and the Owl* 25 (May 1999): 30–38.

Skaggs, Merrill Maguire. *After the World Broke in Two: The Later Novels of Willa Cather*. Charlottesville: UP of Virginia, 1990.

Smith, Helen Zeena. *Not So Quiet . . . .* 1930. New York: Feminist, 1989.

Society of the First Division. *History of the First Division during the World War, 1917–1919*. Philadelphia: Winston, 1922.

Stallings, Laurence. *The Doughboys: The Story of the A.E.F., 1917–1918.* New York: Harper, 1963.

———. *Plumes.* New York: Knopf, 1924.

Stich, Klaus P. "*The Professor's House*: Prohibition, Ripe Grapes, and Euripides." *Cather Studies 4: Willa Cather's Canadian and Old World Connections.* Ed. Robert Thacker and Michael A. Peterman. Lincoln: U of Nebraska P, 1999. 225–43.

Stouck, David. "*The Professor's House* and the Issues of History." *Willa Cather: Family, Community, and History.* Ed. John J. Murphy, Linda Hunter Adams, and Paul Rawlins. Provo: Brigham Young U Humanities, 1990. 201–11.

———. *Willa Cather's Imagination.* Lincoln: U of Nebraska P, 1975.

Stout, Janis P. "The Making of Willa Cather's *One of Ours*: The Role of Dorothy Canfield Fisher." *War, Literature, and the Arts* 11.2 (1999): 48–59.

———. *Willa Cather: The Writer and Her World.* Charlottesville: UP of Virginia, 2000.

Stricklett, "Hap." *The Dud.* Blair, Nebr.: Pilot, n.d.

Stuckey, W. J. *The Pulitzer Prize Novels: A Critical Backward Look.* Norman: U of Oklahoma P, 1966.

Tennyson, Alfred. "Locksley Hall Sixty Years After." *Tennyson's Poetry.* Ed. Robert W. Hill, Jr. New York: Norton, 1971. 467–76.

Trout, Steven. "Telling the Truth—Nearly: Robert Graves, Daniel Defoe, and *Good-bye to All That*." *New Perspectives on Robert Graves.* Ed. Patrick J. Quinn. Selinsgrove, Pa.: Susquehanna UP, 1999. 175–87.

———. "'Where Do We Go from Here?': Ernest Hemingway's 'Soldier's Home' and American Veterans of World War I." *Hemingway Review* 20.1 (2000): 5–20.

———. "Willa Cather's *One of Ours* and the Iconography of Remembrance." *Cather Studies 4: Willa Cather's Canadian and Old World Connections.* Ed. Robert Thacker and Michael A. Peterman. Lincoln: U of Nebraska P, 1999. 187–204.

Urgo, Joseph R. *Willa Cather and the Myth of American Migration.* Urbana: U of Illinois P, 1995.

Van Ghent, Dorothy. "Willa Cather." *Seven American Women Writers of the Twentieth Century: An Introduction*. Ed. Maureen Howard. Minneapolis: U of Minnesota P, 1964. 79–105.

Ward, Christopher. "One of Ours." *Literary Review* 2 (3 Feb. 1923): 435.

Watt, Ian. *Joseph Conrad in the Nineteenth Century*. Berkeley: U of California P, 1979.

"We Will Build the Nebraska Stadium in 1923." Pamphlet. [Nebr.]: n.p., n.d.

Wells, H. G. "The Land Ironclads." 1903. *Selected Short Stories of H. G. Wells*. New York: Penguin, 1979. 98–117.

West, Rebecca. *The Return of the Soldier*. 1918. New York: Carroll and Graf, 1980.

Wharton, Edith. *The Marne*. New York: Scribner's, 1918.

———. *A Son at the Front*. New York: Scribner's, 1923.

White, Hayden. "The Historical Text as Literary Artifact." *Tropics of Discourse: Essays in Cultural Criticism*. Baltimore: Johns Hopkins UP, 1978. 81–100.

Widdowson, Peter. "Hardy in History: A Case-Study in the Sociology of Literature." *On Thomas Hardy: Late Essays and Earlier*. Houndmills, Eng.: Macmillan, 1998. 27–44.

Winter, Jay. *Sites of Memory, Sites of Mourning: The Great War in European Cultural History*. Cambridge: Cambridge UP, 1995.

Woodress, James. "A Note on *One of Ours*." *Willa Cather Pioneer Memorial Newsletter* 37.1 (1993): 1–4.

———. *Willa Cather: A Literary Life*. Lincoln: U of Nebraska P, 1987.

Woolf, Virginia. *Jacob's Room*. San Diego: Harcourt, 1922.

———. *Mrs. Dalloway*. San Diego: Harcourt, 1925.

———. *To the Lighthouse*. San Diego: Harcourt, 1927.

Yongue, Patricia Lee. "For Better and For Worse: At Home and War in *One of Ours*." *Willa Cather: Family, Community, and History*. Ed. John J. Murphy, Linda Hunter Adams, and Paul Rawlins. Provo: Brigham Young U Humanities, 1990. 141–53.

Zola, Emile. *The Debacle*. 1892. Trans. Leonard Tancock. New York: Penguin, 1987.

———. *Germinal*. 1885. Trans. Leonard Tancock. New York, Penguin, 1985.

INDEX